# OLD AGE AND AGENCY

# OLD AGE AND AGENCY

## EMMANUELLE TULLE
### EDITOR

Nova Science Publishers, Inc.
*New York*

**Production Coordinator:** Tatiana Shohov
**Coordinating Editor:** Tatiana Shohov
**Senior Production Editors:** Susan Boriotti and Donna Dennis
**Production Editors:** Marius Andronie and Rusudan Razmadze
**Office Manager:** Annette Hellinger
**Graphics:** Levani Chlaidze and Magdalena Nuñez
**Editorial Production:** Alexandra Columbus, Maya Columbus, Robert Brower,
　　　　　　　　　Vladimir Klestov and Lorna Loperfido
**Circulation:** Luis Aviles, Raymond Davis, Cathy DeGregory, Melissa Diaz, Ave Maria
　　　　　Gonzalez, Marlene Nuñez, Jeannie Pappas, Vera Popovic and Frankie Punger
**Communications and Acquisitions:** Serge P. Shohov

✳

*Library of Congress Cataloging-in-Publication Data*
Old age and agency / Emmanuelle Tulle, editor.
p. cm.
ISBN 1-59033-884-7 (hc)
1. Gerontology. 2. Ageism. 3. Social policy. 4. Older people--Social conditions. I. Tulle,
　　Emmanuelle.
HQ1061.O37 2004
305.26'09182'1--dc22
2004021755

Copyright © 2004 by Nova Science Publishers, Inc.
　　　　　400 Oser Ave, Suite 1600
　　　　　Hauppauge, New York 11788-3619
　　　　　Tele. 631-231-7269　　Fax 631-231-8175
　　　　　e-mail: Novascience@earthlink.net
　　　　　Web Site: http://www.novapublishers.com

*Printed in the United States of America*

# CONTENTS

# PREFACE

This book is about rethinking the ways in which we make sense of social action or agency in later life. The contributions in this collection challenge traditional academic approaches to the study of later life, which, arguably, often deny older people agency. Social gerontology, and the wider society, should be more reflexive and rather than contribute to the continued marginalization of older people, should draw attention to the extent to which the latter's actions may be understood within the set of normalizing discourses which people have to manage and negotiate as they get old. The purpose of this collection is to continue this process, by providing philosophical, theoretical, conceptual and empirical direction for a reflexive social gerontology. This book argues that the management of later life has become complex, caught as it is within a broad discourse which continues to construct old age as a time of decline and dependency but has shifted the burden of responsibility for the avoidance of decline onto individuals.

# INTRODUCTION

Do older people have agency? Is there attrition in agency as we age? This collection is about the search for agency in later life. There is no shortage of empirical evidence to show that as people age they continue taking part in a range of activities and that there is a reflexive engagement with wider structures. By this I mean that growing older does not exempt people from having to manage the structures in which their lives are embedded, be it the structures of institutions in which they may be spending their later years, the political decisions which influence the resources at their disposal or the cultural tools enabling people to make sense of their own experiences. Nor does it erode the ability to act reflexively.

The impetus for this collection is partly theoretical, partly humanistic. In previous work (Tulle-Winton 1999 and Tulle and Mooney 2002). I have explored the broader cultural context in which the lives of older people were conducted and in which a range of interpretations about these social acts were made possible. Two 'lessons' emerged: firstly, what we know about later life is influenced by powerful discourses, such as medicine, welfare and neoliberal ideology and that it is at the meeting point of these discourses that we 'imagine' and produce later life. From these, the dominant narrative (Gullette 1997) of old age has emerged, that is the association of old age with inevitable, wholesale decline, physical and cognitive, as well as social and cultural. Secondly, older people themselves operate within a range of expectations, which are bounded by this narrative. Thus older people are either denied agency because they are engaged in an inexorable process of decline, or if agency does indeed manifest itself, it is used as a way of pushing back decline. Whatever they do, stay active or give in to immobility and inactivity, older people's options are used as evidence that they are devoid of agency. Thus older people appear to be in a Catch-22 – whatever they do, they either postpone decline or have been caught up by it.

If we want to make the case that agency is not the preserve of the cognitively and physically 'able', or even of the physically 'present', we have to start asking different questions and we have to step out of the dominant discourse of age. This approach can only come from the engagement with, and development of, theoretical tools from critical gerontology and social theory which will rescue the study of later life and the search for agency from the unquestioned reliance on well-worn but not particularly liberating assumptions and stereotypes. Thus we need to continue engaging in a critique of the structures which, I would argue, hinder the potential for agency amongst older people. Another important concern, which should underpin this endeavor, is with the liberation of older people from restricted narratives and consequently restricted identities.

All the contributors to this volume have attempted to do just that and they have, in the process, given this book a strong integrity. Thus I am confident in asserting that the book is noteworthy for each individual contribution. What is more, as a collection it is more than the sum of its parts. All the chapters grapple with a similar question – how to rethink agency in later life. We do not deny that aging into the later years increases the risk of physical and cognitive disruption and deterioration. Nor do we deny that these processes of bodily change affect in large part the intimate experience of the later years and self-realization. What we are bringing to light is the paucity of responses, both economic, cultural and personal, which the current discourse of old age allows us to envisage and what impact this restricted imagination has on subjectivities. This suggests therefore the need for a critique – of the contemporary 'problematization' of the later years, of the discourse of old age and of the structures created to 'manage' old age. In other words, we need to critique the narrative of decline, without necessarily invoking its elimination. Thus agency is reconceptualised as the strategies in which people engage, or in which they might wish to engage, to 'resist' decline and, in some cases, we also offer alternative, perhaps more satisfying, strategies for the management of both the external and internal life, often drawn from the experiences of older people themselves. This reconceptualisation is consonant with the desire to expand the field of possibilities in which later life can be imagined and subjectivities created.

## ORGANIZATION OF THE BOOK

The chapters have been organized under broad themes: the broader context for problematising old age, structures facilitating agency as compliance or resistance, micro-strategies of resistance and the internal experience of agency.

The first contributions (Polivka and Longino, Phillipson and Powell) explore the broader cultural and political context in which old age has been problematised.

Polivka and Longino locate their analysis in what they call 'the postmodern dialectic of the new aging experience'. They argue that the broad cultural shifts of the last few decades towards post-traditional and post-modern society present risks but also opportunities for the aging experience, not only for individuals but also for public policy. Thus they bemoan the continued marginalization of frail elderly people in a context where individual freedom is valorized, older life narratives are unsettled, the status of the very old has been lowered and frailty is constructed as the antithesis of agency. On the other hand they perceive some benefits in those changes: the unsettling of expert knowledge, the proliferation of alternative structures of influence, like new social movements, the dissolution of the binaries of modernity and the shaping of new opportunities. They therefore propose a new framework in which agency is not reduced to participation in the market and consumption, nor confined to the physically and cognitively fit, but can be re-imagined as a synthesis between the freedom to act and security. The role of collective forms of support is therefore emphasized. So is the need to allow personal meaning to flourish.

Phillipson and Powell use the concept of risk as defined by Beck to explore changes in modalities of agency in later life. They present an overview of the context in which old age has been constructed in modernity, highlighting particularly its welfarization. They note that the experience of old age became restricted within a welfare/modernist framework and that, although older people were shielded from abject destitution, the opportunities for aging identities beyond retirement, marginalization and dependency were few. Nevertheless the emphasis was on collective responsibility. In postmodernity and neoliberal regimes, the onus is on the self as agent, throughout the lifecourse, facilitated by concerns for demographic shifts and the concommittent shift in the balance between productive social actors and dependent actors. Thus the risk is shifted to the individual and the care relationship is also transformed (marketization, onus on families, etc...). On the other hand, for those who are affluent, consumption is offering a wider range of identities. Nevertheless this is taking place in the context of the management, that is the elimination, of risk, including the risk of bodily dependency. The catch is that neoliberalism and 'the loosening of welfarist notions of age' do reinforce social inequalities in later life. So agency in postmodernity is the individual management of risk, divorced from any sort of collective responsibility to manage neoliberalism and protect various population groups from its worst excesses.

These two chapters are followed by a close and detailed evaluation by Moody, on the one hand, and Katz and Laliberte-Rudman, on the other, of specific structures in which agency can be carried out. Here the understanding of agency as resistance is beginning to take shape.

Moody presents a detailed analysis of two models of older adult education, namely the Elderhostel and the U3A 'movements'. Although these structures have contrasting characteristics, they are however linked by their ethos of providing education to older adults along a set of values, which are different from, and challenge mainstream education. They reject the commodification of education, the reliance on standard curricula, exams, grades and the awarding of diplomas. In effect, they give primacy to the construction of narratives of later life which do not mimic or mirror those of early adulthood. In other words, they encourage the development of new modalities of being. Nevertheless they are not without their weaknesses but I will let the reader discover the full analysis.

Katz and Laliberte-Rudman also critically explore the role of structure in producing particular kinds of agency and subjectivity. Operating primarily within a Foucauldian framework, they show how different narratives embedded in contrasting structural frames, or exemplars, lead to the construction of subjectivities which may reinforce or challenge the dominant discourse of age as it intersects with neoliberal ideology. They show that opting for the retired worker and opportunity-seeker consumer narrative may yield a productive, privatized, individualized and active aging identity, which conforms, to the ideal subject of neoliberalism. This is compared with more collective approaches to aging, such as those embodied by new social movements, like the U3A. The U3A allows people to negotiate their participation within a structural framework which emphasizes a different set of principles, such as those described by Moody, but which may prove more satisfying and less alienating to those who would no longer be able to aspire to neoliberal subjectivities.

These four contributions are therefore linked by their strong critique of neoliberal ideology as it has reshaped the experience of the middle and later years in the last 20 years.

The next set of contributions (Wahidin, Conway and Kontos) focuses on what I would term 'micro-strategies' of resistance, those in which older people themselves, as individuals, engage, reflexively or not, to enable them to live their lives. With the use of innovative theoretical interpretations, the everyday, idiosyncratic acts and thoughts described in these three chapters can be broadened out and given greater collective weight. Here it is older people themselves who engage in the critique of the dominant discourse of old age.

Wahidin's chapter is set in prison and the protagonists are women who either have grown older in prison or were incarcerated in their later years. She shows how the technologies of punishment, intersecting with gender and age, used in the prison focus primarily on the body in ways which compromise identity. The women regain agency – and, in the process, reconstruct their identity - by resisting the obfuscation of their bodies and the imposition of prison time.

Conway uses a case study and a moral economy approach to show how an older woman living her later years in loneliness and social isolation displays her potential for agency. It is not so much in her actions but in her own recollections of significant events in her life that she reclaims her ability to be agentic. In effect her thoughts and recollections provide her with a 'moral' framework within which to compare her past and present life and carve out a meaningful sense of identity. Conway argues that in her appeal for a greater sense of community, solidarity and reciprocity she marks herself out from a selfish and ageist social environment.

Kontos's chapter finds agency where it is traditionally assumed to have disappeared – in people with Alzheimer's Disease. She discusses the work of two 20th Century painters, Willem de Kooning and William Utermohlen, who continued painting right through the onset and development of their illness. According to medical interpretations of AD, cognitive deterioration leads to the erosion of agency and the irrevocable disappearance of self. Thus the disease precludes any artistic intention. Art critics also struggle to admit that the work produced under conditions of illness would have any intrinsic artistic value. She synthesizes Merleau-Ponty's phenomenology which recognizes the importance of pre-reflective action, with Bourdieu's insights into the social and historical dimensions of the body, to argue that agency, in this case the act of creation, is not "the exclusive privilege of cognition" but may originate in the body itself.

The last set of contributions (Hepworth, Hockey and James, and Biggs) focus on agency as an internal process in which bodies, one's own or those of significant others, make their presence felt and inform the work on the self that is permitted within specific cultural contexts.

Hepworth starts from the premise that there continues to exist a tension between the aging body and self and examines key texts to find ways in which this tension can be resolved. This tension, he argues, is a cultural form, that is it has emerged as such in a context in which agency and social value can only be imagined if the body is competent. Thus the declining body of old age shifts the balance of power away from old people to the benefit of younger people. It also presents problems of interpretation for individuals. Hepworth examines in detail the work of Gilleard and Higgs (2000) on the one hand and that of Hallam, Hockey and Howarth (1999) on the other, to show how they grapple with the problem of the declining body. This then leads him to revisit the 'masking' process which takes place as one ages which, he argues, consists of a multiplicity of strategies which may be invoked simultaneously to manage the interplay between the aging body and the self. The consequences of the recourse to masking are nevertheless open to scrutiny and we must turn to Biggs for an examination of its pitfalls.

Biggs takes us on a search for what he terms authentic agency. As such it is a critique of understandings of agency which rely on masquerading or masking the difficulties actors may have in achieving a sense of coherence between the social and psychological conflicts brought on by aging: the felt desire to achieve an authentic sense of self, which is at odds with the demands of the external world which drives people to mask aging by holding on to the pretence of youthfulness, in appearance but also in intention. The result is superficiality and a reduced ability to deal with the challenges of aging. In contrast Biggs sees the later years as offering the potential for accessing depths of emotion, self-knowledge and for achieving continuity in personal narrative.

Hockey and James develop the theme of aging and self by conceptualizing agency in later life as self-authoring, a process in which the body occupies a central place. Their analysis is a critique of orthodox constructions of the aging process which, they argue, are not satisfactory for they do not account for the complexity of what is experienced and they may also mask the potential for different modalities of identity construction as one ages. Thus they start with a very basic question - how do we know we age? - before exploring how aging is experienced phenomenologically, that is in and through the body, and what potential for identity and social action these experiences give rise to. In order to progress their analysis, they rely on anthropological research into aging and change.

I have closed the collection with a set of reflections, informed by my own work to-date on the state of social gerontology and on the potential for agency in later life. My own search for agency has led me to examine the lives on constrasting groups of older people. Firstly I have focused on people who, some time after retirement, moved to what might be seen as 'age-appropriate' housing and appear to have fulfilled the neoliberal project of taking responsibility for their own aging. The second group of people, Masters elite runners, also appear to fulfill the call to remain active: they run regularly and appear to think that running slows the aging process and keeps them healthy. I explore the extent to which agency can be reconceptualized as resistance and I examine precisely what is resisted.

## REFERENCES

Gullette, M. M. 1997. *Declining to Decline: Cultural Combat and the Politics of the Midlife.* Charlottesville, Va: University Press of Virginia.

Tulle, E., and Mooney, E. 2002. "Moving to 'Age-Appropriate' Housing: Government and Self in Later Life." *Sociology 36*:683-701.

Tulle-Winton, E. 1999. "Growing Old and Resistance: Towards a New Cultural Economy of Old Age?" *Ageing and Society 19*:281-299.

# PART 1.
# PROBLEMATIZING AGENCY IN OLD AGE

*Chapter 1*

# POSTMODERN AGING AND THE FUTURE OF PUBLIC POLICY

*Larry Polivka[1]*
*Charles F. Longino, Jr.[2]*

## ABSTRACT

The paper is organized into two sections. It begins with an overview of some of the cultural and social changes and trends associated with the emergence of post-traditional, postmodern society. Those changes will be examined which, we think, have the greatest salience for the future of aging. The second section describes some of the major implications of these changes for public policies related to the elderly. This section also describes the public policy response we think is most compatible with the kinds of lives older persons are likely to experience in the future with an emphasis on the lives of the frail elderly. Most discussions about greater agency and creativity among the future elderly of the baby boom generation, treat physical and mental decline as definitive limits on agency. In our view, it is within these limits and those imposed by the lack of economic resources that public policies should operate to support those who require assistance in order to maintain their freedom and agency.

## INTRODUCTION

The debate over the future of aging in the 21st century and its role of public policy began nearly two decades ago and is likely to become increasingly contentious and central to domestic politics in all Western societies over the next 20 years. A recent *New York Times* article by Robin Toner (2002) described how this perception has become widespread in Congress as both parties work to gain advantage, or protection in current and future conflicts over Social Security, Medicare and Medicaid.

---
[1] Florida Policy Exchange Center on Aging, USF 30437, 4202 E. Fowler Avenue, Tampa, FL 33620, Phone (813) 974-3478, Fax: (813) 974-5788, lpolivka@admin.usf.edu.
[2] Reynolds Gerontology Program, Wake Forest University, Box 7808 Reynolda Station, Winston Salem, NC 27109, Phone: (336) 758-4665, Fax: (336) 758-4664, longino@wfu.edu.

A demographic phenomenon resides at the base of this policy debate: the aging of the populations of industrialized nations, including the United States. Population aging is such a common phenomenon that demographers do not see it as remarkable. In agricultural economies with high birth and death rates, the population is stable. It is destabilized when death rates begin to fall, owing largely to public health measures easily transported from developed nations by non-government organizations. As death rates drop, birth rates fall also, but at a later time. Large families bless the agricultural labor force, but are harder to absorb in an industrializing economy. Birth rates eventually fall to the same lower level as death rates. During the time when birth and death rates are unbalanced, however, the population grows rapidly and becomes younger as the median age falls, indicating the heightened survival rate for babies and children. The explosion of surviving babies moves inevitably up through the ages until they are old, and die out, leaving behind a population that is stable once again, with low birth and death rates.

Western countries, including the United States, moved through this series of transitions during the first half of the 20th century. The U.S. population had reached an all-time low birth rate at the time of World War II. Then in 1946, its birth rate rose for a decade, then it declined to its 1945 low in 1964. This eighteen-year period, 1946 to 1964, is often referenced as "the baby boom generation" in popular literature today. For demographers, however, this reversal is notable because it represents an aberration, a regression to the earlier imbalance between birth and death rates more characteristic of the middle phase of the worldwide population transition. Population aging is a pervasive worldwide natural phenomenon. It is, at least in part, a societal adjustment to the increasing use of birth- and death-related technologies that grow out of the modern era. The policy issues generated or enhanced by population aging, will be debated in every society, not in ours alone.

Characteristic of the era, perhaps, there is no consensus, even on basic terms, to describe our location in societal change. In this paper we attempt to situate these conflicts in the context of broad demographic, social, political, and cultural changes that have swept across Western societies over the past thirty or forty years, after our "baby boom" came of age. Yet we are faced with a choice of competing rubrics: post-traditional society or postmodernism. These two terms are not fully interchangeable in that post-traditional social theorists reject the notion that there is a qualitative difference between modernism and the major tenets of postmodern thought. For them, contemporary societies still operate under the influence of modernism, with its roots in the enlightenment and the birth of science and secularism, only more so during a period that may be called hyper-modernism. For our purposes, these differences are not as significant as the changes and trends in Western society theorized by both perspectives, and that allows us to draw on work by theorists in both camps as we develop our analysis of population aging and public policy.

The paper is organized into two sections. It begins with an overview of some of the cultural and social changes and trends associated with the emergence of post-traditional, postmodern society. Those changes will be examined which, we think, have the greatest salience for the future of aging. The second section describes some of the major implications of these changes for public policies related to the elderly. This section also describes the kind of public policy response we recommend as most compatible with the kinds of lives older persons are likely to experience in the future with an emphasis on the lives of the frail elderly. This emphasis is necessary because the frail elderly have the most at stake in any discussion/debate about changes in public policies related to the elderly, especially health and long-term care policies. We also think it is important to focus on the frail elderly in the context of cultural changes that have tended to valorize individual freedom and agency. We think these changes are at least as significant for the less than fully independent elderly as for the robustly youthful third-ager. Most discussions, however, about greater agency and creativity among the future elderly of the baby boom generation, treat physical and mental decline as definitive limits on agency. In our view, it is within these limits and those imposed by the lack of economic resources that public policies should operate to support those who require assistance in order to maintain their freedom and agency. We do not, in short, see frailty and impairment as the antithesis of agency. It is precisely when the individual begins to experience the erosion of freedom and agency that often comes with impairment and frailty that public policies should be designed to provide the resources needed to resist the loss of agency and allow the individual to exercise as much autonomy as possible under conditions of impairment.

These policies differ from the neoliberal privatization policies that are often associated with a strand of postmodern thought that celebrates the role of the market and self-expression through consumption. We refer to our recommended approach to new policies for the elderly as the "new synthesis" because it gives equal weight to ensuring the economic security of the elderly and creating more flexible self-empowerment-oriented policies that reflect the freedom and individual autonomy created by the emergence of post-traditional, postmodern societies.

## THE POSTMODERN WORLD AND THE NEW INDIVIDUALISM

The postmodern world, or late modernity, is increasingly shaped by conscious, intentional change that tends to radicalize life by *evacuating, disinterring* and *problematizing* tradition. This level of change exposes society and the individual to growing contingency and risk. These trends also produce more opportunities for freedom and creativity for individuals and society. The influence of traditions, and the institutions that embody them, has faded over the last several decades. Accordingly, social organizations and individuals have had to write their own scripts and make decisions about a wide range of issues that were once largely made for them by adherence to strong traditional values and ways of life.

According to Anthony Giddens (1994) tradition is based on a formulaic notion of truth and is managed by priests and guardians through rituals. Formulaic truth uses ritual language that is performative; that is, it does not have referential properties nor does it rely on reasons for justification. Traditions, and guardians of tradition, depend on received wisdom and the ability to interpret symbols and make them meaningful. Expert knowledge, on the other hand, cannot generate meaning, and this has created a "problem of meaning" in our post-traditional world.

Giddens has described some of the major differences between tradition and its formulaic truths and expert knowledge as follows:

> First, expertise is disembedding; in contrast to tradition it is in a fundamental sense non-local and decentred. Second, expertise is tied not to formulaic truth but to a belief in the corrigibility of knowledge, a belief that depends upon a methodical skepticism. Third, the accumulation of expert knowledge involves intrinsic processes of specialization. Fourth, trust in abstract systems, or in experts, cannot readily be generated by means of esoteric wisdom.

> Fifth, expertise interacts with growing institutional reflexivity, such that there are regular
> processes of loss and reappropriation of everyday skills and knowledge.
> *(Giddens 1994:71)*

In modernity, as traditions weaken and fade, we have the task of overcoming the programming built into our early lives (deprogramming our consciousness) as we become more autonomous and responsible for building our own identities and mastering the tools of self-creation—of making our own decisions about values and behaviors. This self-creation does not mean that we make decisions and live our lives independent of others. We often look to others for guidance and support, but they are just as much on their own as we are and the collective expression of values is more likely to take the form of ephemeral fads and fashions than traditions. In place of tradition and the routines of life embedded in them, we have self-reflexivity, i.e., making decisions on our own and in terms of self-generated criteria and rationales. Self-reflexivity, unfortunately, can also create the kind of stress that leads to addiction and other ways of escaping the anxieties of freedom and the loss of transcendent sources of meaning once provided by strong traditions, especially religious traditions. The emergence of the autonomous, self-reflexive individual is the motor of social change in the modern and postmodern era. Scott Lash (1994) has noted that:

> . . . simple modernity is modern in the sense that individualization has largely broken down
> the old traditional structures—extended family, church, village community—of the
> Gemeinschaft. Yet it is not fully modern because the individualization process has only gone
> part way and a new set of gesellschaftlisch structures—trade unions, welfare state,
> government bureaucracy, formalized Taylorist shopfloor rules, class itself as a structure—has
> taken the place of traditional structures. Full modernization takes place only when further
> individualization also sets agency free from even these (simply) modern social structures.
> *(Lash 1994:46)*

The evacuating of traditions tends to make the past emotionally inert. The past can be reconstructed, however, in terms of present needs and desires, as individuals become emotionally and intellectually autonomous, and as personal relationships are more dependent on intimacy, which is largely free of traditional roles and expectations (pure relationships). The succession of generations loses some of its significance in the post-traditional era, as compared to the past, when it was an important means of transmitting traditional symbols and practices. In this way, the processes of detraditionalization tend to diminish the relevance of the old as sources of tradition-based wisdom in postmodern society.

This tendency, however, is countered by the growing sense of many in middle age, who can no longer sustain the illusion of youth, and who have begun to experience the truths of aging: human mortality, fragility, vulnerability, the inherent peril of life, disenchantment with materialism, the realities of love, loss and suffering, the value of kindness, openness and compassion, and the salience of early life memories, especially those of parents and other older relatives and friends. A growing resistance often accompanies these perceptions to purely instrumental values geared to consumerism and materialism.

According to Chris Phillipson (1998), the postmodern society is creating a new definition of what it means to be old:

> . . . in the conditions of advanced modernity, growing old moves from being a collective to an
> individual experience. The notion of an aging society (with social responsibilities) becomes

secondary to the emphasis on aging individuals—the crisis of aging seen to originate in how individuals rather than societies handle the demands associated with social aging. *(Phillipson 1998:119)*

There is no final authority in post-traditional society, including science that is viewed as the foundation of truth and knowledge. Like all other domains of knowledge in late modernity, knowledge claims in science are considered corrigible and subject to constant revision. There may be a greater degree of methodological consensus in science than other fields of inquiry; but, like the rest of postmodern or late-modern life, it has no stable theoretical grounding or set of universal criteria which can assess all knowledge claims.

The individual in post-traditional society increasingly has to decide which expert knowledge to accept, knowing that all knowledge is revisable and subject to a thorough going epistemological skepticism. Trust in knowledge is always provisional and pragmatically given or withdrawn. Many individuals, more or less consciously, appropriate expert knowledge and reconstruct, revise and integrate it to create their own view of the world and sense of self. They use information/knowledge to create their own narratives of the world and their relationship to it—narratives, which are most consistent with their desire to achieve a sense of authenticity. This self-constructed life narrative helps the individual resist the compulsive acceptance of expert knowledge (consumerism) and to protect and valorize their autonomy. The growing importance of autonomously constructed narratives of the self creates the conditions for the proliferation and diversification of cultural perspectives, life style options belief systems, and the eclectic blending of values and behaviors. This trend toward diverse perspectives and openness has major implications for older persons and the retirement experience:

> . . . in relation to retirement as a whole, the scope for decision-making has been drastically widened. Increasingly, people are being called upon to build retirement around their own individual planning, both in relation to finances and the timing and manner in which they leave the workplace. These questions indicate that older age has simultaneously become a major source of 'risk' but also a potential source of 'liberation'. Old age does threaten disaster—poverty, severe illness, the loss of a loved one. But it also can bring the opposite: freedom from restrictive work and domestic roles; new relationships; and a greater feeling of security. People do truly ride a 'juggernaut' in older age, and this is making the period more rather than less central as an issue of concern for social policy.
> *(Phillipson 1998:125)*

This description of the future of retirement might be called "the postmodern dialectic of the new aging experience," which could generate a new synthesis of security (pensions and medical coverage) and freedom. This new synthesis would allow older persons to resist arbitrary closure of "life's journey." New experiences and new identities can be sought and experimented with. Gerontophobes can be challenged creatively across a broad range of social, cultural and political issues. This kind of positive freedom, however, is only available within the new synthesis if based on the security of publicly provided pensions and health care. This is especially the case in minority elderly and women. Postmodern freedom is as dependent on the preservation of Social Security and Medicare, and their enhancements, as it is on cultural openness, individual autonomy, and the other features of the post-traditional society we have discussed here. We will return to this issue, the relationship between security and freedom, in the last section of the paper.

In post-traditional society, reasons have to be given for attitudes and behaviors in the growing absence of tacit assumptions based on widespread acceptance of traditional culture and belief systems. These reasons are increasingly drawn from self-constructed life narratives that open up space for discursive personal relationships and expanded cognitive activity. Individuals bear greater responsibility for articulating their own attitudes, values and behaviors. This need to justify decisions tends to destabilize differentials in power. Power is no longer inherently legitimated by claims on tradition. Rather they are based on revisable expert knowledge and the authority it provides only provisionally. In this context, power differentials are constantly in jeopardy of being dissolved and reconstructed. Power differentials in post-traditional society are increasingly bounded and penetrated by an ethics based on equality. These ethics assume that individual autonomy makes the other as capable and responsible for agency as one's self.

Ronald Inglehart (1997) and his colleagues have been tracking changes in values since the early 1970s in over 25 countries with the use of survey data. In the vast majority of these countries the data indicate movement from materialist to postmaterialist and postmodern values. The shift involves a movement away from values associated with the search for economic security to a growing emphasis on individual autonomy, self-expression, tolerance, human rights, ecological awareness and rejection of institutional and hierarchical authority in all domains. All of these trends are accompanied by a deepening quest for personal meaning and morality, for spiritual development, close affectionate ties with family members and friends, and existential significance in work. Among the many consequences of these changes is:

> . . . a shift away from the overemphasis on instrumental rationality that characterized industrial society, toward a more balanced synthesis of functional rationality and a renewed concern for ultimate ends, in which the pursuit of human well-being and self-expression is a major component.
> *(Inglehart 1997:339)*

In summarizing the overall impact of these changes in values, Ingelhart writes that:

> . . . the publics of advanced industrial societies are moving toward postmodern values and placing increasing emphasis on the quality of life. Empirical evidence from around the world shows that cultural patterns are closely linked with the economic and political characteristics of given societies. The Modernization syndrome is linked with a shift from traditional to rational-legal values; but the emergence of advanced industrial society gives rise to a shift from survival values to postmodern values, in which a variety of changes, from equal rights for women to the emergence of democratic political institutions, become increasingly likely.
> *(Inglehart 1997:339)*

The institutional response to the pursuit of individual autonomy and reflexivity is eroding hierarchical command and control systems throughout society. As it erodes power differentials, it creates greater opportunities for the exercise of autonomy and choice.

Furthermore, the emphasis on autonomy and reflexivity is expanding the scope of ethics in everyday life and making philosophers of us all. We must confront the life and death consequences of our increasingly complex and perplexing technological, cultural and political environments.

These trends toward a post-traditional society, characterized by revisable, contestable expert knowledge, provisional authority, and self-reflexivity, are creating the conditions for the democratization of all forms of social institutions, which must increasingly accommodate individual autonomy as the organizing principle of post-traditional, late modern society. Democratizing processes now operate at every level of society including personal relationships characterized by mutual understanding, intense communication, sensitivity and equality. This democracy of the emotions offers many rewards but also puts relationships under considerable strain. This pressure is not experienced in more traditional societies where the form and substance of relationships are more likely to be inherited than made. The relational pressure in traditional societies tends to arise, to the contrary, from oppressive power relationships.

Democratization is also occurring at the higher levels of institutional life where hierarchy and bureaucratic domination is gradually giving way to continual negotiation among all affected parties. For example, political and professional elites increasingly share decision-making space and authority with social and self-help movements and non-government organizations (NGOs) in the development and response to a widening range of social, political, economic and cultural issues. These movements and groups have their own experts whose knowledge and judgment is frequently contested by their own colleagues who are committed to keeping their organizations as reflexive as possible in response to constantly changing organizational environments. This state of continuous reflexivity and adjustment frustrates the desire for central control and certainty. Members and sympathizers of these loosely structured organizations and groups are agents operating in flexible networks, disembedded from traditions and inflexible, highly structured organizations. Even conventional mainstream political and economic organizations are loosening up. They are becoming more dispersed and flexible as institutional life in general is becoming more fluid and the dualistic models of modernity (autonomy/control, basic/superstructure, culture/economic relations, agency/structure) dissolve with the fading of traditions and their inherited formulaic truths and priests or guardians.

We live, increasingly, in a world shaped by agents, (individuals and groups) of accelerating epistemic change in the cognitive and cultural frames of life. We are moving from the positivistic certainties and technocratic instrumentalism of early modernity toward reflexivity, experimentation, expanding cognitive capacity, cultural openness and complexity, and, of course, individual autonomy. These discursive agents operate in a culture of critical discourse. Further, they create communication societies with competing counter-elites and high levels of contingency. Multiple cultural perspectives are generated by the processes of globalization and detraditionalization. The result is a diffusion of power, and the potential for radical openness. In communication societies, social knowledge and public policy are constructed and deconstructed through a wide range of intersecting and competing networks. These shifting networks are made from relationships that are highly contingent and subject to collapse. This contingency undermines the ability of elites and collective agents to define and control social, political and cultural situations and the policy agenda. This new, emerging reality makes access to the communication apparatus a critical area of conflict. This area will become even more urgently contested in the years ahead as alternative methods, including variants of the internet, are developed just beyond the capacities of corporate organization and governments to control fully.

There is no guarantee that the trends and changes described here under the broad conceptual framework of post-traditional, or postmodern society, will eventually culminate in institutions and cultures that are fundamentally characterized by institutional and individual reflexivity, discursivity, flexibility and openness. Nor is it a certainty that fluctuating networks of power and leveled hierarchies, or that revisable and contested expert knowledge, and a politics and ethics based on unqualified equality and individual autonomy rather than inherited categories and criteria, will prevail. These extensive trends are arrayed against powerful forces, including atavistic nationalism's, religious and ethnic fundamentalism of many kinds, and the drive of transnational corporations to control the global political economy. The probable outcome of this clash of forces over the next several decades will be some unpredictable amalgam, which will not reflect a clear victory for any one side in this complex, multidimensional conflict. It is extremely doubtful, however, that forces associated with the emerging post-traditional society will be vanquished. Currently opposing forces, especially transnational corporations, dependent on information technology, communications, and scientific research are led and staffed by many people who have been deeply influenced by post-traditional values, including self-reflexivity, autonomy, intellectual and cultural openness, methodological skepticism, and an ethics based on equality and self determination.

## TOWARD A POSTMODERN PUBLIC POLICY FOR THE ELDERLY

This brief overview of some of the major tenets of postmodern social theory, or theories of post-traditional societies, is not intended to be comprehensive. Rather, our intention is to use these theoretical tools to identify a few of the more salient trends and changes in Western societies as a prelude to discussing their implications for social policy generally, and policies for the frail elderly in particular. In this section, we will attempt to show that current policies are largely not consistent with our emerging post-traditional society and that this gap will become increasingly evident and difficult to justify as the huge baby-boom generation ages over the next 30 years. This generation is the first to feel the full weight of the change and trends we described in the first section and this influence is likely to effect their expectations of social policy in the future.

The trends and changes caused by the emergence of post-traditional society, and its associated values and behaviors, represent a growing challenge to current social policy. Any effective response to this challenge will require the creation of new conceptual and explanatory frameworks in the development and execution of policies and programs. Frameworks that reflect post-traditional values (autonomy, reflexivity, self-determination, equality) will gain support. Further, perspectives on identity and interpersonal and institutional relationships will take on a postmodern hue in that the need to level power differentials within institutional and organizational contexts will require the dismantling of pejorative binaries embedded in contemporary social policy. These binaries include man/woman, native/foreigner, case manager/client, able/disabled and others that implicitly incorporate assumptions about who has power and who does not. The work of Michael Foucault (1980) on the relationship between knowledge and power is particularly helpful in analyzing the oppressive functions of binary structures, the power relationships they support and the veiled ways in which they are used to exclude groups from the policy development process. Foucault examined how knowledge is used to generate and apply power by the elites, in part by defining what is normal thought and behavior and what is not, and by the use of knowledge/information to create systems of surveillance and disciplinary control. This perspective is easily transferred to social policy discourse. John Gibbens (1998), for example, has noted that:

> Social policy has constructed its own truths and legitimations for its own normalization processes. Deconstruction of the dominant binaries constructed and deployed over recent decades can make way for the invention of alternative, non-binary schemes. Poststructuralism suggests that, in social policy discourse and practice, we should encourage and be prepared to accept more the self-made categories and subjective classification of individuals and groups, such as the practice of 'sexing the self' as a response to the deconstruction and collapse of gender and sex binaries.
> *(Gibbens 1998:42)*

The postmodernist critique of social policy and its underlying binary structure is based on a rejection of many of the fundamental categories of Western through that have dominated thinking about politics and public policy from the enlightenment to the modernisms of the 20th century. More specifically, this critique is based on a rejection of the notion that language directly represents some foundational reality (language is an active agent in the creation of reality(ies), and that knowledge is innocent of power (discourse reflects and often causes oppression), and that any single world view, ideology or knowledge system (metanarrative) is superior (universally valued) to any other that there is an essential human nature.

> If postmodernists reject metanarratives and replace them with multiple narrative disciplines and reject methodological foundationalism and essentialism, so they also reject the ideas of an essential human nature or self; structured lifestyles based on social categorization; and the ideas that values are merely ideological epiphenomena of these primary structure. Rather postmodernists assert that the subject should be seen as essentially decentred or without fixed content; that s/he has few if any fixed, universal or essential characteristics. The self is a multiple personality, with plural, distinct and often conflicting facets and needs, finding expression in ever-changing and highly personalized, eclectic lifestyles, now more usually held together by particular patterns of personalized preferences and values than by the imposition of the dull routine of everyday life or of social-structural and functional necessities. Giddens, Connolly, Taylor and we ourselves have hypothesized that accompanying the 'disembedding' of the self from its traditional social location is a process of the 'reinvention' of the self (Connolly 1991; Giddens 1991a; Taylor 1989). We hypothesize the emergence of new structures of feeling and new patterns of values and preferences amongst western citizens that have an impact on behavior, practices and institutions, including areas considered in social policy
> *(Gibbins and Reimer 1995). (Gibbins 1998:41)*

Abandoning essentialism and foundationalism, binary structures and metanarratives that support the exclusionary normalizing tendencies of conventional social theories and practices, creates space for exploring the diversity, difference and indeterminacy that are inherent in all language, discourse and behavior. In the absence of metanarratives, or grand theories about human behavior designed to generate a consensus around comprehensive controlling social policies, we can begin to recognize the realities of pluralism, fragmentation, diversity of culture and subjective realities, contingency and ambivalence of postmodern life. Gibbins (1998) has noted that:

. . . if social policy has to deal with new selves and groups who are more self-authored, autonomous and assertive, it will need to change its assumptions, aims and practices. . . . How to reconcile the results of the processes of disembedding, pluralisation and empowerment is the problem inherited by postmodern social policy, with which every police force, prison, school, hospital and community must grapple. Changing needs, desires, problems, uncertainties and risks, emerging from the new situations and relationships, also pose immediate challenges.
*(Gibbens 1998:43-44)*

These challenges are also present in the provision of health and long-term care services for older persons.

In responding to these challenges, a new theoretical framework and criteria are needed for the development of social policy:

The outlines of this can be found in various recent texts, which advocate for the future (rather than celebrate the arrival of) the empowerment of citizens: the encouragement of autonomy, self-actualization and expressivism at the individual level; the development of new politics, and new political structures and organizations, such as new social movements, at the group level; the recognition legitimation and support of new types of family, network and lifestyle; the search to craft particular packages of services for particular cases; the prioritizing of particularism (not selectivism) over universalism; the addressing of welfare risks, issues and solution at the global, local and transnational levels; the pluralizing of services; the recognition that a new set of welfare values and principles is needed to deal with a more cosmopolitan and differentiated society; and the exploration of solutions to welfare problems at other levels than and in additional agencies to those of the central and local state.
*(Gibbins 1998:44)*

These are the kind of empowerment-oriented values and realities that should guide the development of postmodern public policies designed to support the new syntheses of security and freedom for older people; they are expansive policies that are flexible enough to be responsive to individual needs and desires. Health and long-term care policies and pension benefits should be universal in scope and particularistic in application.

Chris Phillipson (1998) describes this new synthesis perspective well when he writes that he is not arguing:

. . . for a narrow 'postmodern' view of aging which focuses simply on choice and reflexivity, ignoring the profound inequalities of class, gender and ethnicity which continue to shape the lives of older people. In fact, I wish to draw a middle position between these two: arguing, first for a framework which provides the necessary financial support for older people; but, second, for greater flexibility as regards the way in which older age is allowed to develop within society.
*(Philipson 1998:127)*

In terms of economic security, Phillipson makes the case for a broader, more expansive Social Security system that provides more equal benefits, especially for minorities and women, and that responds to the increasing level of risk experienced by employees in rapidly changing economies across the developed world, including declining private pensions and the growth of pensions based on defined contributions. This means that public pensions should be redesigned to reflect a view of productive activities, such as caregiving, that occur outside the formal marketplace, and that are responsive to the realities of contemporary work, such as multiple entries and exits from formal employment. Flexibility within the occupational system should not come at the price of exclusion from financial provisions for old age.

The new synthesis of the dialectics of aging will require major enhancements in health and long-term care policies in order to expand opportunities for freedom in old age. Out-of-pocket medical expenses under Medicare have grown dramatically over the last 15 years (from 10% to 20%+ of discretionary income) and have put routine medical care beyond the reach of many less affluent older people, especially women. Adding a prescription drug benefit to Medicare would help reduce out-of-pocket costs, but many older people will not have adequate access to healthcare until Medicare copayments and deductibles are substantially reduced and long-term care is made an affordable Medicare benefit. Publicly provided long-term care is now only available to poor Medicaid-eligible elders, the vast majority of whom are in nursing homes. A new synthesis long-term care policy would make care universally available under Medicare (new synthesis: security) and far more flexible than the current Medicaid program. A long-term care policy designed to support the autonomy of impaired elderly persons (new synthesis: freedom) would give them much greater control over the provision of care by allowing them to decide how resources are used. The model of care most compatible with the preservation and nurturing of autonomy under conditions of impairment is consumer-directed care (CDC), which includes allowing consumers to pay their own selected caregivers.

There are multiple strands of postmodern thought, one of which represents a serious threat to the new synthesis (security and freedom) postmodern approach to public policy.

This is celebrationist, Saatchi-style postmodernism, commodified to the gills—regardless of whether the shopping is done in the mall or cyberspace. It sidesteps disparities in wealth just as a group of advertising executives might circumnavigate a homeless beggar on their lunchtime return to the office. In this way it ignores the differential ability of groups to become active consumers and bestows full human status only on those able to choose. Its designation of gender and ethnicity and the like as merely lifestyle choices misses the point that these are also social divisions and still significant sites of inequality. This then is a complacent and selfish postmodernism which, with its hyper-commodification of the cultural realm, serves to exclude the poor just as efficiently as any caste system in history.
*(Carter 1998:21)*

This kind of "celebrationist" postmodernism reduces social, political and public life generally to participation in the market and the citizen to just another consumer whose rights are determined by their power in the market—by their wealth or lack of it. This is a kind of postmodernism that is consistent with neoliberalism and its agenda for privatization of public sector programs and for moving control of tax-funded programs from the public to the private sector where they can be used to generate profits in the name of increased choice and efficiency.

Neoliberal postmodernism is expressly designed to divide the elderly into those who can fully provide for themselves and those who cannot and to dramatically reduce possible support for the latter. According to Gilleard and Higgs (2000):

. . . The relative affluence of occupational and private pension holders separates them out from those older people as primarily welfare benefit recipients. It is the latter group who now constitute the 'problem' of 'old age.' The same dichotomy is played out in relation to health care. Here people are presented with two images; one the physically frail and dependent

'fourth-ager' lacking the necessary 'self-care' skills to sustain a third-age identity, the other the active and health individual producing and consuming his or her 'third age.'
*(Gilleard and Higgs 2000:103-104)*

This is not the progressive postmodern policy agenda that intends to make the capacity to choose and to act autonomously more equal by giving the less affluent greater control over the resources required to meet needs and achieve desires—to experience the freedom and creativity of a postmodern culture on a more equal basis with the affluent by diminishing the power of the market to determine "life options" in old age.

## CONCLUSION

The flexible, reflexive, self-creating lives of many middle-age members of the baby boom generation will change the aging experience over the next 30 years. However, there must be a parallel effort to retain and enhance the security provisions (Social Security and Medicare) of the new synthesis for minorities and women. There must also be vigilance, lest the promise of greater freedom inherent in progressive postmodernism becomes lost in some future culture war or undermined by a diminution of social welfare provisions (security). Social Security and Medicare have greatly increased economic security among older people. These two programs have created the necessary conditions for a new synthesis of aging experiences. This synthesis includes the freedom of a postmodern culture that offers more opportunities for multiple, diverse and creative narratives of the self and personal meaning. Public policies should be redesigned to provide more support for this kind of postmodern aging through greater flexibility and responsiveness to individual needs and desires. This approach, however, is antithetical to neoliberal policies of cutting and privatizing welfare programs and reducing choice to what individuals can afford to consume through the private market, which makes personal meaning a product of individual consumption.

The struggle between progressive and neoliberal postmodernism over the future of public policy for the elderly is likely to play a major role in shaping the direction of American politics for the next several decades and the aging experience of the baby boom generation. The future of Social Security and Medicare has already been placed in great jeopardy by the emergence of huge long-term deficits in the federal budget and the possibility of large, continuing increases in military spending necessary to sustain a long, open-ended war against terrorists and tyrants. These developments could undermine the new synthesis of freedom and security in old age and create the economic, cultural and political conditions for the neoliberal dismantling of health and economic security programs for the elderly as well as others. This would leave baby boomers and later generations with their market-dependent private pensions and privately purchased health insurance. This is not a prescription for freedom, creativity and personal fulfillment in old age for most people.

## REFERENCES

Carter, J. 1998. "Studying social policy after modernity." pp. 15-30 in *Postmodernity And The Fragmentation Of Welfare*, edited by J. Carter. New York: Routledge.
Foucault, M. 1980. *Power/knowledge: Selected Interviews*. Brighton: Harvester Press.

Gibbins, J. 1998. "Postmodernism, poststructuralism and social policy." pp. 31-48 in *Postmodernity And The Fragmentation Of Welfare*, edited by J. Carter. New York: Routledge.

Giddens, A. 1994. Living in a post-traditional society. pp. 56-109 In *Reflexive Modernization: Politics, Tradition And Aesthetics In The Modern Social Order,* edited by U. Beck, A. Giddens & S. Lash. Stanford: Stanford University Press.

Gilleard, C. & Higgs, P. 2000. *Cultures Of Ageing: Self, Citizen And The Body.* London: Pearson.

Inglehart, R. 1997. *Modernization And Postmodernization: Cultural, Economic, And Political Change In 43 Societies.* Princeton: Princeton University Press.

Joyner, R. 2002. Congressional budget battle centers on older Americans. *The New York Times.* January 21. *http://www.nytimes.com/2002/01/21/politics/21/EDLE.html.*

Lash, S. 1994. Reflexivity and its doubles: Structure, aesthetics, community. pp. 110-173 in *Reflexive Modernization: Politics, Tradition And Aesthetics In The Modern Social Order,* edited by U. Beck, A. Giddens & S. Lash. Stanford: Stanford University Press.

Phillipson, C. 1998. *Reconstructing Old Age: New Agendas In Social Theory And Practice.* Thousand Oaks: Sage.

# Chapter 2

# RISK, SOCIAL WELFARE AND OLD AGE

*Chris Phillipson*
Ph.D, University of Keele, UK
*Jason L. Powell*
Ph.D, University of Liverpool, UK

## ABSTRACT

This chapter examines the concept of risk as applied to an understanding of the nature and changing relationship between social welfare and old age in the United Kingdom. We begin by drawing on the sociological work of Ulrich Beck (1992) in order to examine how changes in late modernity have led to what has been coined the 'risk society'. The chapter then assesses historical narratives of social welfare, which positioned older people as 'dependent' individuals and groups in society. We move our attention to examining neo-liberalism in contemporary times as a key feature of the 'risk society' and the recasting of the state, welfare agents and older people. In particular, we observe the rise of managerialism and consumer narratives that are central to neo-liberalism and management of social welfare yet is indicative of the 'risk' society. We conclude by arguing for an interface between risk and critical gerontology. A critical ontodly of risk illuminates the challenges and opportunities afforded to older people in terms of identity performance in welfare policy spaces.

## INTRODUCTION

This chapter analyses the concept of 'risk', which both as a theoretical tool and dimension of modern society, is slowly being developed within the social sciences (Delanty, 1999). Notwithstanding this, the concept of risk and the meaning and implications associated with it, have not been fully explored in relation to critical gerontology. Risk is shrouded in historical and contemporary political debate about whose 'role' and 'responsibility' is it for welfare provision in society –does it reside with the state or the individual? Or some combination of the state, the family and the individual older person? The historical responsibility for the protection and security of older individuals and aging populations gradually shifted towards that of the state, famously epitomized in the United Kingdom by William Beveridge's "cradle to the grave" welfare protectionism of 'dependent' people

(Leonard 1997). In contemporary times, however, this approach has changed with the move from state protectionism to individual responsibility. The shift from protection *of* the individual to self-protection *by* the individual has been claimed to be illustrative of the phenomena of the 'risk society' (Beck 1992). Such a society has been defined in terms of the erosion of traditional values (Giddens 1991) and the desire to allocate accountability and responsibility for personal or social actions (Beck 1992; Delanty 1999; Giddens 1991). Ideas associated with the 'risk society' have, it might be argued, become part of the organizing ground of how we define and organize the 'personal' and 'social spaces' in which to grow old. In what follows we explore this idea both for understanding agency in later life, and for further developing the aims and objectives of a critical gerontology (Minkler and Estes 1998)

The chapter begins by examining some of the arguments put forward by Ulrich Beck (1992) and the relevance of these for understanding how changes in modern society have shaped the welfare identities of older people. To illustrate this, the chapter reviews the historical rise and consolidation of social welfare in the United Kingdom. We assess how risk has impinged on changing forms and modern practices of the 'welfare state'. From this, we trace the welfare transformations to what can be defined as the 'risk society' (Beck 1992) and the impact of this on identity in later life and key areas such as the relationship of older people to the state (Biggs 1999).

The chapter then moves to assessing neo-liberalism as a key feature of the 'risk society' and the re-positioning of older people as 'consumers' and welfare agents as 'managers'. We then evaluate the implications of neo-liberal social policy for older people and professional practices by using the 'risk' framework derived from the work of Beck (1992).

## TRANSFORMING OLD AGE

As a starting point we should note the dramatic change in the institutional structure that has underpinned definitions of age and aging identities. In this context it is important to highlight the way in which old age was transformed in the two decades following the ending of the Second World War (Phillipson 1998). The key development here concerned the way in which, in advanced capitalist societies, growing old was transformed by the social and economic institutions associated with the welfare state, mandatory retirement and inter-generational relationships. These became crucial in shaping the dominant discourse around which aging was framed, and the identities associated with old age. A supporting theme was the re-ordering of the life course into distinctive stages associated with education, work and retirement, with transition to retirement becoming an important element in the development of a new identity separate from that associated with work and paid employment (Best 1980). A final element concerned the role played by health and social services for older people as a symbol of the move to a more civilized society.

On this last element, the debate in the 1940s and 1950s focused on the need to escape the injustice and deprivation endured in the economic depression of the 1930s. Hence, what has been described by historian of social policy Rodney Lowe as the role of the welfare state in moving society to a higher ethical ground. Lowe (1993: 21) suggests in fact that the welfare state was seen as being able to '...elevate society by institutionalising a deeper sense of community and mutual care'.

Older people were integral to this theme of a more inclusive society, one seeking to erase the link between old age and images of poverty and decrepitude. Of course the transformation associated with the post-war welfare state is easy to exaggerate. Beveridge's strictures about avoiding the 'extravagance [of] giving a full subsistence income to every citizen, as a birthday present on his or her reaching the age of 60 or 65' (cited in Macnicol 1998: 381) were taken to heart by most governments (most especially from 1979 onwards). The legacy of the poor law could also still be found in warehouse-like residential and long-stay homes, described to devastating effect by Peter Townsend (1962) in *The Last Refuge*. And older people were the largest single group of those 'rediscovered' as living in poverty in the early 1960s, although governments (abetted by civil servants) were in denial for some time that this could possibly be the case (Townsend and Wedderburn 1965). But the possibility of transforming old age, through more secure provision of health and income, was a significant component of the post-war social contract. Care for older people was viewed, first, as a fair exchange for past work and services (with the sacrifices association with the war still a vital part of folk memory). Second, in evolutionary terms, as a measure of the way in which people were now protected from the hazards of the life course. Third, as part of the intergenerational contract and indicative of the close ties maintained between family groups (Arber and Attias-Donfut 2000).

If the welfare state created -or set out to create- a new identity for old age, it was the transformation in welfare from the 1980s onwards which posed a new challenge to the status and identity of older people. The crisis in aging that took hold from this period reflected, to a significant degree, the loosening of the institutional supports underpinning the life course. Older people were themselves the creation of modernity, reflecting the achievements of industrialism, improved public health and the growth of social welfare (Thane 2000). The steady growth in the proportion of older people in the population was, up until the beginning of the 1980s, largely contained within the dual institutions of retirement and the welfare state.

These, along with the ties maintained between generations, created a social, economic and moral space within which growing numbers of older people could be channeled and contained. In this regard, John Myles' (1984) argument that the welfare state was predominantly a welfare state 'for older people' may be seen as accurate in at least two senses: first, in terms of the way that resources were distributed; second, in relation to the identities and forms of surveillance created. For a period of 20 years or more, moving older people into the zone of retirement and the welfare state, held at bay the underlying issue of securing a place and identity for aging within the framework of an advanced capitalist society. The meaning of later life was, temporarily at least, constructed out of a modernist vision where retirement and welfare were viewed as natural end-points to the human life cycle.

The unraveling of these arrangements can be traced to at least three types of crisis affecting the management of aging populations in the last quarter of the twentieth century: economic, social and cultural. The economic dimension has been well rehearsed, with successive crises from the mid-1970s onwards undermining, first, the goal of full employment and hence destabilizing retirement, and, second, the fiscal basis of the welfare state accelerated with the onset of a privatization from the 1980s onwards (Estes *et al.* 2001).

These aspects led to the development in the social sphere of what Carroll Estes and associates (2001) refer to as the 'crisis construction' and 'crisis management' of aging, with old age now socially constructed as a burden and problem for society (Vincent 1999). At its most extreme, demographic change was itself now viewed as a source of the economic crisis, notably in respect of the apparent imbalance between 'productive' and 'non-productive' sectors in the economy (Longman 1987). Finally, at a cultural level, the modern life course itself came to be viewed as playing a contributory role in the alienation of older people in western society. The cultural historian Thomas Cole (1992: 241) defined the problem as follows:

> The ideal of a society legitimately ordered by the divisions of a human lifetime is now under siege in large part because its view of old age is neither socially nor spiritually adequate and because the social meanings of life's stages are in great flux. Recent critiques of aging in the modern life course have also reflected a dawning awareness that aging is much more than a problem to be solved. In some quarters it is becoming clear that accumulating health and wealth through the rationalized control of the body is an impoverished vision of what it means to live a life.

The sense of unease about the nature of demographic change itself chimed in with a wider discourse about tensions accompanying the transition from a modern to a postmodern world (Conrad 1992). Uncertainties about the benefits of aging are certainly nothing new. Revisionist accounts of the place of older people in past societies have tended to emphasis the punitive character of economic relief, and the marginalization of those lacking gainful employment (Stearns 1977; Macnicol 1998). Both aspects may be found as significant elements in present-day society, for example in the undermining of state pension provision and the assault on retirement amidst fears of 'too few workers' over an 'excess' of pensioners (Vincent 1999). But these historical continuities are given added emphasis in a postmodern age.

Arguably, older people have the most to lose given the restructuring of relationships associated with postmodernity. The extension of individualization may, to take one example, be perceived as highly threatening to identity in the last phase of the life-course. As Biggs (1993) argues, modern life raises at least two possibilities: the promise of a multiplicity of identities on the one side, and the danger of psychological disintegration on the other. Biggs suggests that in response to these circumstances, individual actors will attempt to find socially constructed spaces that lend some form of predictability to everyday relationships. Yet in a postmodern world such spaces may be increasingly difficult to locate.

## FROM WELFARE STATE TO RISK SOCIETY

From the 1980s onwards, the crisis affecting retirement and aging illustrated the way that the problem of social marginality among the old had been contained rather than resolved in the post-war period. Moreover, what a postmodern setting did have to offer -namely the ideal of consumption replacing that of production- seemed only to further marginalize groups such as older people. Bauman, for example, writes of the accelerating emancipation of capital from labor producing a situation where: 'instead of engaging the rest of society in the role of producers, capital tends to engage them in the role of consumers' (Bauman 1992: 111). This transformation in fact reflects a more general shift from the public provision characteristic of what Lash and Urry (1987) refer to as 'organized capitalism', to the more flexible arrangements running though the period of 'disorganized capitalism'.

This development has served to change once again the definition of what it means to be an older person. In the conditions of advanced modernity, growing old moves from being a collective to an individual experience and responsibility. The notion of an aging society with social obligations becomes secondary to the emphasis on the way in which families and individuals handle the demands associated with population aging.

This new development may be seen as a characteristic of a society where the 'social production of risk' runs alongside that associated with the 'social production of wealth' (Beck 1992). As already argued, improved life expectancy may itself be viewed as a consequence of the social transformations associated with modernization. Beck (1992: 21) defines the nature of risk as a *'systematic way of dealing with hazards and insecurities induced and introduced by modernization itself'* (author's emphasis). Of course, older people have been ever present in human history, in roles such as patriarch, beggar, supplicant for poor relief, or grieving widow. But to paraphrase Beck, in the past these could be seen as personal rather than societal tragedies. The impact of older people was limited both by their lack of demographic presence and, crucially, by the relatively superficial nature of the category of 'pensioner' or 'elderly person'. The changes consequent upon modernization transformed both these elements, with aging becoming a new and socially recognized risk.

But in line with Beck's thesis about the nature of risk society are three main developments running through aging populations. First, the globalization of aging is increasingly recognized-all societies (poor as well as rich) are undergoing similar population transformations (albeit with notable exceptions such as those in countries devastated by the AIDS virus). Aging thus becomes simultaneously both a biographical event and one shared with different cultures and societies across the globe (Estes, Biggs, and Phillipson, 2003).

Second, aging experiences are themselves hugely and increasingly diverse. Under the guise of the welfare state, growing old was compressed into a fairly limited range of institutions and identities notably in respect of income and lifestyles. Aging in the post-welfare society, however, has substantially expanded in respect of social opportunities as well as new inequalities and divisions (Gilleard and Higgs 2000; Vincent 1995).

Third, old age is also being changed by what Beck (1992) describes as the era of reflexive modernization. This may be conceived in terms of how individuals and the lay public exert control and influence on the shape and character of modernity. At its core, Beck's (1992: 10) approach suggests the thesis that: '...the more societies are modernized, the more agents (subjects) acquire the ability to reflect upon the social conditions of their existence and to change them in that way'. For older people, this highlights the move from conditions of structured dependency towards the possibility of new, consumer-based lifestyles. On the other hand, this almost certainly goes hand-in-hand with the marginalization of significant groups of older people, trapped in the contradiction between decreasing personal incomes (notably pensions and savings) and the steady withdrawal of support from the state.

These developments confirm the seriousness of the challenge facing older people. In reality in terms of their social position, the old have moved into a new 'zone of indeterminacy' which is marginal to work and welfare. Elderly people experience the world truly as though they were riding (as Giddens 1991:28, expresses it in his description of high modernity) a 'juggernaut': '...it is not just that more or less continuous and profound processes of change occur; rather, change does not consistently conform either to human expectation, or to human control'. This may seem a relatively abstract description of the crisis, which older people may experience but it rather accurately conveys the reality of what may happen to older people in situations of rapid change.

## RISK, SELF-AUTONOMIZATION AND MANAGING OLD AGE: A POST-WELFARE SOCIETY?

Growing old is itself becoming a more social, reflexive and managed process, notably in the relationships between the individual, the state and a range of public as well as private services; this involves the 'political domain'. Coupled with this, processes and relationships in the management of old age are decided by political rationalities (neo-liberalism) that are bound up with ideological and philosophical questions of self-governance and autonomy. Neo-liberalism considers that a welfare society must reflect only the interplay of social and political structures forged out of self-responsibility and consumerism (Leonard 1997; Powell 2001). In recent years, older people as *autonomous* consumers derive their 'care', individually and collectively, from a range of social policies, institutions and sites, so that the organization of care involves market forces, families, and state and care institutions.

The neo-liberal dominance in social policy has been successful because it has identified existential concepts such as self-responsibility; self-governance and self-care that are said to facilitate human action (Leonard 1997). The regulation of personal conduct has shifted from being presented as a responsibility of the state to the responsibility of micro-level social actors such as 'professional experts' and 'older people' as 'consumers' (Biggs 1999). The implications are profound. As Nikolas Rose (1996: 59-60) has pointed out:

> '... the disadvantaged individual has come to be seen as potentially and ideally an active agent in the fabrication of their own existence. Those 'excluded' from the benefits of a life of choice and self-fulfillment are no longer merely the passive support of a set of social determinations: they are people whose self-responsibility aspirations have been deformed by the dependency culture, whose efforts at self-advancement have been frustrated... they are to be assisted as active citizens [through] programs of empowerment to enable them to assume their rightful place as the self-actualizing and demanding subjects of an 'advanced' liberal democracy'.

Here neo-liberalism attempts to define the social policy domain to interpret valid human needs. Under neo-liberalism, the state re-invents itself and its welfare subjects based upon minimal intervention and regulation via a rolling program of privatization, deregulation, and contraction of welfare services (Estes and associates, 2001). Within the 'mixed economy of welfare', there has been the social construction of a market- orientated, consumer-based approach to the delivery of care and the role of older people as consumers. As Leonard (1997) claims the neo-liberal state is being reorganized to include retention of a strong centre to formulate policy but the dissemination of responsibility for policy implementation to managerial regimes. As Gordon (1991: 36) points out:

> 'The fulfillment of the liberal idea ... is a recasting of the interface between the state and society to one of market order. It becomes the ambition of neo-liberalism to implicate individuals as players into the market game administered by managerial actors'.

Care management as an administrative power (cf. Habermas 1992) has been presented as consolidating neo-liberalism by adding 'choice' and reducing 'risks' and 'problems' associated with aging. Biggs and Powell (2000) suggest that care management UK-style can be conceptualized as the co-ordination of welfare services for consumers. The pivotal function of the care manager is seen as being the management of welfare for older clients that draws on services made available through a 'mixed economy of welfare'; a move away from the state as care giver for welfare subjects from "cradle to the grave" to a managerial one of "monitoring" and "assessment" in neo-liberal contract culture. Biggs and Powell (2000) claim:

> 'Care management 'makes sense' as a means of managing a 'mixed economy of welfare' which requires that those who purchase care, or their agents, are separated from those who provide it. Because of the intensification of marketization, this limits the development of cartels, allows purchasers to choose between competing alternatives, thus placing them in the role of 'honest brokers' who assess need, supply information on the alternatives and then co-ordinate purchases. It does not, however, make sense in terms of direct care, intervention or interaction between older people and social workers other than as a sort of 'professional travel agency', advising clientele on the options, best deals and cash options'
> (Biggs and Powell 2000: 46).

The movement away from the traditional counselor role of 'helping professional' to an actuarial role of 'care management' is a feature of the risk society – "helping professions" have had their knowledge base transformed from philanthropic 'caregiver' and 'helper' to 'manager' of budgets, audits and accounting systems (Powell 2001). In addition, older people are the majority group receiving care from the state (Biggs 1999); it would seem unlikely, then, if changes in social policy and professional welfare identity had not been accompanied by changing neo-liberal discourses of aging linked to consumerism and self-autonomization (Biggs 1999; Powell 2001).

In neo-liberal welfare reform, the rise of the care manager as an "expert" has marked a fundamental shift from the social work practitioner to a consolidated managerial role and occupational identity. In emergent neo-liberal managerial regimes, judgement is increasingly bound up with managerial imperatives concerning risk assessment, corporate objectives, purchasing and resource control (Powell 2001). The devolution of managerial responsibilities is intended to empower individuals and to constrain professional autonomy by having such care managers internalize budgetary disciplines and translate social policy imperatives (Leonard 1997).

These imperatives have had a major impact upon social policy and old age. Such neo-liberal reforms were about recasting older people as consumers in a market place to be managed by care managers (Powell 2001; cf. Habermas 1992). Care managers as an administrative power are also 'risk-assessors' and 'enforcers' of the mixed welfare economy, a discourse that leaves older people who engage in the 'care market', on the contradictory and "risky" ground of being simultaneously 'consumers' and potential 'victims' (Biggs and Powell 2001; Powell and Biggs 2000).

Powell (2001) argues that neo-liberalism consistently equates self-responsibility with freedom, with older people presented as active agents in a consumer market. However, divisions associated with class, gender and ethnic position may still leave many poorer older people highly vulnerable - despite the neo-liberal vision of the 'responsible consumer'. Gendered inequalities may be especially important in this scenario. As Nancy Fraser suggests:

'Participants in the 'masculine' subsystem are positioned as *right bearing beneficiaries* and *purchasing consumers of services*. Participants in the 'feminine' subsystem, on the other hand, are positioned as *dependent* clients'
*(1987: 113).*

Further, Biggs and Powell (2001: 110) raise critical questions about the relationship between old age, neo-liberalism and new sources of oppression associated with the risk society:

'Those who do not conform to the utopian dream appear to have been shunted into a non - participative discourse, bounded by professional surveillance or the more palatable yet closely related discourse of "monitoring". In both cases, it could be suggested that a discourse on dependency has been supplemented, and in some cases replaced, by a discourse on risk. The risk of giving in to an aging body, the risk of thereby being excluded from one's retirement community, the risk of being too poor to maintain a consumer lifestyle, the risk of being excluded from participation through incapacity that has been externally assessed, the risk of being abused, the risk of control being taken out of one's hands, and the risk of tokenism in partnership".

## CONCLUSION

By constituting risk as a centrally defining motif of "late modernity" this chapter contributes to new perspective for 'critical gerontology'. This chapter has raised questions about the historical and contemporary understanding of social forces that are an important qualification in understanding the shifting discourses associated with the transformation from the welfare state to the risk society. Older people it might be argued are affected by two major changes in respect of access to support on the one side, and the construction of identity on the other. On the one side, there is the creation of what Estes and others describe as 'no care' zones where community supports may disintegrate in the face of inadequate services and benefits. On the other side, there may equally be the emergence of 'No Identity Zones', these reflecting the absence of spaces in which to construct a viable identity for later life (Phillipson and Biggs 1999).

Older people are now experiencing the argument here is that marginality in a new and somewhat distinctive way. Marginality, for much of the post-war period, could be reclaimed through identities constructed out of an emerging consensus regarding retirement and the welfare state. The collapse of this consensus has exposed once again the vulnerable status of older people. But this vulnerability is not just about the material experience of deprivation; it also reaches into the texture of day-to-day living. For more affluent groups, a temporary solution seems to have been found in the denial of aging and the promotion of new lifestyles. Thus, cushioned from the slights of youth, poverty and frailty, the search for identity may appear as a struggle with bodily betrayal that evaporates with further consumption. However, the social and existential vacuum, which this suggests, reinforces the sense of uncertainty about the identity of older people. The great advantage of the loosening of 'welfarist' notions of age lies in the *possibility* of an alternative social and political construction of old age beginning to emerge which might move beyond traditional welfare structures based on assumptions of dependency (Townsend 1981). This new politics would present a challenge to the constraints placed upon late life development and opportunities for meaningful agency without losing sight of the social threats posed by new forms of risk and insecurity.

# REFERENCES

Arber, S. and Attias-Donfut C., 2000. *The Myth of Generational Conflict*. London: Routledge.

Bauman, Z., 1992. *Intimations of Postmodernity*. London: Routledge & Kegan Paul.

Beck, U., 1992. *Risk Society*. London: Sage.

Best, F., 1980. *Flexible Life Scheduling*. New York: Praeger.

Biggs, S. 1999. *The Mature Imagination*. Milton Keynes: OUP.

Biggs, S. and Powell, J.L. 2000. "Sureveillance and Elder Abuse: The Rationalities and Technologies of Community Care", *Journal of Contemporary Health*, 4: 43-49.

Biggs, S. and Powell, J.L. 2001. "A Foucauldian Analysis of Old Age and the Power of Social Welfare", *Journal of Aging & Social Policy* 12: 93-111.

Delanty, G. 1999. *Social Science: Beyond Constructivism*, Sage: London.

Department of Health, 1989. *Caring for People: Community Care in the next Decade and Beyond,* Cmnd. 849. London: HMSO.

Department of Health, 1994. *NHS Hospital Activity Statistics: England 1983-94 - Statistical Bulletin.* London: Department of Health.

Estes, C. and Associates, 2001. *Social Policy and Aging*. Thousand Oaks: Sage Books.

Estes, C., Biggs, S. and Phillipson, C. 2003. *Social Theory, Social Policy and Aging*. Buckingham: Open University Press.

Fraser, N. 1987. "Women, welfare and the politics of need interpretation", *Hytapia: A Journal of Feminist Philosophy*, 2: 102-121.

Giddens, A., 1991. *The Consequences of Modernity*. Oxford: Polity Press.

Gilleard, C., and Higgs, P., 2000. *Cultures of Aging: self, citizen and the body*. London: Prentice-Hall.

Gordon, C 1991. "Governmental rationality: an introduction", Pp.1-51 in G. Burchell, C. Gordon and P.Miller (editors) *The Foucault Effect: Studies In Governmentality*, Chicago: Chicago University Press.

Habermas, J. 1992. *Postmetaphysical Thinking*, Cambridge: Polity Press.

Leonard, P., 1997. *Postmodern Welfare*. London: Sage.

Lowe, R., 1993. *The Welfare State in Britain since 1945*. London: Macmillan.

Macnicol, J., 1998. *The Politics of Retirement in Britain*, 1878-1948. Cambridge: Cambridge University Press.

Minkler, M and Estes, C. (eds.). 1998. *Critical Gerontology: Perspectives from Political and Moral Economy*. New York: Baywood.

Otway, H., B. Wynne, 1989. *Risk Communication: Paradigm and Paradox, Risk Analysis*, 9: 141-145.

Phillipson, C. 1998. *Reconstructing Old Age*, London: Sage Books.

Phillipson, C. and Biggs, S. 1999. "Population Ageing: critical gerontology and the sociological tradition". *Education and Ageing,* 14: 159-170.

Powell, J.L. 2001. "Theorizing Gerontology: The Case of Old Age, Professional Power and Social Policy in the United Kingdom", *Journal of Aging & Identity*, 6: 117-135.

Powell, J.L. and Biggs, S. 2000. "Managing Old Age: The Disciplinary Web of Power, Surveillance and Normalisation", *Journal of Aging and Identity*, 5: 3-13.

Rose, N. 1996. "Governing advanced liberal democracies". Pp.37-64 in Barry, A, Osborne, T., and Rose, N. (editors) *Foucault and Political Reason*, Chicago: Chicago University Press.

Stearns, P., 1977. *Old Age in European Society: The Case of France*. London: Croom Helm.

Thane, P., 2000. *Old Age in English History: Past Experiences, Present Issues*. Oxford: Oxford University Press.

Townsend, P. and Wedderburn D., 1965. *The Aged in the Welfare State*. London: Bell.

Townsend, P., 1981. "The structured dependency of the elderly: the creation of social policy in the twentieth century", *Ageing and Society,* 1: 5-28.

Vincent, J., 1995. *Inequality of Old Age*. London: UCL Press.

Vincent, J., 1999. *Politics, Power and Old Age*. Buckingham: Open University Press.

Wynne, B., 1987. *Risk Management and Hazardous Waste*. Berlin: Springer.

# PART 2.
## STRUCTURES AND AGENCY

*Chapter 3*

# STRUCTURE AND AGENCY IN LATE-LIFE LEARNING

## *Harry R. Moody*

## ABSTRACT

The practice of older adult education opens up questions about the relation between structure and agency in late-life learning. These questions are illuminated by a close examination of two internationally successful programs: Elderhostel and Universities of the Third Age. Elderhostel, originating in the USA, combines local initiative with a large nonprofit market system to connect older learners with education and travel opportunities. Universities of the Third Age (U3A), originating in Europe, are local mutual-aid groups where retired people are inspired by goals of lifelong learning. Despite different structural arrangements, Elderhostel and U3A exhibit common forms of agency-oriented learning in the tradition of the liberal arts. Neither program has been successful at attracting older people of limited educational backgrounds, but both programs do offer important lessons for adult education and aging policy in the 21st century. To date both Elderhostel and U3A have remained marginal to the social or educational planners. But as forms of older adult education become more popular, they will face the challenge of resisting forces of bureaucratization and commodification: the challenge of remaining true to their own best traditions of self-initiated learning in the later years.

## INTRODUCTION

In the past quarter century, an entirely new kind of education has come into being: called, variously, older adult education, late-life learning, and education for the third age (Fischer et al 1992). Though it arose inside higher education, those same educational institutions have paid little attention to it. In both Europe and America, older adult education has been almost entirely neglected by policy-makers, administrators, and the official voices concerned with education and welfare of the older population. In short, late-life learning, even as it has grown in scale, has remained marginal, even invisible from the standpoint of "official" systems of understanding and control.

This marginality has been a mixed blessing: it has prevented late-life learning from being absorbed under the hegemony of the official educational establishment, including the ascendant ideology of "lifelong learning" promulgated in OECD circles. Being marginal has prevented those who control education from expanding that sphere of control to include the last stage of life. Marginality has inadvertently protected the life-world of late-life learning and permitted older adult education to be free and experimental. Consider, for example, the plurality of courses and programs under the framework of "Universities of the Third Age" or variety of courses in the Elderhostel program.

But there is also a negative side to the neglect and marginality of older adult education. Education for the third age has remained underfunded and has been subject to a lower level of research or documentation than education earlier in the life-course. Perhaps the most negative consequence for the neglect of older adult education has been for the field of gerontology itself. A whole range of issues-- from cognitive changes with aging to the social-structural determinants of the life-course itself-- are illuminated by study of older adult education. As proponents of "critical gerontology" have argued, the dominant paradigms of gerontology remain biomedical model and the social problems approach. We still tend to think of the last stage of life in terms of loss and deficit, hardly ever in terms of freedom or wisdom. Education for the third age, if it were taken seriously by the dominant approach to gerontology, would help to widen our sense of what is possible for human beings in the last stage of life.

In approaching education in later life-- in the period of retirement-- there has been a tendency to reify "retirement" as a simple structural definition of role-- or perhaps to think of it as a "roleless role." Departure from the workforce becomes the dominant factor in understanding retirement. But this characterization unduly privileges structure over individual agency in thinking about both retirement and late-life learning. Indeed, the very categories of economic discourse-- work versus leisure, production versus consumption-- invoke structural elements that may **not** be helpful in illuminating what happens in older adult education. As the life-course itself has become more fragmented and less predictable, the structural boundaries between "work" and "retirement" become less clear. A "postmodern life course" would seem to open greater possibilities for diversity and individual differences, and perhaps for a heightened sense of personal agency (Manheimer 1998).

How far can emphasis on personal agency take us in understanding learning and education in later life? In the current discussion, it will be helpful to look at older adult **education**, which is a more institutionally organized process than, say, "lifelong learning" or "late-life learning." Learning can take place in unstructured ways: for example, through mass media, in libraries and cultural institutions, and from informal interaction, including, increasingly, the Internet. Indeed, some advocates of lifelong learning celebrate such relatively unstructured forms of learning as a triumph of agency and "self-directed learning."

By contrast, the term "education" does imply structure of some kind, as we shall see. In any enterprise we might appropriately call "education" we will not be surprised to find classrooms, teachers, instructional objectives, and so on, not to mention enrollment procedures, class scheduling, financing arrangements, and so on. Structural features of this kind are found, in greater or less degrees, in both Elderhostel and University of the Third Age, to cite two forms of older adult education.

In this chapter we will look at these two different forms of older adult education in the liberal arts. The first, Elderhostel, a national and international organization devoted to retirement education and travel. The second is university-based education that includes both "Universities of the Third Age (U3A)," which have flourished mainly in Europe, and "Learning in Retirement Institutes" in the USA. The University of the Third Age Program based in Cambridge, UK, has been the subject of an illuminating qualitative research study by anthropologist Haim Hazan, summarized in *From First Principles* (1996). In the discussion that follows I draw heavily on Hazan's research, as well as other published accounts of the Universities of the Third Age. I also draw on my own experience over the past twenty years as a teacher, campus coordinator, and member of the Board of Directors of the Elderhostel organization.

Elderhostel and the University of the Third Age represent two very different structures in which late-life learning can flourish. Elderhostel, though legally a not-for-profit organization, is operates on a free market model, which is very different from the pattern of higher education in most countries. The Universities of the Third Age, along with Learning in Retirement Institutes in the USA, are based on a mutual-aid model that largely bypasses the marketplace and provides a very informal approach to teaching and learning for retired persons. Given the very different structural characteristics of these two models, we will want to consider the question "What is the role of structure and personal agency in late-life learning in these two different structural settings?" An answer can be offered when we understand in more detail what Elderhostel and the U3A are like in their actual practice.

## ELDERHOSTEL

Elderhostel was founded in 1975 by Marty Knowlton, a social activist and educator, and David Bianco, Director of Residential Life at the University of New Hampshire in the USA. Elderhostel began as an effort to provide late-life learning opportunities by using low-cost summer dormitory facilities at the university, in keeping with what Bowen called the "economics of unused capacity." For over 25 years Elderhostel has retained the same form adopted at its beginning. Elderhostel programs in the USA are typically 6 days long, with 3 classes each day, drawing on subjects from the liberal arts, broadly understood. There are no tests, grades, or other requirements of conventional education. International Elderhostel programs are typically longer, usually up to three weeks, and may involve more travel. Whether domestic or international, formal classes in Elderhostel are complemented by field trips and cultural events to take advantage of the local environment.

Elderhostel's growth has been extraordinary. The program grew from 220 participants in 1975 to 20,000 five years later (Mills 1993). By the year 2000, Elderhostel was enrolling nearly 250,000 participants each year and had become the largest education-travel program in the world. Despite growth, Elderhostel has retained most elements of the original learning plan: a week or two of organized but informal learning activities sponsored by a host institution (college or university, and increasingly, environmental center, national park, museum, and so on). The national and international Elderhostel network is administered by a nonprofit organization headquartered in Boston.

Both structure and agency have been critical elements in the evolution of Elderhostel. Maintaining a stable structure and commitment to informal, agency-oriented learning has conferred huge advantages on Elderhostel. On the one hand, Elderhostel operates as a franchise, and the term "Elderhostel" is a legally registered trademark. However, the actual functioning of an Elderhostel program is as far from a commercial franchise (e.g., MacDonald's) as one could imagine. Instead of a predictable, cookie-cutter approach to educational offerings, Elderhostel has insisted only on a few essential requirements-- 3 formal class meetings each day, liberal arts orientation, absence of grades or other elements of conventional education, and all costs kept to a minimum. Beyond these elements of quality control, local providers are free to innovate and create programs that reflect local interest and variety. Elderhostel, in effect, is a large-scale enrollment system bringing a wide audience to programs that are locally inspired and created. It is a successful example of the slogan "Think globally, act locally."

Who are the participants in Elderhostel programs? Research shows that their average age is 70 (Culbertson 1997). Nearly two-thirds are female and a similar proportion are college graduates, making the Elderhostel population an elite group. More than half of Elderhostelers have attended graduate school, they tend to be in excellent health, and their average income is comparable to "Gold Card" members of American Express. Further, we must note that, despite its global reach-- Elderhostel now has programs in over 60 countries around the world-- it remains an American enterprise. Almost exclusively, Elderhostel enrolls U.S. citizens for both its domestic and international programs. For the most part, it does not bring non-Americans to programs in the U.S. Nor have other countries created older adult education programs on the model of Elderhostel.

## Motivations for Learning

Why has Elderhostel grown so dramatically? The program, from its inception, has spent virtually nothing on advertising or marketing, relying entirely on word-of-mouth and distribution of its catalog by mail. The reasons for growth must be sought among Elderhostelers themselves and research has shed light on this question. An in-depth study (Arsenault et al 1998) looked at the basis for older adults' decisions to attend Elderhostel programs. As might be expected motives and reasons were diverse: location and dates, program characteristics and course content, accommodations, cost, and so on. Other aspects of the decision-making process suggest that people attending an Elderhostel program are not so much buying a "commodity" as pursuing a particular kind of experience, as we often see in the contemporary "experience economy" (Pine 1999).

A diversity of experience implies as diversity of programs and motives. In keeping with the agency-oriented style by which individuals shape the learning experience to fit their own needs, there is a diversity of "types" of older learners who pursue their learning in an Elderhostel environment. Arsenault distinguishes six distinct types of Elderhostelers: activity oriented, geographical guru, experimenter, adventurer, content-committed, and opportunist (Arsenault 1997). This range of types of older adult learners reinforces the point that structural characteristics of Elderhostel alone do not by themselves preclude or diminish the role of individual agency in shaping the learning experience.

What motivation shapes learning by Elderhostelers? One study looked at this question in terms of adult learning theory and found that Elderhostel participants were motivated to learn in order to achieve a sense of personal control or mastery-- qualities that enhance personal agency. This motivation does not mean that Elderhostelers are all "independent scholars" or purely self-directed learners. Masunaga (1998) found in fact that in a typical Elderhostel program he studied the participants did not plan their own learning but were quite willing to accept control by others, which is in keeping with the careful preparation that tends to make up a successful Elderhostel program. On the other hand, Masunaga found that Elderhostelers did **not** want to remain merely passive recipients of information. They were avoiding the style that Freire characterized as the "Banking Model" of education: that is, deposit and withdrawal of information (Freire 1972, 1985). Elderhostelers prefer to have an opportunity to try out personal ways of constructing meaning from knowledge presented in the formal classroom setting. Thus, group discussion and social interaction outside class becomes of paramount importance for successful Elderhostel programs. In short, the **structure** of a pre-planned program does not necessarily inhibit the sense of individual **agency** experienced by older adult participants in the program.

## Elderhostel and the Marketplace

Elderhostel makes use of a market system for organizing older adult education. Administratively, the Elderhostel central office uses management and computer systems no different from those found in, say, British Airways or any other large commercial enterprise. But the Elderhostel market mechanism is guided by nonprofit principles. Because there is no need to earn a return for stockholders, the bargaining power of the organization is used to keep prices low for participants. State-of-the-art software systems for "customer relations management" now permit enrollment staff to keep track of each individual's program participation history. Enrollment staff can thereby guide participants to appropriate program offerings should the one initially preferred be unavailable.

But Elderhostel is not merely a large-scale travel system. The balance between travel and education is always a matter for judgment. The market structure within Elderhostel is guided by educational values which are not sacrificed for the marketplace. Elderhostel has remained faithful to its mission and committed to liberal arts philosophy. Elderhostel has therefore avoided offerings in skill training or mass entertainment topics that might attract a large audience but would not be in keeping with the historical mission of the organization. In sum, the market structure for Elderhostel has served as a means for permitting transformative learning, not merely a mechanism for matching supply and demand. If Elderhostel were operating as a profit-making business, it would never offer up to 10,000 different local courses and programs but instead would standardize offerings and concentrate on a small number of high-profit "product lines." In that event, profit imperatives would diminish the variety and availability of learning opportunities inspired by values of individual agency and initiative.

The success of Elderhostel offers an important lesson in political economy for the 21st century. A market structure can operate under either for-profit or not-for-profit auspice. Elderhostel is an example of a not-for-profit market system for producing and distributing older adult education. Competitors in the for-profit sector-- such as the Grand Expeditions tour group and similar companies-- operates in the same marketplace but approach customers on a profit-making basis. Elderhostel remains committed to nonprofit values but uses the market mechanism to promote those values. The global lesson is that it is eminently possible to use the market structure for purposes that enhance solidarity and human fulfillment. Elderhostel illustrates a living example of a "Third Way" in the political economy of old age.

# UNIVERSITY OF THE THIRD AGE

The idea for a "University of the Third Age" (U3A) was originally proposed in 1973 by Pierre Vellas and the first experiment along these lines was created at the University of Toulouse in France. Vellas had in mind a new kind of educational enterprise for older adults: an initiative that would enhance the quality of life and strengthen intergenerational ties, while at the same time promoting research in the field of gerontology (Vellas 1997). Since its beginning, the U3A movement has spread to all continents, becoming a global phenomenon and comprising, literally, thousands of locally developed U3A programs of remarkable variety (Swindell and Thompson 1995).

Universities of the Third Age have followed different models but two ideal types predominate: the French model, based on close association with a traditional university; and the British model, which operates more in the spirit of mutual-aid and self-help (Swindell and Thompson 1995). The French model was established earlier (1973) and the British somewhat later (1981). An American version, the Learning in Retirement Institute actually predates both (1962), but dramatic spread of the LIR model across the U.S. did not take place until the 1980s, when Elderhostel committed substantial funding to promote replication of the LIR model. As a result, during the period from 1985 to the end of the century, LIRs in the U.S. increased from 25 to nearly 300-- more than ten-fold increase in growth. A similar process took place in Britain, where the Third Age Trust, a network of local U3As, took responsibility by providing national leadership and calling attention to U3As in the wider educational world. By the turn of the century, there were more than 400 local U3As established in the UK with a total membership approaching 100,000.

U3As inspired by the French model are affiliated with a formal university and tend to look to university resources and faculty for their support (Swindell 1997). Unlike Elderhostel or LIRs in the USA, the U3As on the French model may be funded by the government, with modest support from local sources (Williamson 1997). By contrast the British U3As, guided by a self-help philosophy, need only be loosely affiliated with a university (Withnall and Percy 1994, Laslett 1996).

In the British approach, the U3A is much closer to the LIR model in the USA, consisting of older people who join together both to learn and help others learn (Midwinter 1996). Putting a premium on individual agency and mutual-aid can create a distance from a formal organization, such as a university, which is a pattern we often find in mutual-aid groups. A study of 452 older adults in the LIRs revealed participants to be a group with relatively high socio-economic level and much educational background much higher their age-peers. LIR members are motivated by goals of self-actualization, compensating for gaps in earlier education, and the desire for social contact. However, sheer intellectual curiosity—- "learning for its own sake"-- remains the primary motive (Bynum 1993).

Unlike the Elderhostel model, LIRs are based strongly on a mutual-aid philosophy: "peer learning," where participants themselves are both teachers and students (Clark et al 1997 and Simson et al 2001). In a representative sample of LIR participants it was found that around three-quarters of the "peer educators" were members of the LIR itself, the remaining teachers drawn from members of the local community or college faculty members. The dominant voice and style, then, comes from LIR members who teach one another; the style is one of mutual-aid and solidarity. In keeping with this philosophy, study groups sponsored by LIRs never have tests, grades or academic credits, yet the learning is nonetheless serious: for example, 90% of LIR study groups require "homework" or home preparation. The interactive style of LIRs is reinforced by the fact that over 90% use group discussion, with smaller proportions using lectures or presentations by participants themselves (Simpson et al 2001). The design and operation of LIRs has been codified in a handbook that remains descriptively accurate even a decade after its publication (Fischer et al 1992).

The parallel between the U3A movement and the LIRs in the USA are impressive. In both the British and American models the curriculum is, in a most literal sense, agency-oriented and initiated by the members themselves, not by academic authorities (Minichiello 1992). Despite variations in different national contexts, Picton and Lidgard (1997) have noted that the underlying principles of the U3A movement remain the same, and, despite a different historical origin and trajectory, the American LIR model follows much the same principles.

These principles were best enunciated by Peter Laslett, without doubt the most articulate theoretical voice of the U3A Movement: "The university shall consist of a body of persons who undertake to learn and help others to learn. Those who teach shall also learn and those who learn shall also teach." The reciprocity and equality embedded in U3A principles guarantees that late-life learning in U3A or LIRs will be agency-oriented to a high degree. At one level, the teach-and-learn idea seems utopian, perhaps unrealistic. As Keith Richards, Vice Chair, Third Age Trust, has acknowledged, "This challenging idea is open to misinterpretation and mockery, sometimes from within." Some participants will always prefer a more passive role-- for instance, favoring lectures or tutoring. But Richards believes that a passive role can co-exists with the exhilarating experience of learning for its own sake and drawing on individual life experience. The point is that truly transformative or agency-oriented late-life learning must leave open a path of pluralism and tolerance for learning styles that may outwardly seem passive (e.g., listening to lectures) but are not for that reason any less agency-oriented.

This point about pluralism, along with the difference between the French and British models of the U3A, raises an important question. Are all U3A or LIR programs genuine examples of transformative learning? Claydon earlier raised this critical question by asking whether the U3A is nothing more than a "playpen for oldies" (Claydon 1988). Cusack examined older adult educational programmes from a standpoint inspired by the work of Paolo Freire (1972, 1985) and critical educational gerontological theory (Glendenning and Battersby 1990). Cusack specifically looked at the U3A program in Valletta (Malta) and found it to reflect very traditional mainstream models of educational practice which Freire originally labeled the "banking model:" namely, education as a one-way flow of information from teachers to students. Far from being transformative or emancipatory, Cusack found it to be reflective of oppressive and hierarchical values. No doubt similar examples could be found among LIR groups in the USA, since many of them operate as "clubs" with elite entrance requirements.

The role of social class in older adult education must be acknowledged. Both LIRs and Universities of the Third Age have barriers to access by the broader population that must be noted. Price is far from the only barrier to participation. The production and distribution of educational programs takes place largely outside market mechanisms, though membership fees may be charged. There are some LIRs that charge high fees, but most are quite modest, compared to other leisure-time activity alternatives. It seems to be not the fee structure but other features that constitute barriers to access. Both LIRs and U3As tend to be elitist and attract well-to-do, highly educated audiences, in whatever locality they arise. By contrast, other programs in the USA have succeeded in reaching people of more limited background. Religious congregations have proved successful in promoting greater access, as in congregationally-based Shepherds Centers that offer older adult education and life-enrichment programs to diverse audiences. Something of the same ease of access appears in senior citizens centers that operate under government subsidy. From the limited studies that have been done, it appears that community-based programs are more successful in reaching older people with limited incomes, thereby overcoming some of the barriers to access in both the U3A/LIR model as well as the Elderhostel model.

A few conclusions can be drawn from these observations. First, overcoming class barriers in older education is not easy. Simply keeping entrance fees low is not enough to insure access. Moreover, a philosophy of pluralism means that in many instances older people will, on their own initiative, reproduce elements of the "banking model" of conventional educational practice. Old habits die hard, and teachers who want to promote a more emancipatory or transformative style of older adult learning-- for example, drawing on life-experience or using informal learning modalities-- may find some that elder students themselves resist emancipatory practices. For example, they may complain that discussion groups are not "real" learning. But enough experience has been gathered to show that different structure or setting-- a community-based program-- could overcome many barriers to access that presently limit Elderhostel and U3A/LIR programs to elite audiences.

## INTERPRETING THE EXPERIENCE OF OLDER ADULT EDUCATION

The success and proliferation of older adult education programs over the past generation opens up many questions. What does it mean to create a form of learning in later life independent of the imperatives of conventional education at earlier stages of life? The answer must come from an in-depth look at late-life learning as "late freedom," which expresses the power of individual human agency to learn and grow outside requirements imposed by roles or social structures in which we live our lives (Rosenmayr 1983).

Some of the best description of this agency-oriented late-life learning has come from Haim Hazan (1996). Hazan, writing from a symbolic interactionist perspective, has given an illuminating description of the power of agency in the peer-mediated learning activities of U3A in Cambridge, England. His micro-sociological approach has great value in understanding the motives and behavior of participants in that program.

Many of Hazan's findings can be extrapolated to other U3A programs, but exactly how far they can be generalized remains in doubt. Like LIRs, U3A programs cultivate uniqueness and variety, in keeping with agency-oriented learning. Hazan's study has the great merit of elucidating implicit norms that govern the interaction of participants in the U3A setting. Those norms revolve around agency-oriented education and self-determined learning, but they also underscore the importance of the group and group norms. Similarly, in Elderhostel groups there are also unwritten norms of behavior and discourse: for example, it is regarded as inappropriate to talk about one's grandchildren or to dwell on a previous career; talking about aches and pains is also frowned upon. These norms act as constraints on individual freedom, but they are far from the powerful structural constraints that shape the practice of education at earlier stages of life. Despite Hazan's characterization of a distinctive, sometimes constraining "culture" within the U3A, what emerges from his description is a powerful image of late-life learning as an opportunity for personal growth and agency.

The U3A, I would argue, can be understood partly as a utopian social movement. As Blaikie (1999) notes, the U3A as expressed in the ideas of Peter Laslett has aimed at creating an idealized version of "civil society" among elders. It was an effort at cultural innovation rather than legislative change. Laslett saw the U3A in broader sociological and historical terms related to the "emergence of the third age" in postmodern society (Laslett 1996). In this respect, the utopian dimension of the U3A can be described as a "culture of resistance" among the old. The U3A serves as a protected social space in which elders can escape the ageist influence of the wider culture, and it is also a domain where a positive culture of late-life growth and development can be nurtured. Similar cultures of resistance can be found, say, in the Black Church in the USA or among persecuted minorities in many societies. This culture of resistance or utopian community of the U3A stands in contrast to, say, the culture of Sun City or other commercially-run retirement communities which replicate the norms of conventional middle-class, middle-aged society.

If, on the one hand, the U3A emphasizes the virtues of local community (Gemeinschaft), then, on the other hand, Elderhostel emphasizes the cosmopolitan role of travel as a path to self-discovery and exploration of a wider world. This contrast between the local and the cosmopolitan is worth noting. How is the travel side of Elderhostel to be best understood? In describing the parameters of the "postmodern" quest for identity Bauman juxtaposes the poles of pilgrim (traditional religion) and tourist (postmodern consumer) (Bauman 1996). Elderhostel programs seem to combine both poles. Elderhostel participants frequently travel to places they have always wanted to visit, to locations-- like the city of Jerusalem or a rural wilderness vision quest-- that serve as genuine points for religious pilgrimage. At other times Elderhostels travel in ways that evoke a "Club Med" style of leisure enjoyment: as for instance in a popular Elderhostel program involving a barge that travels down the Loire River, each night stopping at a different chateau to sample the local wines.

We should avoid drawing too sharp a line between liberal arts education, on the one hand, and sophisticated leisure activities, on the other. The prevalence of the marketplace in organizing leisure, as opposed to education, need not be a negative point. The key question lies in the balance between structure and agency in shaping a positive experience of growth in later life. Scholars who analyze the political economy of old age or who write within the framework of critical gerontology tend to emphasize the constraints of social structure, whereas reflexive or narrative gerontology tends to emphasize the power of agency and personal growth over the lifecourse (Hepworth 1996). Those who favor agency are inclined to celebrate the diversity of life-style choices in old age that consumer culture makes possible (Gilleard and Higgs 2000).

But these seemingly opposed perspectives of political economy and narrative gerontology may be incomplete. The phenomenon of older adult education in its variety should give us pause in generalizing or making interpretations. In the USA, for example, there are far more varieties of older adult education than the LIR or Elderhostel models. In one nationwide survey, Manheimer Moskow-McKenzie described a vast variety of late-life learning programs sponsored by community colleges, senior citizens centers, churches (the Shepherds Centers), even department stores (the OASIS program) (Manheimer and Moskow-McKenzie 1995). What is common to all these various "ecological niches" is their marginality, their distance from mainstream higher education.

Older adult education does not occupy the same structural role that conventional education and training does within the larger society. That is, older adult education plays no role in human capital formation nor does it serve to reinforce patterns of social structure or class stratification. Older adult education, as it presently exists, contributes little to the much celebrated goal of "productive aging." Participants are more interested in learning for its own sake than in acquiring skills or contributing to society. By remaining marginal, older adult education has retained the agency-oriented virtues of "learning for its own sake."

Can we argue for more public investment in older adult education as a means of promoting productive aging? What are the implications of seeing late-life education as an investment in human capital formation over the lifespan? If older adult education were to expand in favor of productive aging, it is hard to predict whether that trend would be of greater benefit to middle-class groups or to people of limited backgrounds. Participants in older adult education reflect social class differences, and this comes as no surprise. The most common observation about adult education is that it attracts the very people who are best educated and often has a great problem reaching the adults who "need" education the most. Thus, older adult education, in all its variety remains an enterprise that overwhelmingly attracts people from a middle-class or professional background. This is true for both Elderhostel in the USA and the U3A programs in Europe.

Yet in its internal design older adult education programs, whether in Elderhostel or U3A, seem to owe little to structural constraints of class stratification. On the contrary, there is a strong egalitarian spirit in evidence. Apart from the sense of being part of an elite, there is little evidence of internal hierarchical behavior or competition, such as we find in the secondary and post-secondary educational systems. Moreover, even when older adult educational programs are completely free-- as in the tuition-free/space available programs in most public universities in the USA-- the social class profile of participants looks the same as for Elderhostel or U3A Programs: that is, the same middle-class and professional retirees attend. Price and the market is not the barrier to participation, and in that sense, structural constraints of the marketplace are not relevant.

Is older adult education, then, perhaps just a variety of late-life consumerism, of the kind celebrated by Gilleard and Higgs (2000) or Blaikie (1999)? Not necessarily. For example, there is a curious ambivalence about consumer values in Elderhostel. Elderhostel programs were historically inspired by the spirit of youth hostels: that is, quite opposed to consumer values and affluence of any kind. Elderhostel participants lived in college dormitories, often sharing bathrooms, or at conference center retreats and low-rent motels. Meals and other amenities in Elderhostel programs have tended to be modest; maximum prices are controlled and kept as low as possible to permit retirees of limited means to attend the programs.

In recent years, this anti-affluence mood has begun to diminish. Elderhostel, in response to demand, has permitted more "high amenity" programs. But the programs, and the costs, are still far below what commercial travel operators offer or what prestigious private universities promote as educational travel. Nonetheless, the shift toward permitting more high-amenity programs begins to blur the line between Elderhostel and a commercially-run education-travel enterprise. We can speculate as to whether this shift could bring with it a movement away from agency-oriented learning toward activities driven by market imperatives.

In the case of U3A the opposition to consumer values remains sharp. Elderhostel offerings, are, after all, in some sense "commodified" simply because participants pay a fee and receive a package of services in return. By contrast, in the U3A the "services" themselves are not monetized but are produced by the participants themselves according to the model of a barter or a mutual-aid exchange. True, the French model of U3A does involve association with an elite university sponsor. But regardless of auspice the high intellectual tone of U3A programs insures that they will never become part of the popular marketplace. U3A activities seem represent a pure form of agency-oriented education, closer to the style of independent scholars but flourishing in a group setting.

## CONCLUDING OBSERVATIONS ON THE FUTURE OF OLDER ADULT EDUCATION

This discussion has looked at only two programs, Elderhostel and U3A, from among the wide variety of forms of late-life learning and older adult education. At first glance, programs like Elderhostel and the Universities of the Third Age seem to be polar opposites. "Elderhostel, Inc." looks like a vast travel agency for adult learning, while the U3A appears as a proliferation of self-help groups inspired by utopian goals and a club-like atmosphere of geriatric sociability. Neither of these stereotypes is fair, nor is it true that the two programs are polar opposites, despite structural differences. Indeed, when we look more closely at the kind of learning that actually takes place in these two settings, there are remarkable parallels-- above all, the parallel power of human agency to shape the learning that takes place regardless of structure.

The complex relation between structure and agency in late-life offers lessons for aging in the 21st century. The history of Elderhostel experience should encourage a deeper appreciation of the power of the marketplace as a structure for promoting human agency. The market mechanism is appropriate and necessary for human interaction on a large geographic scale, such as the national or international sphere in which Elderhostel operates. Moreover, markets need not be driven by profit imperatives: a nonprofit marketplace is not a contradiction in terms. A nonprofit market is fully feasible and, in contrast to government bureaucracy, may actually prove a more favorable structure for promoting individual agency. But markets, whether profit-driven or not, are not always the best means of coordinating human interaction. Non-market mechanisms, such volunteerism and mutual-aid, may be more effectively for local, face-to-face initiatives, as in the U3A or LIR. Nor should we imagine that the marketplace and mutual-aid need be in opposition to one another. In the USA, for instance, the LIR and Elderhostel structures have co-existed and actually helped support each other, demonstrating that different structural arrangements can be complementary and facilitative of human agency in different ways.

Acknowledging a legitimate role for the market in older adult education, however, does raise an uncomfortable question. Habermas has spoken about the "commodification of the life-world" in contemporary capitalism and his critique remains persuasive. We may ask: Can market-based older adult education models continue to resist this trend toward commodification? Much of the power of older adult education, in both the Elderhostel and U3A models, reflects the agency-oriented learning that takes place on an informal basis. Successful programs incorporate the life-world of old age-- for example, celebrating birthdays of participants, providing opportunities for informal interaction at meals, and spontaneously refashioning the curriculum to take account of unexpected learning opportunities. It is the power of the life-world, and the intensity and idiosyncrasy of learning, that attracts college and university teachers who are eager to teach in an Elderhostel program. Elderhostel has remained resistant to commodification of its mission by the pressures of the marketplace. Similarly, the U3A, at least in Cambridge, has kept its distance from the official bureaucratic university system, which commodifies learning in its own way.

The values of the life-world are threatened by commodification. Older people participate in older adult education programs not just to acquire knowledge but to experience a sense of belonging and the freedom of individual agency. They often want an experience of learning in which the private and the social spheres are connected and barriers are broken down. At its best, this educational practice becomes emancipatory or transformative learning, along the lines described by Freire and others (O'Sullivan et al 2002).

In this practice of freedom, old age can actually be an ally. Advanced age often brings with it isolation or detachment from earlier social networks due to retirement, bereavement, and other events of later life. But epidemiological research has shown that social networks are key for morale, survival and health in later life (Berkman and Kawachi 2000). Moreover, the positive outcomes of Elderhostel participation lie in the social as well as the cognitive domain (Long and Zoller-Hodges 1995). As the educational enterprise becomes larger, forces of bureaucratization or commodification become stronger and these social network values are put at risk.

As older adult education grows in popularity, it is likely that marketplace forces will grow and the temptation to commodify late-life learning will grow as well. For example, the Walt Disney Company launched a "Disney Institute" (now defunct) to capitalize on potential demand for adult learning. In the USA, Phoenix University, a profit-making higher education institution, has caused widespread alarm among mainstream universities which tend to feel traditional academic values are at risk. Venture capital groups are already looking at older adult education as part of a "Gray Market" with profit potential as the Baby Boom grows old. In all countries, as higher education has grown in scale, patterns of bureaucratization or (in the USA) commodification have emerged. It is not too early to worry that the same trends may overtake older adult education if it becomes less marginal and more popular.

Will older adult education become absorbed as part of the leisure-time industry, along with culture and travel, or can it retain aspirations toward an emancipatory learning? We see today new images of aging centered around so-called "Successful Aging" and "Productive Aging (Moody 2001)." Earlier images of older people as weak or vulnerable-- the "worthy poor"-- have begun to be eclipsed. At the same time the linear life-course with its "three boxes of life" (education, work and retirement) has given way to a postmodern life course (Biggs 1999, Hepworth 1999, Powell and Longino 2001). Commentators celebrate a new diversity in our images of old age, but we should avoid any "cheerful postmodernism" that dismisses questions about purpose and meaning in late-life learning.

## CONCLUSION

In the end, we cannot escape questions about the philosophical presuppositions of education for the last stage of life (Moody 1975). Under new conditions, we need to ask, what kind of older adult education is appropriate for the risks and uncertainties of the postmodern life-course (Jarvis 1994)? The question is not easily answered. Social class barriers to late-life learning remain and need to be overcome. We should by no means resist making older adult education more accessible to groups often bypassed by higher learning. But, on the other hand, we should avoid casting late-life learning as a form of "compensatory education," as if older people were just another set of "victims."

The positive experience of Elderhostel and the U3A is a "culture of resistance" that challenges what Kalish called the "failure model" of old age. Instead of seeing age as deficit, we need to adopt a genuinely developmental perspective which would emphasize gains as well as losses with the process of aging (Guttman 1996)-- such as wisdom or the search for meaning in later life (Carlsen 1999). What is called for instead is a developmental concept of elderhood, perhaps along the lines I have proposed under the framework of "Conscious Aging (Moody 2002)."

This vision of developmental possibilities is by no means merely utopian. We can envisage the future by taking account of the historical accomplishments evident in the best examples of learning in Elderhostel and the U3A in countries throughout the world. In making learning more accessible, we should resist any temptation simply to make it more popular or to define success in terms of numbers alone. On the contrary, we should remember that the quality and the nobility of late-life learning often comes precisely because learning is challenging, provocative, and difficult. As Spinoza said in the concluding lines of the *Ethics*, "All that is noble is as difficult as it is rare."

# REFERENCES

Arsenault, N., G. Anderson, and R. Swedburg. 1998. "Understanding Older Adults in Education: Decision-making and Elderhostel." *Educational Gerontology* 24:101-114.

Arsenault, N. 1997. "Typologies and the Leisure Learner." *Ageing International* 24: 64-74.

Bauman, Z. 1996. "From Pilgrim to Tourist-- or a Short History of Identity." in *Questions of Cultural Identity*, edited by S. Hall and P. du Gay. London: Sage.

Berkman, L.F. and I. Kawachi (Editors). 2000. *Social Epidemiology*. Oxford University Press.

Biggs, S. 1999. *The Mature Imagination: Dynamics of Identity in Midlife and Beyond*. Buckingham: Open University Press.

Blaikie, A. 1999. "Can There Be a Cultural Sociology of Ageing?" *Education and Ageing* 14:127-139.

Bynum, L.L., and M.A. Seaman. 1993. "Motivations of Third-Age Students in Learning-in-Retirement Institutes." *Continuing Higher Education Review* 57:12-22.

Cairns, H. 1996. "The University of the Third Age," pp. 57-60 in *One World, Many Cultures*, edited by D. Jones, B. McConnell, and G. Normie, Cardenden, Scotland: Fife Regional Council.

Carlsen, M. 1999. "Sustaining Power of Meaning," *Generations* 23:27-30.

Clark, F., A.F. Heller, C. Rafman, and J. Walker. 1997. "Peer Learning: A Popular Model for Seniors Education" *Educational Gerontology* 23:751-762.

Claydon, L. 1988. "The University of the Third Age: Playpen for the Oldies or New Community Force?" pp. 243-255 in *Partnerships in Education*, edited by T. Townsend and J. Cowdell. Clayton, Australia: Monash University.

Culbertson, J. 1997. "Elderhostel Serves the Changing Educational Goals of Seniors." *Ageing International* 24:126-132.

Cusack, S.A. 1997. "New Directions in Older Adult Education", *Gerontology Research News* 15:3-4.

Fischer, R.B., M.L. Blazey, and H.T. Lipman. 1992. *Students of the Third Age*. Riverside, NJ: Macmillan.

Freire, P. 1972. *Pedagogy of the Oppressed*. Hammondsworth: Penguin.

Freire, P. 1985. *The Politics of Education: Culture, Power and Liberation*. New York: Bergin and Garvey.

Gilleard, C. and P. Higgs. 2000. *Cultures of Ageing: Self, Citizen and the Body*. London: Pearson.

Glendenning, F. and D. Battersby. 1990. "Why We Need Educational Gerontology and Education for Older Adults: A Statement of First Principles", in *Ageing, Education and Society: Readings in Educational Gerontology*, edited by F. Glendenning and K. Percy. Staffordshire: Association for Educational Gerontology.

Gutmann, D. 1996. "Gerontology Research in the Twenty-first Century: Some Wishful Thinking," pp. 17-25 in *Aging in the Twenty-first Century: A Developmental Perspective*, edited by L. Sperry. New York: Garland Publishing.

Hazan, H. 1996. *From First Principles: An Experiment in Ageing*, Westport, CT: Bergin & Garvey.

Hepworth, M. 1996. "Consumer Culture and Social Gerontology," *Education and Ageing* 11:19-30.

Hepworth, M. 1999. "In Defiance of an Ageing Culture." *Ageing and Society* 19:139-148

Jarvis, P. 1994. "Learning, Ageing and Education in the Risk Society." *Education and Ageing* 9:6-20.

Laslett, P. 1996. *A Fresh Map of Life: The Emergence of the Third Age*. London: Macmillan Press.

Long, H.B. and D. Zoller-Hodges. 1995. "Outcomes of Elderhostel Participation," *Educational Gerontology* 21:113-127.

Manheimer, R.J. 1998. "Promise and Politics of Older Adult Education." *Research on Aging* 20:391-414.

Manheimer, R.J. and D. Moskow-McKenzie. 1995. "Transforming Older Adult Education: An Emerging Paradigm from a Nationwide Study." *Educational Gerontology*. 21:613-632.

Masunaga, H. 1998. "Adult Learning Theory and Elderhostel." *Gerontology and Geriatrics Education*. 19:3-16.

Midwinter, E. 1996. *Thriving People: The Growth and Prospects of the U3A in the UK*, London: Third Age Trust.

Mills, E.S. 1993. *The Story of Elderhostel*. Hanover, NH: University Press of New England.

Moody, H.R. 1976. "Philosophical Presuppositions of Education for Old Age." *Educational Gerontology: An International Quarterly* 1:1

Moody, H.R. 2001. "Productive Aging and the Ideology of Old Age," *Perspectives on Productive Aging*, edited by Nancy Morrow-Howell. Baltimore, MD: Johns Hopkins University Press.

Moody, H.R. 2002. "Conscious Aging: A Strategy for Positive Development in Later Life" in *Mental Wellness in Aging: Strength-based Approaches*, edited by Judah Ronch and Joseph Goldfield. New York: Human Services Press.

O'Sullivan, E., A. Morrell, and M.A. O'Connor (Editors). 2002. *Expanding the Boundaries of Transformative Learning: Essays on the Theory and Praxis*, Palgrave Macmillan.

Picton, C. and C. Lidgard, C. 1997. "Developing U3A", *Third Age Learning International Studies*, 7:219-24.

Pine, B.J., J.H. Gilmore, and B.J.Pine II. 1999. *The Experience Economy*. Cambridge, MA: Harvard Business School Press.

Powell, J.L. and C.F. Longino. 2001. "The Postmodernization of Aging: The Body and Social Theory." *Journal of Aging and Identity* 6:199-207.

Rosenmayr, L. 1983. *Die Spaete Freiheit* [Late Freedom]. Berlin: Severin und Siedler.

Swindell, R. and J. Thompson. 1995. "An International Perspective on the University of the Third Age." *Educational Gerontology* 21: 429-447.

Simson, S., E. Thompson, and L.B. Wilson. 2001. "Who is Teaching Lifelong Learners? A Study of Peer Educators in Institutes for Learning in Retirement." *Gerontology and Geriatrics Education* 22:31-43.

Vellas, P. 1997. "Genesis and Aims of the Universities of the Third Age." *European Network Bulletin* 1:9-12.

Williamson, A. 1997. "You're Never Old To Learn: Third-Age Perspectives On Lifelong Learning." *International Journal of Lifelong Learning* 16:173-184.

# Chapter 4

# EXEMPLARS OF RETIREMENT: IDENTITY AND AGENCY BETWEEN LIFESTYLE AND SOCIAL MOVEMENT

## *Stephen Katz and Debbie Laliberte-Rudman*

## ABSTRACT

Critical perspectives in gerontology consistently fault Western welfare states for constructing later life and retirement as negative stages of decline and dependency. Current cultural theorists point to the emergence of a 'new aging' described as 'positive,' 'successful,' and 'productive,' and represented by images of independence, social mobility and agency. Around these buoyant and optimistic images, lifestyle marketing, health promotion, utopian 'seniors' communities, and fashionable body technologies have rallied. As the welfare states of Western nations retreat from their commitments to lifecourse programs, however, the 'new aging' is also advanced by a bio-demographic politics that infuse everyday life with the ethics and responsibilities of self-care, creating a contradictory culture of aging in the process. On the one hand, middle-aged and older people are led to expect that active and healthy lifestyles will contribute to their acceptability and inclusion within public worlds of social participation. On the other hand, such lifestyles find themselves allied with neoliberal agendas that problematize older bodies and identities as vulnerable, risky, and in need of vigilance. In probing this contradiction, this chapter raises several important questions about the relation between agency and identity in later life by examining two cases: first, the individualized images of the 'retired worker' and 'opportunity-seeking consumer,' as exemplars of retiree identities, are drawn from a Canadian newspaper; second, the image of the Third Age learner in the historical development of the British Universities of the Third Age (U3A) movement is taken up to argue that agency is a potent social force if it is experienced and negotiated as a collective identity. Thus the promise of the 'new aging' and the resolution of debates about agency, identity, and resistance lie beyond the bounds of the privileged site of individual subjectivity to more collective forms of action.

## INTRODUCTION: AGENCY, STRUCTURE, IDENTITY, LIFESTYLE

The field of Sociology, despite its diverse intellectual heritage and divisive schools of thought, articulates its coherence with a tense and durable vocabulary of dualisms – individual/society, macro/micro, positivist/interpretive, and qualitative/quantitative, amongst others. As Stephen Fuller comments, "what this does is to confer on sociology a spurious sense of internal divisions, one due more to lack of communication than genuine disagreement" (1993: 137). Of these, the most salient dualism in recent years is the one connecting 'agency' and 'structure,' along with the social problems, political bearings, and analytical areas which each circumscribe. While agency refers to subjectivity, resistance, action, reflexivity, empowerment, and mobilization, structure evokes constraint, socialization, power, domination, and social reproduction. Furthermore, social thinkers look to 'identity' and 'lifestyle' as the most obvious theoretical connection points between agency and structure. Thus sociological perspectives addressing identity can also be typified according to their position along an agency-structure continuum (Baber 1991; Marshall 1996). At one end of this continuum, structural perspectives such as role theory or functionalism or certain variants of political economy propose that structural features determine the conditions of identity-ascription, over which individuals have little control. At the other end, theories based on the interpretive traditions of symbolic interactionism or phenomenology or ethnomethodology emphasize that individual agents engage in a continual process of negotiating and recreating their identities by drawing upon the social practices and rituals of their everyday worlds (Blaikie 1999; Marshall 1996).

This mix of perspectives on identity has inspired many researchers to approach the agency-structure dynamic by addressing individuals and collectivities as social actors who both shape and are shaped by existing social structures (Baber 1991; Layder 1994; Lee 1990). For example, Gubrium and Holstein propose that although individuals constructively narrate 'selves' using local and meaningful resources, "features of narrative practice may also be formally designated or constrained, especially in a contemporary world replete with formal organizations, interest groups and bureaucracies" (1998: 173; 1995). Sociologist Anthony Giddens, best known for his work on 'structuration theory,' has written extensive critiques of dualistic thinkers and their tendency to privilege either the action of human agency or the dominance of social structures. Central to Giddens' theory is the concept of lifestyle (1984; 1990; 1991; 1999), a sociological problem first identified by Max Weber and Georg Simmel (see Cockerham, Rutten, and Abel 1997; Veal 1993). According to Giddens, the cultural contexts of late modernity and self-identity have become increasingly indeterminate, future-oriented, internally referential, and reflexive. Hence, human agents respond to these contexts by engaging in a 'reflexive project of the self,' a continuous ordering of self-narratives and lifestyle practices within the widening subjective possibilities of post-traditional society. While lifestyle practices appear to flow from individual choice supported by various forms of expertise, Giddens also maintains that such choice is constrained by the structural resources and social systems, which configure life chances. The relationship between agency, identity, and lifestyle, therefore, is bound by the animation of choice and reflexivity as social processes.

The theories of reflexivity which Giddens and his French counterpart, the late Pierre Bourdieu, and their associates advance, have also been criticized especially by feminist thinkers for overlooking those areas where post-traditional gendered identities reinstate, rather than disengage from, traditional patriarchal relations (Adkins 1999; 2001; Jamieson 1999; McNay 1999). Indeed, in the context of gender the politics of the body refigure how lifestyle and identity bridge agency and structure (e.g., Gardiner 1995; McNay 2000). Unfortunately, few feminist theories of agency and structure have crossed over into aging studies (see Bury 1995; Tulle-Winton 1999); nor has the work of Giddens, Bourdieu, and others, who highlight lifestyle as a self-reflexive project or an embedded 'habitus' through which individuals maintain identity, been systematically applied to post-traditional aging and the lifecourse. Giddens does suggest some starting points, however, by stating, "Self-identity for us forms a *trajectory* across the different institutional settings of modernity over the *durée* of what used to be called the 'life cycle', a term which applies much more accurately to non-modern contexts that to modern ones. Each of us not only 'has', but *lives* a biography reflexively organized in terms of flows of social and psychological information about possible ways of life" (Giddens 1991: 14). Thus, "the lifespan becomes more and more freed from externalities associated with pre-established ties to other individuals and groups" (p. 147). Gilleard and Higgs concur, noting that "only in the late twentieth century has the idea emerged that human agency can be exercised over how aging will be expressed and experienced" (2000: 3).[1] These ideas have been further developed by the pioneering work of Mike Featherstone and Mike Hepworth (as our references throughout this study indicate) who investigate the lifecourse as a focal point for the increasingly powerful role of the cultural sphere in late capitalist society. How critical gerontologists have reflected upon the theoretical and cultural conditions of the new aging is briefly discussed below.

## AGING AND THE CRITICAL IMPULSE OF SOCIAL GERONTOLOGY

Over the past three decades the critical impulse within social gerontology has targeted the political and structural regulation of aging populations. 'Structured dependency' theories, the type of political economy framework that dominated critical gerontological discourse throughout the 1970s and early 1980s, described how state policies and institutional practices, ostensibly designed to improve the lives of older people, at the same time reinforced their dependent, marginalized, and disempowered status (Estes 1979; Minkler 1984; Phillipson 1982). Thus, solutions to the problems of aging were sought at the level of structural change and political resistance. The critics also rebuked micro-sociological and interpretive traditions for their neglect of the macro-constraints, ageist economics, and social inequality inherent in capitalist lifecourse regimes. Despite the weaknesses of their theoretical perspectives, however, these micro-traditions expanded the domain of human agency within studies of aging. For example, during this period several gerontological theories arose from research on individuals who maintained their personal integrity while coping with decreased physical capacity or the loss of social roles (Breytspraak 1984; Matthews 1979). Robert Atchley

---

[1] Giddens' ideas have some resonance with the substantial gerontological literature on human agency in developmental and lifecourse studies, and the role of individual action and choice on the trajectories and transitions across the lifespan (see Settersten Jr., 2002). The prolific work of Glen Elder Jr. is strongly associated with these studies beginning with his research on cohorts during the Great Depression in North America (1974). Other gerontologists have specified how human evolution itself would not have been possible without the constant intervention of human action (Dannefer 1999). As both a social and a biological species 'we' have made 'ourselves,' therefore. While this is a significant literature, our study more narrowly focuses on identity and lifestyle as critical agency-structure problems.

applied his 'continuity theory' to show that older adults, within socially structured limitations, still employed information-management and social strategies to maintain a sense of continuity of identity throughout the lifecourse (1989; 1991). Today we also have exciting developments in narrative, performative, biographical, and related qualitative gerontology's that further strengthen the subjective dimension within critical gerontology (Basting 1998; Cole and Ray 2000; Deats and Lenker 1999; Kenyon, Clark, and de Vries; 2001; Twigg 2000).

Clearly the tension between structural and interpretive theories in gerontology reiterates the dualism between agency and structure across the social sciences. Thus leading gerontologists tackle identity in later life by examining the relational and co-constituting interplay of social forces between agency and structure (Birren 1995; Hendricks 2003; Marshall 1996; McMullin and Marshall 1999). For instance, Sharon Kaufman's theory of the 'ageless self,' while posing agency in terms of the symbolic construction of identity through themes of meaning, also asserts that identity-development is a dialectical process between self and culture (1986; 1993). Kaufman contends that the ideational aspect of culture, which consists of shared meanings and symbols, provides an interpretive framework upon which aging individuals selectively draw in order to create a viable and ageless self. Cultural gerontologists have gone further to call for a re-conceptualization of critical gerontology itself in order to take account of the changing culture of post-traditional aging (Andrews 1999; Blaikie 1999; Cole et al. 1993; Gilleard and Higgs 2000; Jamieson, Harper, and Victor 1997; Katz 1995; 2003; Phillipson 1999a; Tulle-Winton 1999). They look at the shaping of new aging identities in the context of the fragmentation of the social institutionalization of retirement, advances in life expectancy and longevity technologies, the expanding affluence of aging groups, the blurring of fixed chronological boundaries, and the shift from production-based to consumption-based economies. In particular, what critical gerontology adds to the structurative framework of Giddens and other sociologists who track post-traditional social forms, is the unique contradiction between personal freedom and structural constraint engendered by contemporary aging. At the heart of this contradiction lies the superseding of ubiquitous images of decline and negative social roles by new positive ideals of activity, independence, and self-care (Hepworth 1995; Katz 2001).

## Positive Aging and the Contradictory Identities of Consumer Society

If, as cultural gerontologists argue, aging persons are increasingly expected to fashion rewarding identities through lifestyle and self-reflexive practices, then we find growing evidence of this development in popular gerontological, biomedical, marketing, leisure, media, and health promotion discourses (Andrews 1999; Ekerdt and Clark 2001; Featherstone and Hepworth 1995b; *Generations* 2001; Hepworth 1999; Laws 1995; 1996; McHugh 2000; Ylanne-McEven 1999). In related academic texts, four common themes feature prominently: 1) A critical attack on the belief that aging is essentially a disease; 2) A focus on activity as crucial to individual happiness and health; 3) A celebration of the possibilities of stretching mid-life and postponing old age; 4) An emphasis on adaptation-skills that reduce dependency on public healthcare systems (Featherstone and Hepworth 1995a, Fisher and Sphect 1999). According to Kevin McHugh, "to be active in aging has now attained the status of a societal mantra. The so-called 'third age' of life is viewed as limitless. Productive activity is the route to happiness and longevity; to live otherwise is tantamount to a death wish" (2000: 112).

Applied gerontological research also underlines the social conditions and individual behaviors that contribute to the attainment of 'successful' aging. Thus, composite professional/popular knowledge has emerged that elaborates the kinds of productive, physical, ethical, and socially interactive activities appropriate for aging lifestyles (Holstein 1999; Katz, 2000).

A deeper problem with this knowledge is that it appears to support a 'tyrannical' positive aging culture that overshadows the difficulties and challenges experienced by many older individuals (Blaikie 1999: 209). Indeed, for those individuals who lack the requisite economic resources, personal skills, and cultural capital to participate in consumer culture in successfully agential ways, or for those who suffer irreversible bodily decline or dependency on others, the new era of aging creates a profound sense of personal failure and social marginalization (Featherstone and Hepworth 1995a; Holstein 1999; Hopflinger 1993; Minkler 1990; 1991). At the micro-level of personal identity, the cultural emphasis on 'new aging' may also heighten the tension between self, identity, and the body for those who live through deep old age and long periods of frailty (Turner 1995). In these cases "the outer body and face can become a rigid alien structure of imprisonment which can mask forever the possibilities of the self within" (Featherstone and Wernick 1995: 2).[2]

Thus, the agential freedoms and arts of lifelong learning, financial planning, and retirement-fitness assumed by the bearers of new aging identities come with a moral edict to live risk-aversion and self-caring lives. This paradox is evidently part of late twentieth and early twenty-first century neoliberal politics, where empowered communities and agential identities are made to subsidize the de-structuring of the public sphere. The social spaces through which agency, structure, identity, and lifestyle are conjoined have been rationalized along the lines of what Nikolas Rose calls 'powers of freedom' (Rose 1999). In short, power works through freedom as well as against it. For this reason, several critics have conceptualized the 'new aging' as a form of governmental rationality, a neoliberal geometry that maximizes individual responsibility in the service of meeting political goals of minimizing dependency and universal entitlements. While the scope of this essay prevents a fuller discussion of the Foucaultian-inspired *governmentality* school of thought that informs this kind of critique, we can use two of its basic concepts – *technologies of government* and *practices of the self* – to refine our observations about the contradictory features of new aging identities based on our cases of 'exemplars of retirement' outlined in the next section.

*Technologies of government* describe and make practicable those ideal identities that best express the fit between political and personal goals (Burchell 1993; Dean 1999; Rose 1992). Such technologies operate through the *practices of the self* around consumer and psychological behavior so as to 'autonomize and responsibilize' individuals potentially at risk of dependency and recast them as active entrepreneurs of the self (Rose 1993; 1999). For example, technologies of government, through consumer campaigns about the need for individuals to secure their 'future,' promote practices of the self that engage in risk-preventive measures such as acquiring insurance or adopting healthy lifestyles (Castel 1991; Rose 1999). At the same time, psychological and behavioral skilling, disseminated through instructional courses, self-help manuals, community programs, and the media, reframe the problems of everyday life into manageable episodes and 'growth experiences' that require regimes of

---

[2] Many of these issues are related to the post-modern remaking of midlife identities and 'midlifestylism' as vital yet indeterminate categories. Biggs (1999), Gullette (1998), and Hepworth and Featherstone (1998) provide excellent discussions of these developments.

conduct commensurate with the norms of an autonomous self. Thus, problems previously (and accurately) understood as social and political issues become transmuted into personal challenges articulated by the therapeutically 'empowering' discourses of professional expertise (Cruikshank 1999). As our examples below illustrate, aging and retirement cultures have become rich environments in which technologies of government and practices of the self operate to idealize prudential human agents who take responsibility for their destinies, lifestyles, and projects of self-discovery.[3]

## EXEMPLARS OF RETIREMENT: THE *RETIRED WORKER* AND THE *OPPORTUNITY-SEEKING CONSUMER*

The following section critically describes two 'exemplars of retirement,' the *retired worker* and the *opportunity-seeking consumer*, from a sample of 138 newspaper articles about retirement life published between 1999 and 2000 in the Toronto Star, Canada's largest newspaper in terms of readership (on-line NADBank Survey 2000).[4] We are using the term 'exemplar' to signify how personal profiles or biographical narratives are transcribed into neoliberal, positive-aging parables about accomplished midlife and older identities.

The *retired worker* is a person who chooses to forego or delay a traditional leisure-based lifestyle by refusing to retire from work upon retirement-age. Instead, she or he selects to continue in a midlife job, find a new job, or change jobs in midlife in order to establish a retirement career for later life. The sample articles are filled with anecdotal testimonials to the psychological, physical, and social rewards of working past retirement, while the *retired worker* is heroized in glowing terms that appeal to readers considering post-retirement work options. For example, work offers "a rhythm and structure to one's life, a sense of identity and purpose, social contacts, and an opportunity to be creative" (Specials, Sept. 25, 1999).[5]

Post-retirement work is also linked to a youthful mind, body and lifestyle, epitomized by a photo caption included in an article describing an 84 year-old office courier which states: "FOREVER YOUNG: Born during World War I, George Pape fought in WWII and vows not to surrender to retirement. He keeps busy now as an office courier" (News, Dec.12, 1999). In these stories happy, busy, and self-fulfilled 'retired workers' are referred to by their 'new' successful work roles, such as the "supermarket man" (Life, Mar. 25, 2000), the "ageless composer" (Specials, Oct.28, 2000), the "performer" (Life, October, 28, 2000), and the "entrepreneur" (Business, Mar.22, 2000). This kind of vocabulary emphasizes the freedoms

---

[3]Foucault's concept of *governmentality* or 'the art of government' (1991: 90) and his essays on the genealogy of liberal rule (1981;1988) have inspired an exciting subfield of governmentality studies (Burchell, Gordon, and Miller 1991; Barry, Osborne, and Rose 1996; Dean 1999; Rose 1999). Such studies elaborate Foucault's perspective on the governmentalization of power to critique neoliberal regimes, insurential and risk-management programs, and the utilization of data-technology and market rationalities in state enterprises. The governmentality literature also emphasizes how personal conduct, freedom, choice, and responsibility are folded into the fabric of 'the social' as political resources (Petersen and Bunton 1997; Cruikshank 1999). Also see the contribution to this volume by Chris Phillipson and Jason Powell, 'Risk and Governmentality: Towards a New Understanding of Neo-Liberalism, SocialPolicy and Aging.'

[4] This research is part of Debbie Laliberte-Rudman's Ph.D. dissertation, 'Active, Autonomous and Responsible: A Critical Discourse Analysis of Canadian Newspaper Constructions of Retirees; 2003, Department of Public Health Sciences, University of Toronto.

[5] References to 'Specials,' 'News,' 'Life,' 'Business,' and 'City' indicate bundled sections of the Toronto Star newspaper, not separate magazines or papers.

that await the entrepreneurial spirit in retirement that overcomes restrictive age-based identities through productive lifestyle choices.

The *opportunity-seeking consumer* is a person who chooses specific lifestyle options in the consumer market that promise to transform retirement into an opportunity and a 'second chance' for self-development and social success; for example, life-long learning courses, retirement 'fitness' skills, internet classes, and leisure travel. Prominent in the newspaper articles are learning and exploring opportunities because these appear to have multiple rejuvenating benefits whereby retirees can "find a new focus for life after work" (Business, Nov.26, 2000), get "another chance in life" (Specials, Sept.25, 1999), and realize the "joys of opening up to new friends and becoming one of the group" (News, Oct.14, 1999). Texts that feature the *opportunity-seeking consumer* stress repeatedly the need to match lifestyle choices with personal desires. For example, an article on 'mature' learners begins: "Bingo and quilting bees are not for Cynthia Aston. 'The drum I beat now is there's more to life than quilting,' says Aston, 71. 'I don't believe in the old stereotype of retirees' " (Specials, Sept.25, 1999).

Both the *retired worker* and the *opportunity-seeking consumer* are exemplary identities which fit the 'new aging' emphasis. On the one hand, they are used to promote different lifestyle agendas and possibilities for agency in later life. For the *retired worker* a production-based identity is central, while for the *opportunity-seeking consumer* engagement in learner-focused and leisure activities are essential. On the other hand, both identities convey to the public how success in later life is an attainable individual responsibility. Readers are provided with the sad 'facts' about the risks and consequences for those who disregard retirement expertise, choose not to acquire appropriate decision-making skills, and delay the consumption of financial and lifestyle products. Hence, there are penalties and the threat of social censure for those who become retired-'unfit.' In an article entitled "Ambition needs redefining," a clinical psychologist advises readers to change their work attitudes: "there is this sobering thought: one recent U.S. study showed that 80 per cent of baby boomers believe they'll be working right through their so-called retirement. In other words, it's no longer a sprint, it's a marathon. If somewhere along that race route, you don't redefine your ambition, you're in trouble" (Business, Oct.7, 1999). Another article warns about retirees that "40 per cent were dissatisfied with retirement." Hence readers should seek "retirement happiness" by participating in retirement workshops and developing "a plan that will meet your needs and your skills" (Business, Nov.26, 2000).

In addition, we find in these texts that persons who triumph as *retired workers* or *opportunity-seeking consumers* are regarded as instant public authorities. For example, in an article entitled "No age limits when it comes to learning," a 66 year-old woman who recently graduated from a college program states, " 'You are never too old to give yourself a second chance in life,' she says. 'But you have to take responsibility for yourself and have a self-generated desire to do something new' " (Specials, Sept.25, 1999). A 58 year-old "social whirlwind" who divorced late in life advises readers that there are "101 places to go" in order to "meet your match" (Specials, April 17, 1999) and a 62 year-old retiree who recently learned how to use the Internet advises readers to "have a little confidence in your ability" (Specials, June 19, 1999). Such expertise also extends to providing guidance on the risks of poverty, a decreased standard of living, inactivity and dependency, and social marginalization, all conceptualized as personal rather than collective problems. The aging individual at risk of inadequate finances is reconstructed as a retired worker who proactively plans a retirement career in a quest to maintain personal financial health, as well as a range of other personal benefits. One article on the advantages of post-retirement work glibly states, "Here's a way to reduce the risk of outliving your money: Don't retire" (Business, Nov.19, 2000). With respect to social marginalization and inactivity, one man who set up a business after retiring indicated that it is "nice to know that you're wanted or needed. I didn't understand that until I found myself retired" (Specials, Oct.28, 2000). A recently widowed woman who learned how to use a computer in her 80s suggests that the computer has been her salvation by keeping her connected" (News, April 29, 2000). The real success for *retired workers* and *opportunity-seeking consumers*, however, is to avoid the risk of aging itself by not succumbing to negative attitudes or behavioral traits that could be interpreted as 'old.' The articles provide readers with a quasi-sociological forum about expanding positive social trends anchored by the truism that one is never 'too old' to do anything; "it's never too late to learn" (News, Oct.14, 1999), "you're never too old to surf…the net" (Specials, June 19, 1999), and age is "no barrier for venture in cyberspace" (Specials, April 29, 2000).

From these newspaper articles and their characterization of successful aging identities we can make three important observations.

First, that such identities exercise their agency in self-reflexive ways. The first step for the opportunity-seeking consumer is to identify "emotional and work-related needs" (Business, Nov. 26, 2000); and the retired worker needs to assess "strengths and weaknesses" (Business, Nov. 19, 2000). The mature life-long learner should first consider how a "lack of confidence" can be overcome through "drive" and the right learning opportunity (Specials, Sept.25, 1999). And retirees of all backgrounds must "work on some feel-good improvements" (Business, Nov. 26, 2000) in order to open "up a whole new world" and satisfy their "yearning for knowledge" (Specials, June 19, 1999).

Second, as our examples above illustrate, successful aging, good health, activity, independence, mobility, and self-support appear as the results of responsible individual choice unencumbered by structural or political constraints. At the same time, risk becomes the inevitable consequence of an individual's irresponsible choice or a refusal to become retirement-fit. Numerous articles provide case examples where good choices make for a good life. A 90 year-old variety store owner is described as keeping "a schedule that would tire a person half his age" (News, Jan.21, 2000), a 101 year-old music composer does not have " much to worry about. A cane given as a gift collects dust in a corner" (Specials, Oct. 28, 2000), and a 75-year old Elderhostel participant recently completed "five days of canoeing, swimming, hiking, rock-climbing and 'wolf-howling' " (City, Oct.1, 1999).

Third, the exemplars of retirement embody the contradictory practices of the self that encompass freedom and power, discussed earlier. Aspiring to be a *retired worker* or an *opportunity-seeking consumer* appears to be an attractive personal exercise, capable of liberating people and the aging process itself from the negative ageism of retirement conventions. However such an exercise also intersects lifecourse and lifestyle in ways that satisfy neoliberal technologies of government that reduce dependencies through enforced individual responsibility without recourse to structural resistance. Just as aging Western populations are growing on an unprecedented scale, governments are decreasing the availability of financial programs to retirees (Battle 1997; Cheal and Kampen 1998; Kalisch and Aman 2001). Just as the retired worker in Canada is promoted as an exemplar identity, policy reform is contracting the use of public pension systems as support to 'early' retirees, while favoring an increase in the retirement age and removal of incentives for early retirement

(Kalisch and Aman 2001; Redvay-Mulvey 2000; Walker 2000). In Canada, just as the economic status of retirees in general has improved since the 1980s (Hauser 1999; Statistics Canada 2000), large numbers of workers in key economic sectors continue to face mandatory retirement regulations and Old Age Security 'clawbacks.' In the case of particular groups such as retired widows, there is also a greater likelihood of living in poverty (Klassen and Gillin 1999; McDonald 1997; Pulkingham and Ternowetsky 1999).

Thus we see that agency in later life, while it is a human quality that is judiciously invested in positive and culturally mandated practices of self-reflection and self-fulfillment, is also an instrument of investment in governmentalized forms of senior and retired citizenry attendant upon such practices. Through their liberating identities and proactive lifestyles our retired exemplars strengthen, rather than resist, the bonds that hold between between agency, structure, consumerism, and neoliberalism in the context of new cultures of aging. The next section looks to a different example, therefore, to question whether these bonds can be better challenged if agency becomes a quality of collective rather than individual action.

## THE BRITISH U3A MOVEMENT:
## AGENCY AND IDENTITY IN A COLLECTIVE CONTEXT

The preceding discussion suggested that the exigencies of neoliberal cultures are narrowly represented through individual exemplars of retirement, whose later life agency is reduced to market ideals around choice and the 'powers of freedom.' Thus, agency, structure, and lifestyle function to turn identity inside-out, so that the internal biographies of selected retired individuals became the externalized heroic cultural narratives of successful aging, or in some cases the anti-narratives of failing individuals who neglect or refuse to become accomplished retirees. The discussion below looks at a different context whereby agency, structure, and lifestyle assemble within a context of collective identity and shared lifestyle. This comparative exercise is worthwhile because it proposes that collective agential identities in aging cultures can negotiate structural relations with different kinds of resources and orientations. In other words, perhaps the agency-structure problem is due to the heavy focus of its theorists on privileged, self-reflexive, individual identities to the disregard of collective identities and actions geared to social change.

To clarify this point further, this section of the study looks at Universities of the Third Age or U3As as they are called in Britain. Part mutual-aid society, part social movement, part educational facility, and part lifestyle culture, U3As are a unique organization that gives new definition to the 'third age' itself, a rapidly changing and expansive lifecourse space which, as Blaikie notes, "the term 'retirement' does not wholly elucidate" (1999: 70). Indeed, the age markers of the third age, recognized as beginning sometime after 55 or 60, are less relevant than the freedoms and accomplishments that are assumed to distinguish it from younger second and older fourth ages. Part of the uniqueness of the U3As is that they constitute a *new* social movement in the sense that they bear little relation to traditional 'gray' lobby or protest movements based on pension reform, social security entitlements, and health benefits.[6] In this

---

[6] Gray lobby movements and pension politics have a complex international history and impressive record of debates about the making of aging identities (Clifford 1990; Haber and Gratton 1994; Orloff 1993; Pratt 1993; Vincent 1999).

sense the 'senior power' behind the U3A movement shares many of its characteristics with that of other contemporary groups who use local and diverse strategies to connect political goals with lifestyle practices in an era of diminishing social supports. Our analysis here complements Rick Moody's chapter in this volume on 'Structure and Agency in Late-Life Learning.' By examining the dilemmas of agency and structure in Elderhostel, U3As, and other learning-in-retirement organizations, Moody clearly illustrates how post-traditional aging embodies both an agential and egalitarian anti-ageist culture of resistance and a structural reinforcement of dominant social relations. Hence, Moody provides an important opportunity to think about what kinds of late-life learning, given its marginality, can ensure the promise and accessibility of personal growth and experimentation for retired learners. In our case study of U3As we focus more directly on the making of collective identity within a third age social movement with the goal of broadening sociological and gerontological theorizing about agency and structure.

Third Age movements in general have also demonstrated that older populations do not necessarily constitute an unified 'interest group,' 'voting bloc,' or 'senior citizenry' (Street 1999), and political participation is often a result of a lifelong interest in all aspects of public culture rather than simply the onset of older age (Jirovec and Erich 1995; MacLean, Houlahan, and Barskey 1994). Group memberships crosscut by existing gender, ethnic, regional, and class differences are as consequential in shaping collective identities as those based on age. Most importantly, the politics and 'agency' of older people are not necessarily socially progressive or critical of state policy, as Robert Kastenbaum's poignant account of retired senior voters in Arizona who opposed the creation of a Martin Luther King Jr. holiday in the United States demonstrates (1991; 1993). "Chances are that gerontologists will continue to find employment in exposing and combating ageism for a long time to come. But one never reads or hears about older adults as themselves practitioners of bigotry, racism, discrimination" (Kastenbaum 1993: 166). Thus agency is not as an essential condition of being aged; rather, agency is exercised in various ways because it is an effect of how older groups of people utilize the contingencies of social life as practical resources.

British Universities of the Third Age may or may not be based in a university. They are programs organized by and according to the interests of people usually over the age of 55. The first U3A or *université du troisième age* was established in Toulouse, France in 1972, followed by the establishment of The International Association of Universities of the Third Age (AIUTA). The first British U3A, inspired by the French model, began at Cambridge in 1982. Unlike Universities of the Third Age in Europe and in North America associated with university facilities, the British groups are uniquely built on a self-help, mutual–aid ethos recalling a more traditional concept of sociality (Midwinter 1984; 1996; Swindell and Thompson 1995). Branches are self-governed, decisions are collectively made, and sessions are held in local community spaces and members' homes. No pre-requisite experience or educational qualifications are required for membership, nor are credentials, certificates, or degrees offered. Since the initial U3A in Cambridge, the movement has expanded rapidly and as of this writing (June 2002), currently stands at 501 U3A groups consisting of 121,892 mostly female members, who study, teach each other, and discuss their interests in thousands of 'courses' spanning hundreds of topics ranging across disciplines and cultural experiences.

At first glance U3As seem to be an unequivocal success not only as an opportunity for an inventive and inexpensive adult education, but also as a forum for local social reform. They are a fascinating example of how identity and agency meld as participation in Universities of the Third Age creates the conditions under which one becomes a Third Ager, a character in a new stage of life where, as the late Peter Laslett and founder of the British U3A movement says, "blanket phrases, which include 'the Elderly,' 'Senior Citizens,' 'The Retired,' and so on, have ceased to be appropriate now that the vital necessity of recognizing differentiation during that lengthy phase of life has become apparent" (1995:10). For these reasons, Laslett (1989) and other key figures in the movement such as Michael Young (Young and Schuller 1991) have been accused at times of advocating 'Third Ageist' cultural and lifestyle priorities over economic and political issues, and for glorifying the positivity of the Third Age at the expense of the Fourth Age (see Blaikie 1999: 184-187; Biggs 1997; Gilleard and Higgs 2000: 38-42). Haim Hazan's ethnography, *From First Principles: An Experiment in Ageing* (1996), elaborates the interpersonal discourses and rituals through which Cambridge U3A participants rethink their identities as a kind of "buffer zone" between middle-age and old age (p. 33). Members are encouraged to experiment and "abandon conventional parameters of time, space, and meaning and to reconstruct their own" (p. 51). For Hazan, this experimentation also encourages an anti-aging and death-denying atmosphere so that agency leads away from social realities, historical time, and educational enlightenment to a symbolic culture based on "the code of the existential state of the speakers" (p. 148).

Despite the criticisms made of Third Ageism, few studies examine how the establishment of a Third Age identity within the U3A enterprise has been a process of ongoing negotiation and change, and how agency emerges as an overall property of collective action. To illustrate these points the remaining part of this chapter outlines three tensions through which identity, agency, lifestyle, and structure dynamically interacted during the U3As' formative years of development. These tensions are central vs. local politics, research vs. non-research activities, and commercial vs. educational interests. Most importantly, these tensions, rather than limiting U3A organizers and participants, have inspired them to conceive of new solutions to the demands for lifelong learning in an aging society where it is estimated that 14.8 million people are over 55 years old (Midwinter 1996: 26). Thus we see the U3A learner as less of an individualistic exemplar of retirement than as a person contending with lifecourse continuity within a larger social movement aimed at rattling second ageist educational systems.

## Central vs. Local Politics

In February 1981, Cambridge scholar Peter Laslett, Lord Michael Young (who was also instrumental in establishing Britain's Open University) and Eric Midwinter (talented writer and director for the Centre for Policy on Aging) met at Cambridge for a seminal discussion of U3As. Later that year in July, Midwinter publicized in a BBC radiobroadcast the U3A idea of local groups of retired and elderly people meeting to teach and learn from each other. He asked for responses and he immediately received 400 letters. On the basis of this enthusiastic reaction and Laslett's drafting of a formational document, *Objects and Principles*, the U3A founders established a National Committee, secured a Nuffield Foundation donation, began an experimental 'Easter School' at Cambridge with 75 participants, and initiated a newsletter in 1982. By 1983 The Third Age Trust, to which all U3As belong, was registered as a charity with eight U3As. It was still a low-key organization, with the first meeting of the National Committee taking place in Michael Young's car in 1982 (on the road from Cambridge to London) and the first executive secretary, Dianne Norton, running the organization out of her home office. As the movement grew throughout the 1980s, administrative challenges ensued. For example, struggles for financial support led to the need for members to contribute modest membership fees. The expanding numbers of U3As also required a permanently staffed, central coordinating office and a small London office was founded in 1988.

In 1989 a general meeting was called to revise the Constitution of the Third Age Trust, with the result that the Cambridge U3A along with three other groups withdrew from the national organization. Concerned about the centralization and bureaucratization of the U3A movement and vexed that the planned expansion of The Third Age Trust would have few benefits for the largish Cambridge U3A, then Cambridge U3A Chair, David Clark, wrote to the Third Age Trust outlining the Cambridge decision to separate. Since that time another group whose trajectory fell outside the national organization was the Cornwall U3A Forum. These separations signaled that the U3A movement, as with other social movements, had matured to the point where it was being shaped by the tension between central and local politics. Hence, locality began to play a key role in determining what kind of structural form the U3As would take and how memberships could be identified. In the late 1980s and early 1990s, the National Office moved to larger premises, launched a Travel Club, and established new sub-committees on services, conferences, and finance. Today the U3A has expanded its informational and organizational programs through the Internet (http://www.u3a.org.uk).

As the U3A movement continues to grow and becomes, no doubt, one of the largest universities in the world, will this development require more centralization or create more tension with certain local U3As? How can the U3A movement, premised as it is on self-help communitarian and popular democratic principles, continue in its accelerated growth to meet a multiplicity of visions and directions without risking groups opting out? These issues lead to a second tension about U3As as research units.

## Research vs. Non-Research

Peter Laslett's seventh U3A objective from his founding "Objects and Principles" document is "to undertake research on the process of aging in society" (in Cloet 1993: 16-18). Laslett believed that U3A members are in an ideal situation to undertake research and publishing that would counter not only the predominance of second age-generated literature on the aging process, but would also conform to one of his initial objects to "assail the dogma of intellectual decline with age." True to his word, Laslett helped to write the first piece of U3A research at Cambridge in 1984, the text *The Image of the Elderly on TV*, that looked at the negative effects of TV ageist stereotyping (Lambert, Laslett, and Clay, 1984). Later in 1990 the Harpenden U3A members undertook a similarly critical project to scour daily newspapers for images and references to old age and later analyze the results (Midwinter 1996: 37). One of the most interesting research projects was in early 1985, when the Centre for Policy on Ageing and the Community Education Development Centre advised the BBC on its twelve part series of Dickens' *The Pickwick Papers*. Sixteen U3A discussion groups organized by Eric Midwinter agreed to watch and evaluate the series. They drew up documentation that the BBC took very seriously and while the groups enriched their education in Victorian drama, the BBC learned something new about images of aging by working with some sharp Third Age media critics.

Other research efforts that have come out of the U3As include local historical projects documenting village antiquities and joint programs with the former *DesignAge* of London's Royal College of Art that ran competitions for product innovations geared to elderly consumers. However, most groups produce no research. Afterall, they are seeking an education apart from formal accreditation institutions and Laslett's mandate to create an alternative, Third Age research base appeared to be daunting. As David Clark, former Chair of the Cambridge U3A admitted in an interview, research "means going through an awful lot of papers and counting things and messing around with adding machines ... and we're not going to do that sort of hard work."[7] Research, for Clark as well as for others, remains an academic career activity and not something that should be foisted on those learning for pleasure, at leisure. (For Hazan (1996), this anti-research stance is another example of the U3A ideological denial of the objective realities of aging).

Hence a second tension emerged between those groups and leaders who promoted scholarly production and political engagement, and those who do not. Part of this tension hinges on how the U3As envisioned their impact on the wider society and their role in representing the Third Age as a social-demographic force. These issues point to a third tension between commercial and educational interests.

## Commercial vs. Educational Interests

On the one hand, with the growth of the U3A movement the concept of the Third Age has become respectfully popular as a signifier of a new literate citizenry. The multivolume *Carnegie Inquiry into the Third Age* (1992-93) did much to publicize the cultural, health, and economic profile of this citizenry, and, according to the Inquiry, "was prompted by one of the great social achievements of the 20th century – for the first time people have 20 or 30 years of active life ahead of them after finishing full-time work, rearing a family, or both" (*The Carnegie Third Age Programme* brochure). A more telling illustration was the story about then 80-year old Lord Michael Young's new baby in the British newspaper *The Independent* headlined with "Father of the Third Age" (Jan. 20, 1996) without further explanation of the term. On the other hand, the concept of the Third Age spread into commercial categories as Third Agers were presumed to constitute a homogeneous and prosperous market group. For the U3A groups, there also developed a number of enterprising activities such as a volunteer-run translation service (The Int/Tran Service) begun in 1992, Dianne Norton's establishment of The Third Age Press in 1994, and a widening network of international leisure, travel, and skills-exchange programs.

Such networking was not always desirable by U3A members who felt increasingly vulnerable to their redefinition as a marketing target. For example, in 1994 Saga Insurance offered the National U3A Committee a deal whereby the company would take on the costs of running and updating the newsletter, *Third Age News*, in return for free advertising space. The deal was decided by a membership vote that favored the Saga offer for a two-year trial period. Nevertheless, the incident triggered a widespread debate and internal division between those who wanted to keep U3As free from commercial interests and those who saw productive

---

[7] Interview with co-author Stephen Katz, January 18, 1996. On the academic role of older researchers in non-British UTA and other programs see Glanz and Neikrug (1997) and Lemieux (1995).

partnerships with the private sector as beneficial to the growth of the movement. In the words of Marion Bieber, one of the founding organizers of the London U3A:

> When you've worked for ten years without ever even considering payment, when you sweated to do everything on a shoestring, and have done it successfully, and when you know that there are the skills and abilities out there in U3A that could run that newspaper standing on their heads ... why do we suddenly have to have paid journalists to write articles? We should always limit ourselves to what we can do within the philosophy, which we represent. If we can't do it then let's not try.[8]

While the 'Saga saga' (as it was called) was eventually resolved, and since 1998 there is a also a new U3A bulletin called *Sources,* Marion Bieber's 'philosophy which we represent' is still a relevant indicator of the kind of agency/structure tensions upon which the U3A identity was being forged.

To the three U3A tensions we have been describing – central vs. local politics, research vs. non-research activities, and commercial vs. educational interests – one could add others; for example, political vs. non-political actions, or homogeneous vs. heterogeneous memberships. In all these cases agency and identity derive from an expansive set of collective practices riven with the internal tensions of defining a Third Age way of life as well as resisting those external structures that would marginalize it. In a rapidly aging country like Britain, we have the exciting opportunity to observe how the problems and prospects of British U3As, with their modest origins and now celebrating their twentieth anniversary, are part of a reordering of the relationship between demographic, social, educational, and experiential spheres and a rethinking about what aging and learning can mean to each other. Criticisms are acknowledged, as Eric Midwinter notes, there is "a muted flat note among the melodious songs of praise for U3A. It may be that its very success has allowed the perilous thought to permeate that it is *the* answer" (1996: 15).

## CONCLUSIONS

This chapter began by reflecting on the theoretical fit between agency and structure, identity, and lifestyle within the practical context of retirement and Third Age cultures. By examining two illustrative cases – Canadian 'exemplars of retirement' and British U3A lifelong learners – we can suggest that this theoretical fit is multidimensional, relational, uneven, and contingent. In the first case, the layering of neoliberal technologies of government with idealized practices of the self creates identities stretched between anti-conformist, inventive lifestyles and the 'powers of freedom' that constrain them. In the second case, the making of identity through collective struggle and local educational politics has resulted in a new social movement whose growth and success overflow the bounds of enforced neoliberal individualism and its ethics of responsibility and self-care. From both cases we learn that this new stage of life – retirement or third age or 'fresh map of life' (Laslett 1989) – is an indeterminate identity-zone, where the tension between agency and structure can be observed anew in a society that remains largely hostile to the emergence of genuinely meaningful and empowering older identities. As Chris Phillipson remarks, "the

---

[8] Interview with co-author Stephen Katz, November 14, 1995.

secure place on which to make one's stand may depend, not on the shifting sands of consumer identity, but through the creation of a protected inner core and an external environment that provides both an adequate material base while remaining sufficiently secure to allow experiments with social identity to emerge" (1999b: 165). If the coexistence of security, material adequacy, and experimentation is the ground upon which the contradictions of aging identities are to be worked out, then, as sociologists of aging we have an obligation to contribute our critical skills to this new stage of life upon which a shifting constellation of political, cultural, scientific, commercial, professional, and biographical enterprises is already making claims.

## REFERENCES

Adkins, L. 1999. "Community and Economy: A Retraditionalization of Gender?" *Theory, Culture & Society* 16: 119-139.

Adkins, L.. 2001. "Risk Culture, Self-Reflexivity and the Making of Sexual Hicrarchies." *Body & Society* 7: 35-55.

Andrews, M. 1999. "The Seductiveness of Agelessness." *Ageing and Society* 19: 301-318.

Atchley, R.C. 1989. "A Continuity Theory of Normal Aging." *The Gerontologist* 29: 183-190.

Atchley, R.C. 1991. "The Influence of Aging or Frailty on Perceptions and Expression of the Self: Theoretical and Methodological Issues." Pp.207-225 in *The Concept and Measurement of Quality of Life in the Frail Elderly*, edited by J.E. Birren, J.E. Lubben, J.C. Rowe, and D.E. Deutchman. New York: Academic Press.

Baber, Z. 1991. "Beyond the Structure/Agency Dualism: An Evaluation of Giddens' Theory of Structuration." *Sociological Inquiry* 2: 219-230.

Barry, A., T. Osborne, and N. Rose, editors. 1996. *Foucault and Political Reason: Liberalism, Neo-Liberalism and Rationalities of Government*. London: UCL Press.

Basting, A. D. 1998. *The Stages of Age: Performing Age in ContemporaryAmerican Culture*. Ann Arbor: University of Michigan Press.

Battle, K. 1997. "Pension Reform in Canada." *Canadian Journal on Aging* 16: 519-552.

Biggs, S. 1997. "Choosing Not to be Old? Masks, Bodies and Identity Management in Later life." *Ageing and Society* 17: 553-570.

Biggs, S. 1999. *The Mature Imagination: Dynamics of Identity in Midlife and Beyond*. Buckingham: Open University Press.

Birren, J. E. 1995. "New Models of Aging: Comment on Need and Creative Efforts." *Canadian Journal on Aging* 14: 1-7.

Blaikie, A. 1999. *Ageing in Popular Culture*. Cambridge: Cambridge University Press.

Breytspraak, L.M. 1984. *The Development of Self in Later Life*. Boston: Little, Brown and Company.

Burchell, G. 1993. "Liberal Government and Techniques of the Self." *Economy and Society* 22: 267-282.

Burchell, G., C. Gordon, and P. Miller, editors. 1991. *The Foucault Effect: Studies in Governmentality*. Chicago: University of Chicago Press.

Bury, M. 1995. "Ageing, Gender and Sociological Theory." pp. 15-29 in *Connecting Gender & Ageing: A Sociological Approach*, edited by S. Arber and J. Ginn. Buckingham: Open University Press.

Castel, R. 1991. "From Dangerousness to Risk." pp. 281-298 in *The Foucault Effect: Studies in Governmentality*, edited by G. Burchell, C. Gordon, and P. Miller. Chicago: University of Chicago Press.

Cheal, D. and K. Kampen. 1998. "Poor and Dependent Seniors in Canada." *Ageing and Society* 18: 147-166.

Clifford, C. G. 1990. *Canada's Fighting Seniors*. Toronto: James Lorimer.

Cloet, A. 1993. *University of the Third Age (U3A): The Rank Fellowship Report*. London: The Third Age Trust.

Cockerham, W.C., A. Rutten, and T. Abel. 1997. "Conceptualizing Contemporary Health Lifestyles: Moving beyond Weber." *The Sociological Quarterly* 38: 321-342.

Cole, T. R., W. A. Achenbaum, P. L. Jakobi, and R. Kastenbaum, editors. 1993. *Voices and Visions of Aging: Toward a Critical Gerontology*. New York: Springer.

Cole, T. R. and R. E. Ray, editors. 2000. *Handbook of the Humanities and Aging (Second Edition)*. New York: Springer.

Cruikshank, B. 1999. *The Will To Empower: Democratic Citizens and Other Subjects*. Ithaca and London: Cornell University Press.

Dannefer, D. 1999. "Neoteny, Naturalization, and Other Constituents of Human Development." pp. 67-93 in *Self and Society in Aging Processes*, edited by C. Ryff and V. W. Marshall. New York: Springer.

Dean, M. 1999. *Governmentality: Power and Rule in Modern Society*. London: Sage.

Deats, S. M. and L. T. Lenker, editors. 1999. *Aging and Identity: A Humanities Perspective*. Westport, CT: Praeger.

Ekerdt, D. J. and E. Clark. 2001. "Selling Retirement in Financial Planning Advertisements." *Journal of Aging Studies* 15: 55-68.

Elder, G. H., Jr. 1974. *Children of the Great Depression: Social Change in Life Experience*. Chicago: University of Chicago Press.

Estes, C.L. 1979. *The Aging Enterprise*. San Francisco: Josey-Bass.

Featherstone, M. and M. Hepworth. 1995a. "Images of Positive Aging: A Case Study of 'Retirement Choice' Magazine." pp. 29-48 in *Images of aging: Cultural Representations of Later Life*, edited by M. Featherstone and A. Wernick. London: Routledge.

Featherstone, M. and M. Hepworth. 1995b. "The Mask of Aging and the Postmodern Lifecourse." pp. 371-398 in *The Body: Social Process and Cultural Theory*, edited by M. Featherstone, M. Hepworth, and B. Turner. Thousand Oaks, CA: Sage.

Featherstone, M. and A. Wernick. 1995. "Introduction." Pp.1-15 in *Images of Aging: Cultural Representations of Later Life*, edited by M. Featherstone and A. Wernick. London: Routledge.

Fisher, B.J. and D.K. Specht. 1999. "Successful Aging and Creativity in Later Life." *Journal of Aging Studies* 13: 457-472.

Foucault, M. 1981. " 'Omnes et singulatim': Towards a Criticism of 'Political Reason.'" pp. 223-254 in *The Tanner Lectures on Human Values, vol. 2*, edited by S. McMurrin. Salt Lake City: University of Utah Press.

Foucault, M. 1988. "The Political Technology of Individuals." pp. 145-162 in *Technologies of the Self: A Seminar with Michel Foucault*, edited by L. H. Martin, H. Gutman, and P. H. Hutton. London: Tavistock.

Foucault, M. 1991. "Governmentality." pp. 87-104 in *The Foucault Effect: Studies in Governmentality*, edited by G. Burchell, C. Gordon, and P. Miller. Chicago: University of Chicago Press.

Fuller, S. 1993. "Disciplinary Boundaries and the Rhetoric of the Social Sciences." pp. 125-149 in *Knowledges: Historical and Critical Studies in Disciplinarity*, edited by E. Messer-Davidow, D. R. Shumway, and D. J. Sylvan. Charlottesville: University Press of Virginia.

Gardiner, J. K., editor. 1995. *Provoking Agents: Gender and Agency in Theory and Practice*. Chicago: University of Chicago Press.

*Generations*, special issue on "Images of Aging in Media and Advertising." Fall 2001.

Giddens, A. 1984. *The Constitution of Society: Outline of the Theory of Structuration*. Cambridge: Polity Press.

Giddens, A. 1990. "Comments on the Theory of Structuration." *Journal for the Theory of Social Behaviour* 20: 75-80.

Giddens, A. 1991. *Modernity and Self-identity: Self and Society in the Late Modern Age*. Stanford: Stanford University Press.

Giddens, A. 1999. *Runaway World: How Globalization is Reshaping Our Lives*. London: Profile Books.

Gilleard, C. and P. Higgs. 2000. *Cultures of Ageing: Self, Citizen and the Body*. London: Prentice Hall.

Glanz, D. and S. Neikrug. 1997. "Seniors as Researchers in the Study of Aging: Learning and Doing." *The Gerontologist* 37: 823-826.

Gubrium, J. F. and J. A. Holstein. 1995. "Individual Agency, The Ordinary, and Postmodern Life." *The Sociological Quarterly* 36: 555-570.

Gubrium, J. F. and J. A. Holstein. 1998. "Narrative Practice and the Coherence of Personal Stories." *The Sociological Quarterly* 39: 163-187.

Gullette, M. M. 1998. "Midlife Discourses in the Twentieth-Century United States: An Essay on the Sexuality, Ideology, and Politics of 'Middle-Ageism.' " pp. 3-44 in *Welcome to Middle Age! (And Other Cultural Fictions)*, edited by R A. Shweder. Chicago: University of Chicago Press.

Haber, C. and B. Gratton. 1994. *Old Age and the Search for Security: An American Social History*. Bloomington: Indiana University Press.

Hauser, R. 1999. "Adequacy and Poverty Among Retired People." *International Social Security Review* 52: 107-124.

Hazan, H. 1996. *From First Principles: An Experiment in Ageing*. Westport, CT: Bergin & Harvey.

Hendricks, J. 2003. "Structure and Identity– Mind the Gap: Toward a Personal Resource Model of Successful Aging." pp. 63-87 in *The Need for Theory: Critical Approaches to Social Gerontology for the 21st Century,* edited by S. Biggs, J. Hendricks, and A. Lowenstein. Amityville NY: Baywood.

Hepworth, M. 1995. "Positive Ageing. What is the message?" Pp.176-190 in *The Sociology of Health Promotion*, edited by R. Bunton, S. Nettleton, and R. Burrows. London: Routledge.

Hepworth, M. 1999. "In Defiance of an Ageing Culture." *Ageing and Society* 19:139-48.

Hepworth, M. and M. Featherstone. 1998. "The Male Menopause: Lay Accounts and the Culture Reconstruction of Midlife." pp. 276-301 in *The Body in Everyday Life*, edited by S. Nettleton and J. Watson. London: Routledge.

Holstein, M. 1999. "Women and Productive Aging: Troubling Implications." pp. 359-373 in *Critical gerontology: Perspectives from Political and Moral Economy*, edited by M. Minkler and C.L. Estes. Amityville, NY: Baywood.

Hopflinger, F. 1993. "From Ageism to Gerontologism? Emerging Images of Aging in Gerontology." pp. 90-97 in *Images of Aging in Western Societies: Proceeding of the 2nd 'Images of Aging Conference,'* edited C. Hummel and C.J. Lalive D'Epinay. University of Geneva: Centre for Interdisciplinary Gerontology.

Jamieson, A., S. Harper, and C. Victor, editors. 1997. *Critical Approaches to Ageing and Later Life*. Buckingham: Open University Press.

Jamieson, L. 1999. "Intimacy Transformed? A Critical Look at the 'Pure Relationship.' *Sociology* 33: 477- 494.

Jirovec, R. L. and J. A. Erich. 1995. "Gray Power or Power Outage? Political Participation Among Very Old Women." *Journal of Women & Aging* 7: 85-99.

Kalisch, D. and T. Aman. 2001. "Maintaining Prosperity in an Ageing Society." *Organization for Economic Co-operation and Development Aging Working Papers*. Paris.

Kastenbaum, R. 1991. "Racism and the Older Voter? Arizona's Rejection of a Paid Holiday to Honor Martin Luther King." *International Journal of Aging and Human Development* 32:199-209.

Kastenbaum, R. 1993. "Encrusted Elders: Arizona and the Political Spirit of Postmodern Aging." pp. 160-183 in *Voices and Visions of Aging: Toward a Critical Gerontology*, edited by T. R. Cole, W. A. Achenbaum, P. L. Jakobi, and R. Kastenbaum. New York: Springer.

Katz, S. 1995. "Imagining the Life Span. From Premodern Miracles to Postmodern Fantasies." pp. 61-73 in *Images of Aging: Cultural Representations of Later Life*, edited by M. Featherstone and A. Wernick. London: Routledge.

Katz, S. 2000. "Busy Bodies: Activity, Aging, and the Management of Everyday Life." *Journal of Aging Studies* 14:135-152.

Katz, S. 2001. "Growing Older Without Aging? Positive Aging, Anti-Ageism, and Anti-Aging." *Generations* 25: 27-32. pp. 15-31

Katz, S. 2003. "Critical Gerontological Theory: Intellectual Fieldwork and the Nomadic Life of Ideas." In *The Need for Theory: Critical Approaches to Social Gerontology for the 21st Century,* edited by S. Biggs, J. Hendricks, and A.Lowenstein. Amityville NY: Baywood.

Kaufman, S. R. 1986. *The Ageless Self: Sources of Meaning in Later Life*. Madison, Wisconsin: University of Wisconsin.

Kaufman, S. R. 1993. "Reflections on 'The Ageless Self.'" *Generations* Spring/Summer: 13-16.

Kenyon, G., P. Clark, and B. de Vries, editors. 2001. *Narrative Gerontology: Theory, Research and Practice*. New York: Springer.

Klassen, T. R and C. T. Gillin. 1999. "Heavy Hand of the Law: The Canadian Supreme Court and Mandatory retirement." *Canadian Journal on Aging* 18: 259-276.

Lambert, J., P. Laslett, and H. Clay. 1984. *The Image of the Elderly on TV*. Cambridge: Cambridge University of the Third Age.

Laslett, P. 1989. *A Fresh Map of Life: The Emergence of the Third Age*. London: Weidenfeld and Nicolson.

Laslett, P. 1995. "The Third Age and the Disappearance of Old Age." pp. 9-16 in *Preparation for Aging*, edited by E Heikkinen, J. Kuuisinen, and I. Ruoppila. New York: Plenum.

Laws, G. 1995. "Embodiment and Emplacement: Identities, Representations and Landscape in Sun City Retirement Communities." *International Journal of Aging and Human Development* 40: 253-280.

Laws, G. 1996. " 'A Shot of Economic Adrenalin': Reconstructing 'the elderly' in the Retiree-based Economic Development Literature." *Journal of Aging Studies* 10: 171-188.

Layder, D. 1994. *Understanding Social Theory*. Thousand Oaks, CA: Sage.

Lee, R. L. M. 1990. "The Micro-Macro Problem in Collective Behaviour: Reconciling Agency and Structure." *Journal for the Theory of Social Behaviour* 20: 213-233.

Lemieux, A. 1995. "The University of the Third Age: Role of Senior Citizens." *Educational Gerontology* 21: 337-344.

MacLean, M. J., N. Houlahan, and F. B. Barskey. 1994. "Health Realities and Independence: The Voice of Elderly Women." pp. 133-163 in *Gender, Aging and the State*, edited by B. Nichols and P. Leonard. Montreal: Black Books.

Marshall, V. W. 1996. "The State of Theory in Aging and the Social Sciences." Pp.12-30 in *Handbook of Aging and the Social Sciences* (4th edition), edited by R.H. Binstock and L.K. George. San Diego: Academic Press.

Matthews, S. H. 1979. *The Social World of Old Women*. Beverly Hills, CA: Sage.

McDonald, L. 1997. "Invisible Poor: Canada's Retired Widows." *Canadian Journal on Aging* 16: 553-583.

McHugh, K. E. 2000. "The 'Ageless Self'? Emplacement of Identities in Sun Belt Retirement Communities." *Journal of Aging Studies* 14: 103-115.

McMullin, J. and V. W. Marshall. 1999. "Structure and Agency in the Retirement Process: A Case Study of Montreal Garment Workers." pp. 305-338 in *Self and Society in Aging Processes,* edited by C. Ryff and V. W. Marshall. New York: Springer.

McNay, L. 1999. "Gender, Habitus and the Field: Pierre Bourdieu and the Limits of Reflexivity." *Theory, Culture & Society* 16: 95-117.

McNay, L. 2000. *Gender and Agency: Reconfiguring the Subject in Feminist Social Theory*. Malden, MA: Polity Press.

Midwinter, E., editor. 1984. *Mutual Aid Universities*. London: Croom Helm.

Midwinter, E. 1996. *Thriving People*. London: The Third Age Trust.

Minkler, M. 1984. *Readings in the Political Economy of Aging*. Amityville, NY: Baywood.

Minkler, M. 1990. "Aging and Disability: Behind and Beyond the Stereotypes." *Journal of Aging Studies* 4: 245-260.

Minkler, M. 1991. "Gold in Gray: Reflections on Business' Discovery of the Elderly Market." pp. 81-83 in *Critical Perspectives on Aging: The Political and Moral Economy of Growing Old*, edited by M. Minkler and C. Estes. Amityville, NY: Baywood.

NADBank Survey 2000. Toronto: Newspaper Audience Databank Inc. www.nadbank.com.

Orloff, A. S. 1993. *The Politics of Pensions: A Comparative Analysis of Britain, Canada, and the United States, 1880-1940*. Madison: University of Wisconsin Press.

Petersen, A. and R. Bunton, editors. 1997. *Foucault, Health and Medicine*. London and New York: Routledge.

Phillipson, C. 1982. *Capitalism and The Construction of Old Age*. London: MacMillan.

Phillipson, C. 1999a. *Reconstructing Old Age: New Agendas in Social Theory and Practice*. London: Sage.

Phillipson, C. 1999b. "Population Ageing and The Sociological Tradition." *Education and Ageing* 14: 159-170.

Pratt, H. J. 1993. *Gray Agendas: Interest Groups and Public Pensions in Canada, Britain, and the United States*. Ann Arbor: University of Michigan Press.

Pulkingham, J. and G. Ternowetsky. 1999. "Neo-Liberalism and Retrenchment: Employment, Universality, Safety-net Provisions and a Collapsing Canadian Welfare State." Pp.84-94 in *Citizens or Consumers? Social Policy in a Market Society*, edited by D. Broad and W. Antony. Halifax: Fernwood Publishing.

Redvay-Mulvey, G. 2000. "Gradual Retirement in Europe." *Journal of Aging and Social Policy* 11: 49-60.

Rose, N. 1992. "Governing the Enterprising Self." pp. 141-164 in *The Value of the Enterprise Culture, The Moral Debate*, edited by P. Heelas and P. Morris. London: Routledge.

Rose, N. 1993. "Government, Authority and Expertise in Advanced Neoliberalism." *Economy and Society* 22:283-299.

Rose, N. 1999. *Powers of Freedom: Reframing Political Thought*. Cambridge: University of Cambridge Press.

Settersten, Jr., R. A. 2002, editor. *Invitation to the Life Course: Toward New Understandings of Later Life*. Amityville, NY: Baywood.

Statistics Canada. March 6, 2000. "Income Levels, Income Inequality and Low Income among the Elderly: 1980 to 1995." *The Daily*.

Street, D. 1999. "Special Interests or Citizen Rights? "Senior Power," Social Security, and Medicare." pp. 109-130 in *Critical Gerontology: Perspectives from Political and Moral Economy*, edited by M. Minkler and C. L. Estes. Amityville, NY: Baywood.

Swindell, R. and J. Thompson. 1995. "An International Perspective on the University of the Third Age." *Educational Gerontology* 21: 429-447.

*The Carnegie Inquiry into The Third Age (9 Reports)*. 1993. Dunfermline: The Carnegie United Kingdom Trust.

Tulle-Winton, E. 1999. "Growing Old and Resistance: Towards a New Cultural Economy of Old Age?" *Ageing and Society* 19:281-299.

Turner, B. S. 1995. "Aging and Identity: Some Reflections on the Somatization of the Self." pp. 245-260 in *Images of Aging: Cultural Representations of Later Life*, edited by M.Featherstone and A. Wernick. London: Routledge.

Twigg, J. 2000. *Bathing – The Body and Community Care*. London and New York: Routledge.

Veal, A. J. 1993. "The Concept of Lifestyle: A Review." *Leisure Studies* 12: 233-252.

Vincent, J. 1999. *Politics, Power and Old Age: Struggles Over Old Age and Ageing*. Buckingham: Open University Press.

Walker, A. 2000. "Public Policy and the Construction of Old Age in Europe." *The Gerontologist* 40: 304-308.

Ylanne-McEven, V. 1999. " 'Young at Heart': Discourses of Age Identity in Travel Agency Interaction." *Ageing and Society* 19: 417-440.

Young, M. and T. Schuller. 1991. *Life After Work: The Arrival of the Ageless Society.* London: Harper/Collins.

# PART 3.
# MICRO-STRATEGIES OF RESISTANCE

# Chapter 5

# RECLAIMING AGENCY –
# MANAGING AGING BODIES IN PRISON

## *Azrini Wahidin*

## ABSTRACT

The central focus of the chapter is to demonstrate how female elders who are in prison negotiate and resist the omnipresent power of the disciplinary gaze. It is by engaging with Foucauldian thought that one is able to illustrate how elders in prison transgress ageist and gendered discourses. Moreover, it is through a discussion of the body and the role of time–discipline that we can come to understand how the 'old body' is performed in prison. The work of Foucault is crucial in understanding the nature of power in prisons and how it affects the identities of elders in prison.

The spaces occupied by older women in prison demonstrate how time, space and techniques of punishment in the ordering of prison life are disrupted, destabilised and transformed. The elders demonstrate how the use of power and how the capillaries of punishment in prison are directed in a specific way at the female body. They choreograph their own bodies by transgressing or reinforcing typifications of age and femininity and in turn the elders thwart the process of institutionalisation. It is the ability to resist and reclaim aspects of their outside self which enables elders to survive prison life.

**Key Words:** Time, Bodies, Prison, Agency, Aging, Identity.

## INTRODUCTION

'…. After one week of prison, the instinct for cleanliness completely disappeared from me. I wander aimlessly around the washroom when I suddenly see Steinlauff, my friend aged almost fifty, with nude torso, scrub his neck and shoulders with little success (he has no soap) but great energy. Steinlauf sees me and greets me, and without preamble asks me severely why I do not wash. Why should I wash? Would I be better off than I am? Would I please someone more? Would I live a day, an hour longer? I would probably live a shorter time because to wash is an effort, a waste of energy and warmth …we will all die, we are all about to die…Steinlauf interrupts me. He has finished washing and is now drying himself with his cloth jacket, which he was holding before, wrapped up between his knees and which he will

soon put on. And without interrupting the operation he administers a complete lesson. This was the sense, not forgotten either then or later: that precisely because the Lager was a great machine to reduce us to beasts, we must not become beasts; that even in this place one can survive, and therefore one must want to survive, to tell the story, to bear witness'.
*(Primo Levi, 1996:8)*

In this chapter I propose to synergise theories of agency and embodiment to describe and interpret how female elders negotiate time and space in prison. This chapter serves to map moments in prison demonstrating how 'old' female bodies transgress the disciplinary gaze of the prison. I will be drawing upon the work of Foucault to understand the nature of power in prisons and how the technologies used to exert power affect the identities of elders in prison. A central implication of the Foucauldian perspective is the way that the sites for the operation of power simultaneously become sites for resistance, so that the ultimate impact of incarceration upon the identities/sense of self of the women is an outcome of what the women do with the time and the body discipline imposed on them. It is by applying a Foucauldian gaze and as demonstrated throughout my data, that prison power can be viewed largely in terms of the management and production of the body through various time-disciplines, so that the subversion of time-discipline and self-(body) regulation become key modes of resistance.

The work of Foucault is central to understanding penality and how various institutions, practices and techniques serve to discipline the body (Bourdieu, 1978, 1981; Bordo 1990). The term 'performativity' will also be used to demonstrate that the impact of prison on women involves a combination of enforcement and denial of stereotypical femininity (e.g: 'feminine modesty' is over-ruled in the strip-search; the 'feminine' role of nurturance is asserted through the practice of expecting elders to nurture the younger women). In addition femininity itself, and more specifically aging within femininity, is viewed in society in terms of the presentation of the body. Butler (1990) has shown that the performative nature of gender can be subversive as well.

The term 'capillaries' will be used in this chapter to reflect the finding that the power to shape the elderly subject is dispersed; that it results from the whole spectrum of routines, forms of treatment, disciplines, attitudes of other inmates, the women themselves and the outside culture; and that the effect is very much the reconstruction of the subject as opposed to the mere punishment of the illegal act. Although Foucault does not identify age as a defining construct (constituent of identity), one can apply his theories to understand how ageist discourse is implicated in policing a particular cohort.

By giving voice to the elders in prison, I hope to draw out the contradictions and dilemmas which they experience as older women in prison, thereby illustrating the relationship between time and the performance of time in a total institution. By looking at the role and meaning of time we can come to understand how female elders in prison reiterate and negotiate the identity 'prisoner' within the discipline of 'the time of incarceration'. The focus of this chapter will be on inserting the words of female elders[1] into debates about the body, identity and the potential for agency in prison.

---

[1] The data from which this is drawn arises from research done by Azrini Wahidin; Unpublished doctoral thesis, *Life In The Shadows - A Qualitative Study Of Older Women In Prison', 2002.*

## LOCATING THE FIELD – NEGOTIATING ACCESS

During the course of the research sixteen prisons were contacted[2] and visits made to both male and female prisons, including the Elderly unit at HMP Kingston and the only female prison in Northern Ireland. To obtain permission from the 'gate-keepers' (Goffman, 1961), I decided to contact individual governors, deputy governors and other governor grades or both rather than approach the Home Office. The aims and objectives of the research were outlined and access was requested. This proved to be a successful way of opening the prison gates to an 'outsider'. Being a young female researcher without being 'Home Office approved', was beneficial and, perhaps, this persona afforded greater access, with many people going out of their way to be helpful, given the assumed non-threatening position of my persona. Moreover, by approaching individual governors rather than the Home Office, I kept the research as near to the ground as possible.

## SERVERS OF TIME

By examining the total institution, I will demonstrate how time is used by the prison to mark the body. The aim of time-discipline is to train the body and by its own construction emit socially defining and confining norms (Butler, 1990; Foucault, 1977a). Inevitably, in this process of prison time-discipline, the corporeality of time and the use of time in prison transcends the subject/object dualisms. It is by understanding the multi-faceted nature of time and the aging body that we can come to understand how time is a constituent part in the construction of our identities.

It is by examining how female offenders survive the prison time machine that this chapter will reveal how the prison apparatus inscribes the aging body. As I will argue, older women in prison are not passive objects but find ways of governing time. Butler (1979) argues that 'gender is not written on the body as the torturing instrument of writing in Kafka's 'In the Penal Colony'; inscribing itself unintelligibly on the flesh of the accused. The question is not: what meaning does that inscription carry within it, but what cultural apparatus arranges this meeting between instrument and body, what interventions into this ritualistic repetition are possible?' (1997:186).

Many elders find themselves trapped in a series of routines, ruled by prison clock time. An awareness of repetition makes many of the elders in the study negotiate the strictures of institutional time. It is by re-imagining the boundaries of the body that we can begin to understand how time-discipline 'inscribes itself unintelligibly on the flesh of the accused'. This can be done through looking at both the meanings of its inscription for women and the disruptive agentic repetitions in the daily practices in which women engage.

## BODY, POSITION AND AGENCY

The tendency in some sociological work on the body (Falk, 1985) to valorise the objective body as distinct to the subjective body leads to a false dichotomy based on the

---

[2] At the time of writing there were 16 female prison establishments.

Cartesian dualism. In contrast, by engaging with Foucauldian theory one can illustrate how the capillaries of power, or techniques of discipline, pervade all areas of life. Foucault (1977b) proffers that power 'reaches into the very grain of individuals, touches their bodies and inserts itself into their actions and attitudes, their discourses, learning processes and everyday lives' (ibid: 39).

As this chapter shows the body is not a passive site on which social codes are inscribed; rather it is an active component of being. It is through embodiment, that is the lived aspects of corporeal being, that I will access agency, suggesting a more fluid relation between body and subjectivity.

The prison places the aging body and other bodies in a political field where power relations have an immediate hold upon those held under the prison gaze. The work of Merleau-Ponty (1966), on the phenomenology of the body is of interest here, allowing a broader concern with the understanding of everyday life, in that the body can be seen as a reciprocal agent working from within, modifying, and modified by, particular structures.

One must remember that bodies never act in isolation; they are always part of networks/systems, which involve other bodies and cultural phenomena. It is not the case that we just have bodies, but that we are involved in the development of regimes which govern our own bodies. For example, women body-builders, women who have eating disorders or women who self mutilate are resisting normalized forms of hegemonic femininity by re-inscribing and transgressing the limits of their body. They are reversing the gaze. In a similar vein, Kate deploys techniques which enable her to subvert forms of disciplinary control.

'Those that leave the handcuffs on, I'll embarrass them in the hospital. I would hold my hand up and make sure that everybody in the hospital saw them. The screws take them off in the end because they [are] embarrassed. I don't let them get away with it. You just have to play them at their own game, don't you?'[3]
*(Kate Age: 53)*

The above example demonstrates how the symbiotic nature of punishment is experienced and managed by the elder by appropriating the jailers' tools as she moves from the private sphere of the prison to the public arena of the hospital. The process of being punished in a public space, the hospital ward, can be subverted by reversing the public gaze onto the jailer. Rather than surreptitiously cloaking the visible signifiers of punishment, her counter technique is to make them public. This is a good example of how the 'profaned bodies' of elders constructed by the judicial-stare and purloined looks of the outsider gaze can be reversed (Wahidin, 2002a). It illustrates how power is in a state of flux, providing the disempowered with a means of controlling the onlooker's gaze and the prison officers' actions.

Such activities could be said to differ from other forms of body project: body-building, dieting, etc., involve the celebration of the ideal physique rather than the techniques involved in subverting hegemonic norms of femininity. The example above demonstrate how elders in the study became the object of their own gaze, in order to maintain a degree of control over their bodies in an environment where private lives become public property. In becoming the object of their own gaze they become powerful in being 'invisible as the source of the gaze'. In other words they are the ones who are looking without being looked at (Tsëelon, 1995:68).

---

[3] Pseudonyms have been given to protect the identity of the women.

'Somebody said to me once you know, because I used to get very upset when I had to strip and they said to me, what you do is; if you do it really quickly, you peel off all your clothes right, you quickly rip off your knickers and hand it, and as you're handing your knickers just twirl around and you're in *control* of the knickers, the spin, whatever. That day I had this white lacy body on me, all in one thing, so I slowly took off my clothes, peeled off my blouse, peeled off my leggings.' (emphasis in original)
*(Wan-Nita, Age: 52)*

It is through these bodily practices that the elders in the study transformed their gendered habitus, thus creating new identities and new spaces in the carceral machine.

'I stood for a moment in this white lacy body and I thought I'll just let them see how well I look for the age of fifty, and then I peeled it right off and handed it, twirled around, carried on laughing and that is the first time ever I've dealt with a strip like that. Whereas before I used to get really distressed and everything.'
*(Wan-Nita Age: 52)*

## Bodies Do Matter

The more we problematise the body the less sure we can be of what the body is and what the body represents (Falk, 1994; Featherstone 1991; Frank 1990, 1991). The body in its material form has been taken for granted, absent as a source or tool of agency or forgotten in gerontological literature (Öberg, 1996). We only begin to think about the body when it begins to break down mechanically. Thus the role of the body in gerontology has for some time focused on the failing body and the political response to 'old' bodies.

## The Absent Body

There is one common fact about human beings: we have and are bodies.

'Human beings are embodied, just as they are enslaved. Our everyday life is dominated by details of our corporeal existence, involving us in a constant labour of eating, washing, grooming, dressing and sleeping'
*(Turner 1984: 37).*

To neglect this governance of the body and the subject as embodied we would be neglecting the importance of the body as a receiver and emitter of signs. There has been a plethora of publications relating to the body[4] in the Social Sciences. Nonetheless, we do not possess a coherent and comprehensive account of the huge range of problems relating to the issue of human embodiment, such as the role of corporeality, the gendered, sexualised and racialised body; body image and how the self is produced through the control of the body, that is, through 'technologies of the self'. The questions about the gendered nature of power have been facilitated by feminist and gay writing on the body.

The sociology of the body has been important in challenging the welfarist and biological model of the body purely in terms of categories such as sickness, disease and illness (Turner,

---

[4] See Michel Feher, 'Fragments for a History of the Human Body', (1990)

1984; 1987). The body is crucial to the whole debate about the social construction of medical and bio-medical categories. Within this chapter the body will be likened to a Möbius strip oscillating within and between a number of different discourses: the biological and the social; the collective and the individual; the discourse of structure and agency. Bauman, (1992) averred that the 'postmodern strategy of survival', compared to 'traditional ways of dabbling with timelessness,' is that:

> 'The ambiguous nature of the body may be formulated by means of a number of binary oppositions which all posit the body in a double role. The body is both the Same and the Other; a Subject and an Object, of practices and knowledge; it is both a tool and raw material to be worked upon'
> *(1992:50).*

By querying the role of the body through the penal time machine one can move away from the two perspectives which locate the body respectively within the naturalistic and the social constructionist framework (Frank, 1990, Tulle, 2000; Wahidin, 2002b; Wahidin and Tate 2001). The phenomenological perspective, adds a richness to the literature by examining embodiment and corporeality (Falk, 1985; 1995). It places the body not as a passive materiality that is acted upon but one that negotiates the capillaries[5] of power enabling the body to be always in the process of becoming through the *experiences* of its embodiment (Castorialdis,1987; Heidegger, 1978).

On entering the prison landscape, the elders reinvent their identity through the tensions and contradictions that emerge between self, the aging body and the expected roles that the older women are required to play in prison. This in turn allows the subject to resist, negotiate or acquiesce time-discipline. Thus there are moments of both submission and resistance as the elders renegotiate the prison world.

## CHOREOGRAPHY OF AGING

Questions of age, the experience of age and the passing of time confront us all on a daily basis (Biggs, 1999). This section examines how elders negotiate, internalize, relate to the abstract gauging of age in relation to their subjective experience of the aging process (Biggs 1997; Featherstone and Hepworth 1991: Phillipson and Biggs 1998). In other words, it explores the subjective interpretation of the experience of aging, as distinct from the prescriptions of chronological age (Featherstone and Wernick 1995).

Age in prison, as I will demonstrate, becomes an amplified variable, which defines elders and their role in relation to younger women. Elders in the study are positioned as careers (maternal figures), disciplinarians, yet by the same token they become invisible as individuals because they are perceived to lack the traditional feminine markers of sexuality and

---

[5]   A phrase from Foucault, a biological metaphor in fact, used to denote a kind of power which reaches into every part of the 'body' of society. Capillaries (literally) are a multitude of small intersecting fibrous channels (the word comes from 'hairs') through which blood circulates, and this idea is meant to shift our attention away from large-scale centralized power of the state towards the less visible operation of decentralized networks. Foucault says this is the most important kind of power characteristic of modern societies, which he illustrates by, among other things, the discourses and practical knowledge of various professions and academic disciplines, etc (Wahidin 2004).

reproductive capabilities. A good example of essentialising discourses in operation is the practice of separating older men from younger men in prison but, as yet, there are no facilities to separate older women from younger women, and this difference appears to be based on socially constructed roles of femininity and masculinity. The separation of older men from younger men is based on discourses which serve to construct a masculinity on the assumption that older men are predatory in nature and thus are more likely to corrupt younger men. It is within this space created by the expectations of the disciplinary machine, the interpolation of age by the prison estate, that other techniques of control and punishment emerge.

This space opens up a room for women in later life, as Flo argues, potentially to be victimised and:

'To [be made fun] of behind your back and [to be]call[ed] names. To me - for an older woman [being] in prison is lonely. It's a lonely time for an older woman because they don't take an older woman on like, you know? You can start a conversation [and they] ignore you and just walk away.'
*(Flo, Age: 59)*

Foucault's account of the relationship between penal practice and a disciplinary society is important in understanding how discourses and subjugation are not only confined to the criminal justice system and overt disciplinary techniques of control but pervade all areas of life, 'with the aim of producing and shaping an obedient subject' (Foucault, 1977a:33). Foucault uncovers the ways in which knowledge and power are constituted in each other, and especially in the ways in which this mutual interdependence effectively exercises social control.

'Power and knowledge directly imply each other.... there is no power relation without the correlative constitution of a field of knowledge, nor any knowledge that does not presuppose and constitute at the same time power relations'
*(Foucault, 1977b: 27).*

Technologies of carceral power are imbued in the process of regulating, and manufacturing a type of human behaviour which in turn accelerates the aging process by rendering invisible the needs and voices of women in later life (Rose, 1990).

In order to do their time quietly and to avoid situations that may lead to confrontations, women in later life remove themselves from public spaces in prison to the 'private' realm of their cells.

'It is egg-shell time, all the time. I think and that's how I view prison anyway. A continuous walking on egg-shells. It's hard. It's mind blowing sometimes, and I just like retreating into my room. I mean, I spend more time in my room than I do anywhere.
*(Olivia, Age: 60)*

The quote below is a good example of the effects of punishment on the body showing how Pat has become alienated and at times separated from her body.

'Inside I don't feel old. But my body feels old. Health wise - I have no energy and my bones ache all the time. When I was at home on a morning I'd be as bright as a button. Looking forward to the day. But here, it's such an *effort*. You seem to be *dragging* your body around

all the time. You are *conscious* of *your body.* You know, it feels heavy all the time. *Your heart is heavy all the time.* Your feelings are all – there is no light heartiedness.' (my emphasis)
**(Pat, Age: 51)**

It is her body which feels old. It is her body which she is conscious of, dragging her body with her rather than it being part of her. For Molly it has meant:

**A.W**: 'In terms of health would you say ..'
**M**: '*Deteriorated badly.* There is nothing else I can say. The sheer boredom in prison. I came in to prison at nine stone, which is one stone overweight than I should have been. I was a healthy person; I was active, I played a lot of games, badminton and tennis. When I came to HMP Durham I went from nine stones up to sixteen stone. That was sheer comfort eating. I have rheumatoid arthritis, which has meant that when I have gone out and all the things I have dreamed of doing whilst all these years inside, I just can't do now.' (emphasis in original).
**(Molly, Age: 53)**

For others the techniques of power employed by the carceral realm become a tool to negotiate, resist, modify and in a sense arrest the effects of the system, the sentence, and the environment in its process of metamorphosing the body under the prison's gaze. The youthful body is positioned in terms of sexuality and desirability. Youth and the desire to recapture youthfulness through wearing certain clothes, becomes a conduit which captures the feel good factor. Kate feels this paradox between what she wears and how it makes her feel and how others on the outside may perceive her:

'I try to keep as young as I can. The only thing I'm frightened of is being mutton dressed as lamb. I mean I've got the CATS[6] on. I mean how many fifty year old women wear CATS? Not many.'
**(Kate, Age: 53)**

The role of the body, the way it looks rather than the way it feels, is important in how women in later life resist the institutional inscriptions written on the body. This was clearly articulated when Wan-Nita stated:

'I'm going to get a job in a gym, so that when I go out of jail I'll be quite fit. I want to, that's what I focus on you see is that I'll be fit. I won't be *fat* and *old* when I get out.'
**(Wan-Nita, Age: 52)**

The gendered body in prison is a discursive site in which power is produced, acted upon, engaged with and received. These aspects of power allow spaces for resistance to emerge, enabling power to be both positive and negative. The extract below shows how Emma was able to enlist the help of others, to make up for the lack of provision for those elders who are immobile or disabled. Carmel recollects in general how women with age-related illness are not catered for in the prison environment by giving this particular example:

**C**: 'Like when Emma was here, I think she could have perhaps done a little more than she perhaps did. I was on the yard when she broke her hip about two years ago, she fell on me. She was in hospital for a few weeks and then she came back here and was in her cell. Really she should have been on a prison hospital wing. But there are no facilities for that, here at

---

[6] CATS is the brand name for Caterpillar clothing and accessories.

HMP Durham. I think that's really bad to say it is a long-term wing. I was saying about Emma, when eventually Emma came back to the wing she was put on the 'two's'[7] 'cause we have no cells on the flat here. It wasn't ideal, people were having to carry her flask and people were getting fed up of carrying her things up for her.'

C: 'I mean eventually she got stronger and I think perhaps she could have done a little bit more that she did. But it was with difficulty. She had crutches to begin with, and then we got her onto a stick. Um, but it wasn't ideal. She should have had a cell on the ground floor. Um, this is the problem with anybody who is *infirm and in prison*, I suppose. God I hope it never – listen to me (laughs).'

*(Carmel, Age: 60)*

In the extracts below the women are positioned into roles that are defined by state mechanisms of control. The essentialising of their identity as women and as elders serves to further the pain of imprisonment. Wan-Nita describes the additional responsibilities placed on elders in prison:

'It's hard being an older woman in prison because so much is expected of you. The prison expects so much, you're supposed to think differently to the younger ones.'

*(Wan-Nita, Age: 52)*

It is the expectation versus the realities which place older women in a position of cumulated jeopardy.

'Expecting us to be able to put up with all the shit that we have to live with around us, to live in the drug situation and expecting better of us because we're older. We have to put up with it. They just expect so much from us you know, they expect - they'll put a smack head or a noisy one on this house, hoping that the older ones on this house will calm them down. *We're here to do our own sentence not to do somebody else's and that shouldn't be expected from you.*' (emphasis in original)

*(Margot, Age: 54)*

The extract below demonstrates how women in the study collude with and utilise this construction of age as different to survive in prison. For Yvette, as a first time offender, her first night in prison,

Y: 'Prison was my worst nightmare'. I started to cry and this girl came up to me and she asked me what I had done. Another girl came in and because I had cigarettes on me she began asking for a light, and then for my cigs. But she was asking cigarettes from everybody. A big girl says don't get hassling her, she's my auntie.'

A.W: 'Did it bother you being called auntie?'

Y: 'No. You could say it acted like a shield.'

*(Yvette, Age: 53)*

Here ageist discourse creates a protective force when age is interpreted in terms of vulnerability. This also illustrates the effect of the meanings ascribed to age in serving the interest of the offender, who is consequently colluding with patriarchal and ageist discourse. The intersection of class and the role of age as a signifier of a claim to respect is important in conditioning understandings and interpretations of the aging process and the performance of the body in prison.

---

[7] Two's is a term used to denote the second landing.

For others, their lives before prison govern and inform their performing role in prison, positioning younger women in prison under a benevolent gaze. Beatrice, a grandmother of 62, found herself in trouble for the first time. The quote below illustrates that although placed beyond the walls, a mutually benefiting relationship can and does emerge across generations:

> **B:** 'I'm always looking at these girls and thinking how young they are and I think about my grandson straight away - comparing them. And if there is any way that I could help them I do. The two young girls came on our house and I said, 'don't do that', don't go mixing with those women and if there is anything you want come and ask me. And if I can help you, I will.'
> **A.W:** 'So you look after them?'
> **B:** 'Yes, yes. I think I do. But they say they look after me now.' (Laughs).
> *(Beatrice, Age: 62)*

Although prison homogenises women in terms of their criminal label, it is the women who recognise the differing needs of women through various stages in the lifecourse. Ellen comments that:

> 'In Holloway, if they saw you walking up a landing with say a mop and bucket, a youngster will come along and take it off you and say, 'let's take this down to your room for you or something like that.'
> *(Ellen, Age: 73)*

The experiences and the tacit knowledge of life before prison, the life threads of familial responsibilities, motherhood, becoming a grandparent, the role as a carer inseminate life in prison, which in turn enables or disables the success of performance of survival on the prison stage. Anna argues:

> 'Well really, I like to do it anyway because these kids in here are the same age as my own children. That could be one of my children, you know, in prison. I'd like to think that, I mean God forbid, but you know, say one of my kids went into prison. I'd like to think they'd got somebody they could talk to and you know somebody who could help them.'
> *(Anna, Age: 50)*

The body is constantly operating within fields of temporality, in which mobile networks of relations produce and transmit power/knowledge to the object subject (Butler 1992). Thus the body operates within fields of power and within the realm of signs (Baudrillard 1982:180). It has been argued that time and identity in prison consist of a multiplicity of discursive elements that come into play at various times, thereby existing in 'different and even contradictory discourses' (Foucault, 1967: 100-102).

## DOING HARD TIME

The use of the word 'time' is deliberately ambiguous. In discussing prison time I hope to demonstrate the multiple temporalities used in prison. Time is used against elders in prison as an additional form of punishment, and in turn re-appropriated by them through techniques of resistance. Here, I will explore how conceptions of time in prison are structured and controlled, and how they are resisted by elders. I will interrogate the meanings of time in prison and explore how it becomes dispersed and contested. By using the words of elders to explore the meaning of time I will attempt to make time visible, and examine how prison time becomes, 'body time': that is, a time of the construction of identities.

By interrogating prison *time* we can see how time-discipline is based on intensifying efforts, in the move towards maximising speed and efficiency, rehabilitation through disciplining the body via the art of time governance (Foucault 1977b; Gurvitch 1990; Hassard; 1990). Identities have the ability to reach beyond physical time-space boundaries, an ability which becomes crucial to prisoners in resisting the effects of dislocation from a familiar time and space order (Berthelot, 1986; Giddens, 1981). To survive, elders in this study phantasmically grasp onto the familiar.

In the voices of the women we hear that in order to survive the new order they create transgressive spaces in which they can suspend the outside world but in an unprecedented fashion float between the prison and the outside world. In order to survive, elders in the study take on an automatic mode of functioning regulated and punctuated by the calls for check[8], medication and meals.

As the outside world recedes many elders like Anita find ways of resuming those life threads:

'You have to try and visualise and remember. Like at nights, when I start saying my prayers, it is as if I go home. I go through my front door and I go round the house and then finally go up stairs and into the bedroom and I get into my own bed. Being with the person that you love, you don't forget how that feels. But you forget what it's like to just get up and go and have a *bath. Or a shower. To cook a meal. Or* just to put the kettle on and make a drink. Instead of having to drink out of a flask. A luke-warm drink out of a flask. *Just to be able to choose what you eat. Eat when you want to eat and food that you want to eat.'* (emphasis in original)
*(Anita, Age: 62)*

The extracts below show how the conscious subversion of prison time becomes immensely symbolic as an act of self, and of resistance to the loss of will. It also represents the construction of a personally meaningful project (e.g. to avoid being institutionalised), which gives form and sense to daily existence:

'Um..... I still try to retain thoughts about outside. I mean obviously, um I think you have *to work hard* at *not becoming institutionalised*. Because you see people *being* institutionalised. And sometimes you are finding *yourself*. I mean sometimes you go for a shower at the same *time* every day, because you know you've only got so much time left. And sometimes I'll say to myself, *'I'm not going for a shower tonight'*. Just because I know I always go at such a *time* and sometimes it just *stares* you in the face. I think you fill your flask at a certain *time* because it is ten minutes before lock in. And I think, 'Oh, no' and you know it's a *battle*. It's *a battle* not to become institutionalised because everything is regimented.'
*(Ros, Age: 54)*

Although many of the elders in the study actively resist the synchronised movements of disciplinary time they find themselves slipping into the rhythms of prison time. Cath found that the only way she could resist the inculcation of prison mores in her battle to survive was as follows:

---

[8] Prison colloquialism for when they are called to sign the check list.

'I am fighting - actively by tuning into the World Service - I am forcing myself to read. So you've got to keep reminding yourself that 'Averbergion, and the earthquake in Afghanistan - people are really suffering much worse. So - it's vital. Vital. It's a form of *psychological survival.*' (emphasis in original).

Although, she says:

'This is *life* after a while, the outside world recedes and this is more real.'
*(Cath, Age: 55)*

In these circumstances, prisoners have to sustain their lives in some way and look around for ways of marking time (Zerubavel, 1990). Whilst forced to 'mark time' in terms of serving their time, most attempt to make prison time meaningful. Each woman finds ways of making the passage of time flow faster by differentiating and dividing time. The elders in the study interact with time by making time digestible, ticking months off, weeks off and even days off, placing time around visits or parole dates. Throughout the research I found that they built their own subjective clock in order to protect themselves from the terror of prison time. Flo, makes the months seem shorter:

F: 'Oh yes, yes, I was crossing them off and then I was leaving them to the end of the month. I've got my calendar and I thought to me now I've left it, I've marked half of March off. Tonight I'll mark the other page off and turn the page off to April and see if it goes any quicker that way by doing it at the end of each month instead of doing it day by day you know.'
*(Flo, Age: 59)*

# DE-MASKING TIME

Time use in prison is embodied in the institution's philosophy, practice, and types of punishment which are inflicted upon the body under the prison gaze. Time is neither tangible nor real but an ontological curiosity that divides 'reality' into seconds, minutes, hours, days and years (Adam, 1990; 1995). However in its myriad of forms, the capillaries of time in prison govern possible 'freedoms, representing the 'past', 'present', the 'now' and possible futures. This exploration will take us into the triple edged world of time in prison, where time is a measurable, tradeable commodity, a form of 'currency' and further punishment. Wan-Nita, argues that:

'[Time, in here is] quite different because you're *watching* the clock inside prison whereas you don't necessarily *look at* the clock on the outside. I mean the clock was there and you might glance at it, but here *clock time* means *everything.*' (emphasis in original)
*(Wan-Nita, Age: 61)*

The penal inscriptors of time change the rhythms of the body, most evidently seen in the cessation of menstruation and the growing susceptibility to age-related illnesses (Biggs, 1997, Featherstone and Hepworth, 1983, 1993, 1991). These indicators are described by the elders as evidence of the aging process and their physical deterioration under the penal gaze. The process of penal time reinvents the body, which in turn carries its own evidence of time passing and time in progress; yet is experienced as time in stasis whilst in prison. Time passes and stands still as elders are temporally and spatially isolated from wider society. Their normal patterns of life are both materially and ideologically severed. This time of incarceration, time standing still yet passing away, permeates the self through the severance of life threads to the outside world, creating a new temporal order.

In this extract Wan-Nita discusses how within this island of prison time (i.e. prison structural time), she becomes lost within seas of timelessness (subjective prison time), separated but aware of time passing and time changing on the outside:

'My life on the outside has already *gone* because from the very first day when you come into jail; first of all you are on remand time, you live in a *make believe world*, because you think you're going home. So for that year, you think you're going home. Then you get sentenced and you've got a year where you know you're not, you're still undecided as to what's going to happen to you. You know you've got a life sentence but you don't accept it. You see you still think a miracle is going to happen, and each day your life slips away from you a little bit and then one day *you wake up in the morning and it's all gone and that's the worse day of all, when everything before has gone.* I was writing, it was like a diary effect, I was writing about present day and past and it was all mingled in together, it sort of made you cry and laugh at the same time, and that's what happened to me along that way. It *all* just slipped away. *You can't keep it, you can't hold it.* It's like my Clare, my baby, who's not a baby anymore. Toni's a young lady. You can't hold that life there because it doesn't mean anything.' (emphasis in original)
*(Wan-Nita, Age: 52)*

In terms of 'the outside', the prison structuring of time usurps the time ordering of what was known and familiar. Molly, an elder who has served the longest time in prison of the cohort, poignantly describes the severance of outside life threads, as not seeing 'a whole of anything'. By being in prison, she was cut 'off completely from the outside world':

'We were in this old castle, the windows are way up at the top, so you never saw out unless you were on the top floor. You never saw a whole sparrow. So you never saw a whole tree or a whole sky, you *didn't* see a whole anything, it was like a patchwork quilt. It shut you off completely from the outside world.' (emphasis in original)
*(Molly, Age: 53)*

One must stress that matters of time, work, privacy, freedom and deterioration are also serious issues for those on the outside; however they lack the salience they have for the elders in the study. It is not purely their sense of time passing which is problematic but their relationship to the prison world. The pain of prison time arises from the tension between self, prison self (the effacement of self) and reality.

The analysis of time in prison, in effect, becomes a discussion of the presentation of identities in, through and by time. However, time in prison is constructed within the boundaries of the institution, imposed from above by a system of explicit formal rules. The routine of daily activities comprises a single rational plan, which has been designed to fulfil the official aims of the institution rather than the needs of individuals. It is the use of time as imposed that eliminates choice, which in turn disables the self to create meaningful and symbolic relations with prison time and external/outside time. Time as discussed above has been constructed to discipline and bring about the social death of the outside self through temporal and sensory deprivation (Cohen and Taylor, 1992; Foucault, 1977b).

Although aware that their prison time consists of time in waiting, and that the lost time can never be replaced, the post-release period of new time, of post-work, post-menopause brings new freedoms, new roles, new opportunities and new fears (Hockey and James, 1993). Molly, although 'raring to get out and to start living', eloquently describes her anxiety about being released:

> 'When we get out, that's when we start our sentence. That's when we really start our sentence. Are we going to be accepted? Will we be found out? Will they find out what we did? Will we be able to assimilate without too much difficulty? *That's when it starts!'*
> *(Molly, Age: 53)*

The meanings and experiences of living beyond the walls, inside and outside of prison, connect women in later life to the outside world by which they manage meanings and nuances of time discipline of the prison world. Identity management is vital in order to survive the inmate culture by providing a means to recede from the prison gaze. This tacit knowledge recreates women in later life as knowing agents within a system which attempts to suppress the sense of self by recreating meaning with the aim to 'produc[e] and shap[e] an obedient subject' (Foucault, 1977b).

The body is a malleable receptacle, that is acted upon, receives but also produces mechanisms which aim to reinforce, preserve and protect elders even in the most extreme conditions. Molly recalls her induction into prison life.

> 'At Durham we had to slop out it was disgusting. We were potty trained again. We had a bucket of cold water, you had your flask and if you came on - *god help you.* There was nothing you can do about it. You couldn't clean. You couldn't do *anything.* You can't have a woman who is on and not clean. Privacy was non-existent because the officers could come round when you were sitting on a bucket. It was disgusting - it was so degrading. We had to be searched every single week and all your belongings, clothes were on the corridor for all to see.' *(emphasis added)*
> *(Molly, Age: 53)*

The inscriptions placed on the outside of her body through such violations constitute an assault on her sense of identity via personal and intimate intrusions. She is aware that with the passing of time, prison life has scorched her body. Punishment consists not only of the deprivation of liberty but, as described by the elders, it is also the continued and continuous assault whilst in prison.

> 'I expect people to find fault with me all the time. I am on the defensive all the time and thinking I have to justify myself, which I would never have done. Like a teacher, you give your orders and command respect, and I lost everything like that'.
> *(Molly, Age: 53)*

As the carceral reality ambushed her physical and spiritual being, she resists the penal recoding of her body by retreating from her body to the recesses of her mind.

> 'They took away all my self esteem, self-dignity. At least they can't take away my mind, they can't take away my academic achievements. They can take everything else away. But it is hard to respect yourself when you have to undress in front of people. It is hard when you have to be searched every single week, and your possessions are touched by people and every letter

is looked through. Day after day you are reminded you can't be trusted, you can't have any responsibility, it wears away after twenty years. I don't think I'll ever really lose that'.
*(Molly, Age: 53)*

The strategies of subversion employed provide a means to shield the inward face from the prying judicial gaze by immersing her prison world into an abstract world. Other women cope with the prison regime by reinventing and distributing the humiliating and degrading experience into one which temporarily enables them to control the prison gaze, the violation and the situation.

'The [first time you] strip off. It is a *really degrading thing*. For a long time it used to bother me. If I knew I was due for a search, I'd think, *'oh God, they'll be coming in a minute. They'll be coming and I have to take my clothes off*. You see how I have changed. I've changed and I've become stronger and I think to myself, I whip it off. And they say, 'don't take your bottoms off before you put your top back on'. I think, well, *blow you* because what's the difference I'm being stripped stark naked. So I just throw everything off now. I can't say I like doing it. But it's my *bravado*. If you do it like that really quickly I feel they as if *they* take a step back. They are *more embarrassed than I am*'.
*(Carmel, Age: 60)*

The presentation of self in this instance (a woman controlling a strip search) is in the meaning attributed to the mode of survival in prison. The strip searches are a degrading technique of punishment, reinforcing the lack of control elders have over those who survey, gaze, police and govern the most intimate surfaces of the body. The profaned bodies, as constructed by the corporeal regime of the prison, negotiate the disciplinary gaze into purloined looks. The performance is a process of negotiation which clearly illustrates how elders can regain control. This performance becomes a series of tactical game–like moves to ensure survival. It becomes an end in itself and a means to an end.

As argued above, the body is nebulous in form, and is always in the process of becoming. The contours of the body outline a visible but transitional object. But as Butler (1997) argues there is no surety of what the body is. What one can argue from listening to the voices of the elders what the body becomes the liminal space in which the subject's lived experience of the world is incorporated and as such can never be purely understood. The body is in situ, placed within various temporal and spatial fields of power. In Elizabeth Grosz's words (1994), the body is a 'transitional entity'.

## CONCLUSION

The application of a Foucauldian perspective brings a richness to understanding how networks of power operate upon and within the body. Moreover it is by incorporating Butler's concept of 'performativity' in relation to the composite role and configuration of the body which I have sought to show, that the internal essence of gender is manufactured through the repetition of acts, positioned through the gender stylisation of the body. In this way, it shows that what we take to be an 'internal' feature of ourselves is one that we anticipate and which is produced through and by certain bodily acts.

She notes, 'just as bodily surfaces are enacted as the natural, so these surfaces can become the site of a dissonant and denaturalized performance that reveals the performative status of the natural itself' (186:1990). Gender's performative nature can turn back on itself: when bodies perform gender incorrectly, when they make 'gender trouble', then they attack the idea that gender performances must immediately follow from inborn genders, and therefore question the expressivity of gender.

It is by examining the body through the idea of embodiment and corporality, that identity comes to be seen as a set of embodied potentialities rather than as an externally imposed set of constraining norms. The voices of elders, draw out the contradictions and dilemmas which they experience, thereby illustrating the relationship between time and their involvement as 'servers of time' in a total institution (see Goffman 1961, 1963). The body, as we have seen, is not a static surface to be worked upon, but is in a constant state of being re-imagined as the lifecourse scripts blur, and the inevitable happens, that of aging itself.

The discussion has demonstrated how time-discipline works upon and within the body. Furthermore it is by examining the role of corporeality through the voices of the elders that we can see how elders in prison reclaim agency by managing their aging bodies through re-appropriating the power of the disciplinary gaze.

In one way or another we are all 'serving and doing time' and writing about time symbolically represents a form of de-masking; time becomes the mask of discipline. Time-discipline can be impersonal, dispassionate or very subjective; it can appear as a mask, the most neutral image of which is the clock, a mask which threatens, denies, suppresses and expropriates people in and outside of prison.

# REFERENCES

Adam, B. 1990. *Time and Social Theory*. Cambridge: Polity Press.

Adam, B. 1995. *Time Watch - A Sociological Analysis of Time*. Cambridge: Polity Press.

Bauman, Z. 1992. *Mortality, Immortality and Other Life Strategies*. Cambridge: Polity Press.

Berthelot, J. 1986. "Sociological Discourse and The Body." *Theory Culture and Society* 3, 155-164.

Biggs, S. 1997. "Choosing Not To Be Old? Masks, Bodies and Identity Management in Later Life." *Ageing and Society* 17, 553 - 570.

Biggs, S. 1999. *The Mature Imagination Dynamics of Identity in Midlife and Beyond*. Buckingham: Open University Press.

Bordo, S. 1990. "Feminism, Postmodernism and Gender Scepticism." Pp in *Feminism/Postmodernism* edited by L. Nicholson. New York, Routledge.

Bourdieu, P. 1978. "Sport and Social Class." *Social Science Information* 17: 819-40.

Bourdieu, P. 1981. "Men and Machines." Pp 304-313 in *Advances in Social Theory and Methodology Toward An Integration of Micro-And Macro-Sociologies* edited by K. Knorr-Cetina and A. Cicourel, Boston, Routledge and Kegan Paul.

Butler, J. 1987. *Bodies that Matter on the Discursive Limits of 'Sex'*. Oxford: Clarendon.

Butler, J. 1990. *Gender Trouble: Feminism and the Subversion of Identity*. New York: Routledge.

Butler, J. 1997. *Excitable Speech: A Politics of the Performative*. New York: Routledge.

Castorialdis, C. 1987. The Imaginary Institution of Society. Trans. Kathleen Blamey. Cambridge MA: MIT Press and Cambridge.

Cohen, S. and Taylor, L. 1992. *Escape Attempts: the Theory and Practice of Resistance to Everyday Life*. London: Routledge.

Falk, P. 1985. "Corporeality and its Fates in History." *Acta Sociologica* 28: 2:115-136.

Falk, P. 1994. *The Consuming Body*. London: Sage.

Falk, P. 1995. "Written in The Flesh." *Body and Society* Vol. 1, No.1: 95-105.

Featherstone, M. 1991. *Consumer Culture and Postmodernism*. London: Sage.

Featherstone, M. and Hepworth, M. 1991. "The Mask of Ageing and the Postmodern Lifecourse." Pp 371 - 390 in *The Body, Social Process and Cultural Theory*, edited by M. Featherstone, M. Hepworth and B. Turner. London: Sage.

Featherstone, M. and Wernick. A. 1995. *Images of Aging - Cultural Representations of Later Life*. London: Routledge.

Feher, M. 1990. *Fragments for a History of the Human Body*. New York: New York Press.

Foucault, M. 1967. *Madness and Civilisation: A History of Insanity in the Age of Reason*. London: Penguin.

Foucault, M. 1977a. *The History of Sexuality Vol. 1*. London: Penguin.

Foucault, M. 1977b. *Discipline and Punish - The Birth of the Prison*. Translated by A. Sheridan, London: Allen Lane.

Frank, A. 1990. "Review Article - Bringing Bodies Back in A Decade Review." *Theory, Culture and Society* 7: 131-162.

Frank, A. 1991. "For a Sociology of The Body: An Analytical Review." Pp 60- 70 in *The Body Social Processes and Cultural Theory*, edited by M. Featherstone, M. Hepworth and B. Turner. London: Sage.

Gurvitch, G. 1990, "The Problem of Time." Pp 35 – 47 in *The Sociology of Time,* edited by J. Hassard. London, Macmillan.

Giddens, A. 1981. "Agency, Institution and Time - Space Analysis." Pp 161-174 in *Advances in Social Theory and Methodology Toward an Integration of Micro and Macro Sociologies* edited by K. Knorr-Cetina and A.V. Cicourel. Boston: Routledge and K.P.

Goffman, E. 1961. *Stigma - Notes on the Management of Spoiled Identity*. Englewood Cliffs: Prentice-Hall.

Goffman, E. 1963. *Behaviour in Public Places - Notes on the Social Organisation of Gatherings*. New York: Free Press.

Grosz, E. 1994. *Volatile Bodies: Towards a Corporeal Feminism*. Bloomington and Indianapolis: Indiana University Press.

Hassard, J. 1990. *The Sociology of Time*. Basingstoke: Macmillan.

Heidegger, M. 1978. *Being and Time*. Oxford: Blakewell.

Hockey, J. and James. A. 1993. *Growing Up and Growing Old - Ageing and Dependency in the Lifecourse*. London: Sage.

Levi, P. 1996. *If This Is A Man - The Truce*. London: Abacus.

Öberg, P. 1996. "The Absent Body - A Social Gerontological Paradox." *Ageing and Society* 16: 701-719.

Merleau – Ponty, M. 1966. *Phenomenology of Perception*. London: Routledge & Kegan Paul.

Phillipson, C. and Biggs, S. 1998. "Modernity and Identity: Themes and Perspectives in the Study of Old Adults". *Journal of Aging and Identity*. 3: 11-23.

Rose, N. 1990. *Governing the Soul*. London: Routledge.

Tsëelon, E. 1995. *The Masque of Femininity the Presentation of Women in Everyday Life,* London: Sage.

Tulle, E. 2000. "Old Bodies." Pp 64-83 *The Body, Culture and Society: An Introduction,* edited by P. Hancock, L. Jagger, B. Hughes et al. Open University Press: Buckingham.

Turner, B. 1984. *The Body and Society: Explorations in Social Theory.* Oxford: Blackwell.

Turner, B. 1987. "Ageing, Status Politics and Sociological Theory." *The British Journal of Sociology* 40: 589-605.

Wahidin, A. and Tate S. 2001. *Time And The Geography of Exclusion – Time Given, Time Taken Away:* The British Sociological Association Jubilee Conference 9-12th April. Unpublished Conference Paper.

Wahidin, A. 2002a. *Life in the Shadows: A Qualitative Study of Older Women in Prison.* Keele University: Unpublished PhD thesis.

Wahidin, A. 2002b. "Reconfiguring Old Bodies in the Prison Time Machine." *The Journal of Aging and Identity* 7: 177-195.

Wahidin, A. 2004. *Older Women in the Criminal Justice System: Running Out of Time,* London: Jessica Kingsley.

Zerubavel, E. 1990. "Private Time and Public Time." Pp 168-178 in *The Sociology of Time* edited by J. Hassard. London: Macmillan.

# Chapter 6

# AGENCY IN THE CONTEXT OF LOSS AND BEREAVEMENT: A MORAL ECONOMY OF AGING?

## *Steve Conway*

### ABSTRACT

Following ideas that aging can be understood as a fundamentally moral enterprise, this chapter explores how this is played out within the very adverse circumstances of loss and bereavement. The agency reflected in the beliefs discussed is shown as a response to this particular experience. The chapter focuses upon agency through the pursuit of virtue and is based upon the idea that in describing the experience of growing into the 'fourth age' (Laslett 1987 1989), it is the lifecourse paths that people follow which shape their sense of social identity. Social identity is shown to be constituted through the use of narratives. Therefore the analytical approach adopted uses narrative analysis in conjunction with a lifecourse approach. Two key findings emerge. Firstly, there are striking parallels between 'moral economy' arguments and the beliefs of the case study. Thus ideas about reciprocity, interdependence and community are reflected in the data. Secondly, it is concluded that understanding beliefs needs to be related to the 'social' as a reflection of a micro-politics of experience.

**Keywords:** beliefs, moral economy, social identity, agency, virtue.

## INTRODUCTION: A MORAL ECONOMY OF AGING

The dominant way in which aging is conceived takes the dependency of 'the old' as natural and reflects a form of thinking which regards 'old age as an illness' (Kirk 1992). 'Moral economy' takes a very different view; thus professionals, organizations and wider social processes, such as individualization, are held to construct much of the dependency of older adults (Minkler and Estes 1991; Robertson 1997). In other words, old age is regarded as a social construction that reveals there are alternatives. Working largely within the political economy tradition, moral economy posits that the way conceptualization the 'needs' of older adults is influenced by the relationship between political decisions and economic interests. Therefore for political economy, the structural position of 'old age' is shaped by the outcome of conflict between and within the state, business and labor, and the role of the economy (Estes and Linkins 2000: 155). However, moral economy leads to a deeper understanding of the nature of the relationship between the individual and society. As Kohli (1991: 274, cited in Robertson 1997: 433-4) puts it, 'speaking of moral economy not only shifts the emphasis from individual motivations – to the system of reciprocal relations . . . [but also] allows us to extend the argument beyond the political and economic sphere in a narrow sense . . . into an analysis of the moral structure of the economy itself.' Thus it is argued that need should be politicized (Robertson 1997: 425) in terms of moral obligation, solidarity and reciprocity (Kohli 1991; Vincent 1996). Needs are said to be conceived by market-based rather than moral obligations. For example, it is noted that the 'biomedicalisation' (Estes and Binney 1991) of aging has done much to obscure non-medical factors relevant to growing old; such as, existing retirement and pensions policy that exclude and disadvantage older people (Phillipson 1982, 1998). Indeed, conceptualizing growing old as a medical issue has influenced research, policymaking and the way it is considered in everyday life (Estes and Binney 1991: 118).

In general terms, the disempowering nature of the dominant 'institutionalized thought structure of the field' (Estes and Binney 1991: 118) is called into question by moral economy on several grounds. Thus the dependency of older adults is shown to be fostered and constructed by a false dichotomy between need and dependency that is underpinned by individualism (Johnson 1995; Kohli 1991; Phillipson 1982, 1998; Robertson 1997; Vincent 1995). As Kohli (1991: 275) explains, '[moral economy reflects] collectively shared basic moral assumptions constituting a system of social relations.' Indeed, Johnson (1995 cited in Robertson 1997: 425) calls for an 'essentially moral' transformation of aging related policies, which reprioritize 'human solidarity and reciprocity as central features of our social order'.

The idea of a moral economy of aging is based upon a long term and deep view of giving and receiving. It has been used to analyze areas including pensions and other entitlements (Minkler and Cole 1991), health care policy (Holstein and Minkler 1991), and the 'scapegoating' of older adults for taking up scarce resources (Minkler 1991; Vincent 1995). It also draws upon historical scholarship of social change succinctly summarized by Vincent (1996: 20). For example, participants in 18th century food riots were reacting to increased food prices based upon market imperatives rather than previously long standing values of custom and need. They felt that long term moral agreements of their rights were being ignored. What binds all of the ideas about moral economy together when applied to aging is the proposition that the needs of older adults should be grounded in moral precepts with a long term understanding of giving and receiving, rather than short-term and individualizing market-based imperatives. Indeed, at the level of intergenerational relations, there is empirical evidence of long term forms of social and economic exchanges between the generations based upon need rather than self-interest (Finch 1987). Moreover, there is evidence that demonstrates public support for cutting military budgets rather than programs for older adults (Minkler 1991).

As a way of summarizing, then, a moral economy of aging extends the arguments of political economy. Political economy concentrated on the role of the polity and economy in constructing old age. Moral economy develops this critique and argues that old age is understood via moral precepts derived from market-based principles of reciprocity. As a challenge to neo-liberal ideology, which Rose (1993) describes as having invested a great deal in the idea of the existence of free individuals, moral economy places community at the centre of any understanding of reciprocity. In so doing, the fundamental interdependence of individuals is therefore acknowledged. As Roberston (1997: 437) succinctly notes, 'the fact that we live in communities means . . . that we are interdependent'. However, such individualizing notions that old age is an illness encourages the assumption that displaying need in later life is a sign of individual failing. In other words, the Western notion of the individual is framed in a network of social, political, economic and cultural relationships. In reality no person is completely independent of another and we 'live within complex webs of mutual dependence or interdependence' (Robertson 1997: 437). Put simply, there is no such thing as an individual and we are all part of interdependent communities.

The dominance of neo-liberal ideology in aging related policies is, then, called into question by moral economy on conceptual, theoretical and empirical grounds. Nonetheless, this chapter is based upon the proposition that however well intentioned moral economy may be, it can also be thought of as a largely 'top-down' perspective on aging that would benefit from a more 'bottom-up' approach. In other words, moral economy is an expert voice on behalf of older people that could be given greater credibility if their voices were also heard in an interpretive way. Therefore this chapter follows the idea that if the moral economy of aging argues for reciprocity, there is a need for consistency from its proponents in gerontological debate and critique, and the voice of experience of older adults also needs to be recognized as well as that of the gerontologists. If the aim of moral economy can be considered as re-establishing the idea of reciprocity based upon community, then surely it would be helpful and salient to adopt more inclusive and interpretive ways of achieving this?

# I. Methodology

The data examined in this paper is from one case study drawn from an interpretive analysis of twenty-six older adults living in and around a city in North East England. The research was concerned with beliefs about aging, illness and death and involved focus groups, and individual biographical interviews. The case study (Hettie) discussed in this paper was chosen for two reasons. These will be elaborated upon in the analysis of data, but for the purposes of introductory clarification they are summarized here. Firstly, Hettie was suffering from loss and bereavement, and in this context her circumstances can be considered to be more adverse than the other interviewees are. Secondly, despite this significant level of adversity, her beliefs reflect a substantial amount of agency in the way she actively constructs and makes sense of both, her life at particular moments, and her own sense of identity.

As the interviews were exploratory in nature, a qualitative interviewing strategy was adopted in order to identify and explore emergent themes, rather than simply test ideas conceived before data collection took place (Britten et al 1995). Each interview was tape-recorded and transcribed in full. Hettie was interviewed twice. The first interview was very open and she was asked to talk about her life generally in relation to issues of aging and health. The second interview was more structured and themes and points needing clarification were explored. The general format of interviews drew on the core principle of a biographical approach; that is, phenomena like values, beliefs and attitudes need to be examined in biographical context (Bertaux 1981; Dant and Gearing 1990). Therefore interviews took the form of a life history.

The use of case study material needs to be judged from different criteria normally used in social research. For example, empirical representativeness is not an issue. Biographical material can be justified by its richness and in its capacity to reveal and bring together the uniqueness of experience with broad social themes central to the lives of particular individuals (Bertaux 1981; Evans 1993). In other words, it illustrates the merits of the idea of 'theoretical generalisability', helping to apply and examine theoretical problems within an empirical context (Mason 1996). In so doing, it illustrates the interplay of social processes and biography. Thus an individual's biographical account can illuminate the emotional meaning of the conventional sociological wisdom that we are 'socially constructed' (Jerrome 1994). The position taken in this chapter is that an individual case study needs to be considered in its own terms. It is not intended to serve as illustration of a typical life. The case study discussed in this chapter aims to illustrate how the interviewee constructs and makes sense of her own identity at a particular moment, in ways that reveal her own agency. To draw upon Jerrome (1994), in terms of validity, the plausibility of my interpretations cannot be examined through a dialogue with the interviewees, as only a selection of the data is available. The test of validity lies in the readers' response to this chapter. The recognition of a plausible and credible analysis (Hammersley 1992) would indicate an understanding that derives from a robust methodology and interpretation.

Furthermore, the data examined below are regarded as 'narrative reconstructions' that represent complex interpretations of experience that can be understood in terms of the relationship between the final stage of life or the 'fourth age' (Laslett 1987, 1989) and society (Williams 1993, 1996). In this context, the data are seen to represent forceful and fundamentally moral expressions of social identity in relation to the interplay of agency/structure. Such expressions, therefore, may be thought of as conventional ethical distinctions produced by traditional discursive formations, such as religion or the law, on how to make judgements about what is right and virtuous, and so on. Alternatively, they can be understood in sociological terms, as expressions of social identity reflecting change across the lifecourse through each differing social situation and status (Hepworth 1995: 176). In this second interpretation morality is conceived of as something that is framed and constructed in social relations with others in different situations and at different moments throughout the lifecourse. Thus to paraphrase Goffman, who brings the two explanations together (1968a 1968b, cited in Hepworth 1995: 176-7), morality provides methods for judging oneself and others, reflecting the fact that any given society establishes means for classifying what are normal and abnormal attributes of persons in different categories. Therefore, the moral conception of social identity derives its meaning from what is thought of as typically normal and acceptable in any prescribed category of person. Thus to categorize oneself and others is essentially a moral process.

Following this sociological way of thinking, it is argued that identity is a characteristically social and moral property that brings together person and society. Thus in a sociological explanation of social identity established by Jenkins (1996) he refers to meanings of the term being constituted in human social relations as a way of establishing both uniqueness and collective similarity. Hettie's expression and construction of identity can be conceived of as both unique and collective. It may be regarded as unique as none of the other interviewees appears to share both, the adverse circumstances of bereavement and loss, and they did not appear to emphasize agency, to the same degree as Hettie. On the other hand, it can be regarded as an expression of collective identity. It reflects the pursuit of an 'imagined community', which is replicated across the whole sample. Hence there is what can be described as a very strong sense of collective identity or even 'communion' with other community members with whom the sample are not able to communicate, or come into contact with on a face-to-face or everyday basis, such as dead partners, friends, work colleagues, famous people from popular culture, history, and so on (Conway 2003). More relevant to this chapter, and in relation to the arguments of moral economy, Hettie's active pursuit of identity can be seen to parallel the views of the academic gerontologists in ways which reflect a desire to be connected within reciprocal social relations based upon the principles of community.

## Contextualising Agency

As noted above, this chapter is using a case study approach because of the particularly unique circumstances of loss and bereavement. There are also some parallels between the case study and the whole of the sample from which the material is drawn, and this is elaborated upon elsewhere (Conway 2003). However, a useful way of introducing Hettie's beliefs here is to contextualise them in wider contexts. Therefore the following section elaborates more upon the limitations of the dominant thought structure of the field as a way of providing further evidence for a lifecourse approach. Furthermore, illustrations of the way in which older adults can respond to the emotional and socio-structural constraints of 'old age' in active and non-passive ways are illustrated by reference to other data from the sample. Finally, it will be useful to provide further explanation of narrative analysis with reference to the concept of 'vocabularies of motive' (Mills 1940).

If we are to make sense of people's beliefs as they age into the fourth age, then it has to be recognized that they cannot be reduced solely to the concepts of 'activity' or 'disengagement'. Such concepts, which were pillars of the gerontological theorization of 'adjustment', have been criticized as being depressing, fatalistic and individualizing in ways which reflect mainstream thinking (Fennell et al 1988: 42; Estes and Linkins 2000; Katz 1996). However, the reality of life for older adults is not the heroic overthrow of powerful social processes that disempower them, but the day-to-day struggle of everyday living.

On another level, the argument that people are denying they are 'old' for reasons of vanity is often misplaced (Thompson, Itzin and Abendstern 1990, 1992). Thus the expression of the preferred styles of adaptation to the final stage of life and the methods used in everyday living can be understood as moral practices and micro-political acts of refusal to lie down, or surrender to the 'times-up' narrative (Conway and Hockey 1998). It is within this context that many beliefs of older adults are grounded in both temporal and moral senses within life histories. As one man said to me: 'I still tip my hat to the ladies and I get riled for it', and 'I am still living under the good Victorian influence of my mother.' This suggests a sense of collective identity with an historical culture that is perceived to be morally virtuous and in stark contrast to everyday living in contemporary society. Thus in pursuing this view and against the odds of being 'riled', his agency is revealed. When I asked another man about what he did after retiring, he told me he worked in a garage, sweeping up and serving customers on an almost full-time basis for several years. I asked how much he received in wages and he replied, rather nonchalantly, that he was paid in kind. The contact with people in their cars and the way the owner of the garage befriended him was payment enough for him! Again a sense of agency is revealed. He actively followed the 'busy ethic' (Ekerdt 1986) by keeping himself occupied through his employment in the garage, even though his reward was not conventionally financial. Thus a sense of moral community between the work ethic and retirement is revealed in his actions.

The interviewees in the study seemed to draw on a range of narratives and vocabularies that allowed them to express attitudes they conceived of as morally right and virtuous. On some occasions, this also appeared to be micro-political in its outlook. As another woman from the same study said to me: 'when people treat you as if you are daft because you are old [and they say] we will take you . . . for a cup of tea and a sticky bun' and her friend adds: 'we do not want a cup of tea and a sticky bun, our brains are the same as what yours are . . . they think pensioners and they think you are stupid [laughs]' (Conway and Hockey 1998: 482). However, we need to be cautious about the capacity of older adults to act upon the constraints they face in everyday life. Their dependency and pain, whilst greatly fostered by institutions in the political and economic systems of advanced capitalist societies (Bond and Coleman 1990; Phillipson 1982), is something they have to live with and in this sense can be overwhelming and unbearable. As the woman whose beliefs are examined in detail below says: 'It's a very long uphill struggle . . . But the fear, the apprehension. It can be too much. I can be perfectly alright one day, but the next day can be awful.'

The beliefs examined here are not simply matters of individual motive. They represent the influence of 'vocabularies of motive' which include dominant narratives and ideologies in society (Mills 1940) on particular biographical contexts. That is to say, the view of social identity can be considered as a form of theorizing that is shaped by the lifecourse. Moreover, as Gubrium and Wallace (1990: 131) have written: '...striking parallels can be found with the theorizing of ordinary men and women concerned with aging and their more celebrated gerontological peers.' This chapter will show that there are parallels between beliefs about aging which reflect the constitution of a moral identity, with arguments for moral economy.

Moralizing and an essential sense of identity are something that has been highlighted by many writers as a strong theme amongst the beliefs of older adults (Eckerdt 1986; Fontana 1977; Hepworth 1995; Williams 1990). Thus as Jerrome (1992: 142, cited in Hepworth 1995: 181) states, old age is 'a matter of virtue and moral strength . . . To be happy and make the best of things in spite of pain and hardship is a moral and social obligation'. In terms of both the ethical and sociological explanation of morality offered above, coping with aging, then, becomes a fundamentally moral activity. It also parallels Foucault's (1988) idea of the 'care of the self', which he traces back to the Judeo-Christian tradition. This appears to provide an ethic which helps older adults cope with the adversity caused by the physical and sometimes emotional pain that aging can involve. However, and more relevant to this chapter's focus upon agency, it can be posited that the pursuit of virtue is a form of resistance to hostile and ageist, social and cultural forces. To understand this more fully, and to reiterate my own position, the arguments of moral economy for a communitarian based categorization of old age could be given greater credence, if the beliefs of older adults were to be taken much more seriously.

## THE CONSTRUCTION OF A MORAL IDENTITY IN THE LIFE OF AN OLDER PERSON

Hettie (her name has been changed) is a seventy eight year old woman who lives alone and is widowed. She has arthritis and back pains, and her general physical health is deteriorating. She is also bereaved and suffering from the loss of all of her close family. The town in which she lives is a market town and commuter belt for many working in a nearby city. It also contains a small proportion of socially and economically deprived people who live largely in a nearby council estate. The estate is known as a high crime area and she told me she had suffered a number of attacks, some youths had threatened her with a knife and, 'three months later', she was woken in the middle of the night by the sound of a stolen car 'being rammed into the house opposite'. On other occasions a bottle was thrown through her front window, and she had been spat upon and sworn at by some youths in a nearby alley. These incidents and her bereavements had left her very shaken. After transcribing the interviews I sent typed copies to Hettie (which were approved in full).

### Collective Identity in the Context of Family

Throughout the interviews Hettie gave an impression of wanting to be connected. This theme was prominent when she talked of how lonely and traumatized she was because of her bereavements. The deaths of her close family had cast her off from the support network of her family and left her, feeling like what she called a 'lonely ship'. Thus her rationale for wanting to be safely connected seemed to be based upon the idea that, without the protection of something collective, she was open to attack. She was also very traumatized by her loss.

> ...and it is a hell of a thing to come to terms with, it really is. ((pause))[1] I am very lonely for a start. And ((pause)) you miss the warmth you miss the companionship. ((pause)) You see, Mother and Aunty Mary used to live their life through me. They used to say: ((excited voice)) 'Now then love, what have you got to tell us?' I'd say: 'I've seen Mrs So and So' and she said: ((quizzical voice)) 'So and So'. OH[2], we were all so very close. My mother, my husband, aunty Mary and I. ((pause)) We were a little world on our own, ((pause)) and when you lose the lot it's... ((pause)) Well I hope it doesn't come to you, but it's not very nice...

Her sense of identity, therefore, is collective, being constituted within the context of her immediate family: 'We were a little world on our own'. As Lyotard (1984) has argued, the twentieth century has been characterized by a growth of little or local narratives and a demise of the grand narratives of institutions such as science and religion. The 'little world' of her family appears to be a key vocabulary of motive. She had a pivotal role in this world as a carer and represents her Mother and Aunt as living their lives through her.

When asked to talk about herself, Hettie highlights the importance of her role as carer for her own sense of well-being:

---

[1] Double parenthesis contain author description.
[2] Capitals indicate especially loud sounds and pronounced definition relative to the other talk.

Hettie:   Well, what actually do you want to know? I mean, do you want to know what I have
          just been saying?
SC:       Well, I just want you to tell me about your life in your own terms [really[3]
Hettie:   ((quiet voice)) [yes . . . I felt then [after the bereavements] ((pause)) like a lonely
          ship. I had looked after people for so long. I'd done a lot of caring for other people.
          Anyhow, I do a lot of charity work. I help people and I do charity work. I help
          people and I go to hospital [to befriend patients and families]...

In overall terms the above extracts show Hettie is emphasizing the vocabularies of motive
of reciprocity and community. Giving to others, especially her family, made her feel secure.
She stresses her pivotal role in the family as a contact with the outside world for her mother
and aunt. In return she received 'warmth and companionship'. Elsewhere in the interviews
she talks of how she 'nursed' all of her close family members prior to their deaths. Thus she
also gave as a carer, perhaps in recognition of the 'little world' or community her family gave
to her

### Role models for a collective social identity
I was interested in what she did to pass the time in everyday life. I asked if she watched
television:

Hettie:   Oh, yes.
SC:       Do you use it a lot?
Hettie:   No, not now . . . Was it Martin Lewis who said, and he got scorned for it, 'Lets have
          a bit of good news instead of all this bad news'. I mean, WHY NOT? There is some
          good news. There must be. BUT we get... And it makes me so depressed. Not when I
          live on my own. When you have got somebody to talk to and you thresh it out. Well,
          THAT'S THAT. But, I mean, when you live on your own, it really affects you.

After her relatives died she was unable to reconstruct herself in the protective social
relations they gave her. Thus accounts of violent atrocities on television made her
'depressed'.
Hettie also liked 'good' books by 'good' people.

I like reading biographies and autobiographies. I used to love murders, but just recently I have
gone off them. I have just been rereading, because I think she is marvelous, Dorothy Sayers ...
They are very good at the library. I also like that Dick Francis, Queen Mother's jockey. I
really read books that give me a lift. You want something a bit uplifting, not like the news on
TV.

Therefore, aside from her dead family, Hettie has other role models. In the extracts above
she is aligning herself with TV presenters who promote a 'little world' view of good rather
than bad news and writers of books that give her 'a lift'. Such nice people, then, belong to her
collective identity. She has her heroes and they are virtuous people. Looking for heroes can
be seen as an attempt to transcend routine, repetitive and mundane aspects of everyday life
(Featherstone 1992). Hettie finds her heroes 'uplifting', they lift her out of her loneliness and

---

[3] Left brackets indicate the point at which the speaker's talk is overlapped by another's talk. For example:
Text in square brackets contain author explanation
          SC: For some [time
          DD.            [people have been saying

depression, and they help her return to her 'little world'. In this world she can connect with people who share her moral beliefs.

## Purity And Danger

Concerns about hygiene and dirt were also prominent in Hettie's beliefs. Douglas' seminal work (1995) on the symbolic properties of dirt is a useful source of understanding here. For Douglas, what constitutes dirt reflects beliefs about potential pollutants and dangers to order: 'dirt is essentially disorder . . . [it] offends against order. Eliminating it is . . . a positive effort to organize the environment' (Douglas 1995: 2).

Hettie's concern with domestic order and cleanliness reflects her ideas about purity.

SC:     Do you ever let things go in the house?
Hettie:     Oh no . . . NNNo, Never. [I] wouldn't like to see it get dirty . . . I am ((pause)) very tidy. It annoys me intensely to see things untidy.

Perhaps also revealing the influence of gender as a form of regulation over her (Arber and Ginn 1991a, 1991b), she also told me that her deceased husband, whom she talked about a lot, had said: 'he liked to come downstairs to a clean and tidy house in the morning'. She told me she had kept to that wish since his death.

Hygiene and dirt were symbols for purity and danger. Thus in describing her working life as a civil servant, the signs of danger she encountered were things that traumatized her. Working in social security, she was, 'shocked' by some of the clients, and 'had no idea that there was this side to life'. Their 'smell', as was their bad language: 'HER LANGUAGE . . . OH, IT WAS SHOCKING', were signs of impurity and danger. Other signs included neglecting children. The extract below provides further illustration of her ideas about purity and danger:

. . . I went on a training course in Leeds and I was sat next to a lady who was really lovely, working with the sick and elderly . . . She said: 'Don't you work with the sick and elderly?' I said: 'For every sick person or elderly person we have 99 of the scroungers and the scum of the earth'. She said: 'Where do you ((aristocratic type pronunciation)) *come* from'? 'XXX', I said. 'Where do you come from'? ((Aristocratic type pronunciation)) *'Oh, Harrogate'.* But it has been noted as the worst this side of Liverpool. They were nearly all seafaring persons you see. And every Friday on the *counter* somebody would be refused money because they had already had it on the Monday. They would say: 'well, you can take the kids'. Then they would leave them on the counter and the child fellow ((pause)) well, he would take them into custody . . . I didn't last very long. I went to the other side. To the, err, insurance side.

The 'other side', then, by implication was regarded as a place of normality, away from all the signs of danger or impurity she describes in her experiences. An earlier encounter with otherness was also recounted with disdain when she talked of a school trip to Lourdes in France. On this visit Hettie had been 'shocked' by the commercialism that she claimed to have witnessed. She regarded herself as a 'normal', a 'nine to fiver', who had been put into an 'abnormal world' on the trip. Her sense of other, which is outside of this spatial metaphor, is implicated by her language and intonation: 'TRASH', 'INJURED', 'ILLNESS', 'SICK PEOPLE'.

Err, and you see, they couldn't understand why I was getting so upset at all of these things . . .
but you see this was beyond my ken, you see. That they could have TRASH ((pause)) sell
trash for a very, very special reason . . . Can you understand that? . . . the terrible people. On
the awful INJURED, ILLNESS, SICK PEOPLE. Playing on them.

Reflecting, therefore, a creation of a collective and moral identity, within which Hettie
positions herself, she associates order and cleanliness with purity. When she has had to step
out of this and encounters *the other*, such as the 'scroungers and scum of the earth' that she
met in her working life, or those she derided for being involved in the commercialism she
observed on her school trip to Lourdes, she has been traumatized and morally outraged at the
signs of impurity or danger she witnessed.

## 'Too Old for the Times in Which We Live'

Hettie's metaphoric use of the term disease to criticize the contemporary social world
(Sontag 1978) reveals how she feels as if she is living out of her own social time.

> Yes, the times in which we live. ((pause)) I am too old for the times in which we live . . . It is
> all embracing, is this disease. ((pause)) I mean, they can't keep their hands off anything. I
> mean, did I tell you - the other day somebody pinched a pint of milk off me . . . it is
> symptomatic of the times in which we live . . . Once upon a time you would never have
> pinched somebody's bottle of milk.

Further illustration of the issue of temporal displacement comes when I was trying to
explore her feelings about the bottle being thrown through her window and the youths that
had attacked her.

> Yes, the times in which we live. ((pause)) I am too old for the times in which we live. I was
> saying this to a fellow across the way the other day. He said: 'well, I can give you forty years
> my dear, and *I'm too old for the times in which we live'*. ((laughs)) No, not nice at all. I mean,
> you have to lock your doors as if you live in Fort Knox. Well, my next-door neighbor [an
> older person] was burgled. (my emphasis in bold)

For Hettie, it was difficult to belong to the present because the past had been so different.
She was 'too old for the times in which we live', as was her neighbor and, by implication,
other older adults. The metaphor of 'Fort Knox' also indicates her assertion of a tight closed
boundary around her identity. People in the past were much more humane and nicer than
people in the present.

> Well, before I lived here . . . he [her doctor] was very good, very good . . . Now doctors
> ((pause)) treat the symptoms. ((pause)) They don't treat the patient . . . You see, when you had
> the other fellows they would say: 'that's because you tend to get a little bit too heat up a little
> too quickly'. These folks say: 'oh I will give you a tranquilizer' ((pause)) You see they
> haven't time. But, you see ((pause)) the old family doctors, they had surgery in the morning,
> visiting in the afternoon; they say they haven't time. But the old family doctors would have a
> surgery in the morning, they would have visiting in the afternoon and have a surgery in the
> evening, they did midwifery during the night. ((pause)) These don't. They do surgery in the
> morning, a bit of surgery in the afternoon and the evening and then, ((pause)) Bob's your

Uncle. ((pause)) If they are not on duty at that time then . . . No . . . ((sighs)) It is a sign of the times, I suppose.

'Old family doctors' were also part of her collective and moral identity. By contrast, present day doctors were seen as mechanistic and dehumanizing in the way they treat 'symptoms' rather than 'the patient'; another 'sign of the times' in which she felt she had no place. I wondered if leaving a career in the civil service to look after her sick brother had contributed to her sense of vulnerability. Looked if she 'lost any confidence' after she left work to look after her brother? Her response was as follows:

No, my mother used to run lots of charity events for people in need, and we used to have garden parties . . . We used to do all sorts of things. We used to have whist drives, bridge drives [sounded like] . . . You name it we did it. As mother got older I took more and more control . . . fashion shows . . . Oh, we had wonderful things as a family. We raised about £15,000 [in 1943].

Three vocabularies of motive, then, seem to be important here: gender, reciprocity and community. These are all being used to justify her actions and to demonstrate virtue. Firstly, the gendered idea of women as much more 'natural' careers than men appears to have been embraced by Hettie without question. Thus she leaves work to look after her brother and does not feel any wrench. Quite the contrary, Hettie's example of her involvement in charity work with her mother, which was long before she left work to look after her brother, appears to show that she is emphasizing giving, but this has returns for her: they 'had wonderful things as a family'. Yet again therefore she appears to be stressing community.

Moralizing and an essential sense of identity are therefore prominent in her account. Pursuing virtue appears to be the key way she is presenting herself and her social identity. Hettie's positioning of herself within a collective identity is also generationally situated (Mannheim 1952). The past is highlighted as a better time than the present. Her memories are a great comfort. She also told me how she looks at old photographs and birthday cards, anniversary cards and Christmas cards from her dead husband that she keeps in a box. Looking through such symbolic representations of her memories serves as a release from the stresses of the present: when she looks at them she has a 'really good weep'. The past is gone in that her family are dead and doctors who simply 'treat the symptoms' have replaced the good 'old family doctors'. However, she maintains a sense of continuity with her memories by connecting with the past by an adherence to what she believes are its moral principles. This is her key method of actively pursuing virtue.

To refer back to the sociological explanation of morality mentioned earlier, what makes her moral is not doing 'good' in any essential meaning of the term, but adhering to a set of principles that regulate her life and shape her aspirations. These, conveniently enough, allow her to interpret what is going on around her. Thus she highlights how she was brought up to believe in God and to do good work through charitable activities which she continues to adhere to in the present. Her dead husband, a former District Commissioner for the Boy Scouts, would be 'very pleased' with the good work she does for the Scouts in the present as she is 'Chairman of the Executive Committee.'

## Maturation and the Importance of Independence

On another level, Hettie associates aging with spiritual maturation. As she grows older, she gains more insight into what she sees as the workings of God because 'the veil', the boundary between this world and the next, gradually opens: 'As we get more mature, the veil parts a little bit.' For example, after describing her late husband's spirituality, she talks about an experience of seeing behind 'the veil' herself.

> ...it's a spiritual thing. It's your spirit calling to another spirit . . . I had the most enormous experience. I mean, it was there and it was gone. The veil moved aside for a split second . . . It was a lovely summer's afternoon . . . and I just looked up, and it was a wonderful experience . . . The feeling that I had seen a little bit behind the veil.

Two narratives of aging seem to be important to Hettie. First, as the previous section illustrated, growing older is seen to result in feelings of temporal displacement: the values and beliefs that older people are thought to feel an affinity with are held to belong to the past and are out of date in the present. By contrast, aging is seen to involve the gaining of spiritual maturity, helping her to maintain and build a moral sense of identity. Hettie's use of these contradictory narratives, one negative and the other positive, illustrate narrative reconstruction, in that she is drawing upon competing sets of ideas in the way she conceptualizes her beliefs.

I suggested that she might consider moving to sheltered accommodation, with its offer of independence and added comfort of extra security. Her response was as follows:

> ...I have got friends who I can talk to. And, as I told you, the clergy have been excellent. No, I don't need anybody else, thank you very much. There must be... Well I know there are thousands like me. ((pause)) I have got a wonderful book by Dr Clare Weeks on ((pause)) self-help for your nerves she was on TV. After her first talk on TV she received 1200 letters from sufferers. ((pause)) Wonderful books, filled with such confidence and encouragement.

Even though she feels vulnerable and alone, she refuses to think of herself as being old in terms of the negative sense of being dependent. As she puts it, 'I don't need anybody else.' Her friends, the clergy and writers of wonderful books are all she needs. Therefore in emphasizing the vocabulary of motive of independence, her agency is revealed. However, the attacks she has suffered and the failure to find satisfactory help for her own deteriorating health are involuntary exchanges with a society that represents a major threat to her independence. Such dangers have led Hettie into the urgent pursuit of a collective and moral identity, which protects her. The areas where she manages to achieve control are in her mundane activities and in the inner world of her own beliefs. By contrast, the areas where she has little or no control, as they involve powerful and external social forces and institutions, serve to both illustrate, and provide evidence of, the sociological idea that modern society brings about a paradox of making people more independent, but also making them more dependent on society (Durkheim 1984: 7).

## AGING AND THE PURSUIT OF VIRTUE:
## FROM THE COLLECTIVE TO THE MORAL

My impression of Hettie was of a highly virtuous and moral person. Almost everything she said was underpinned by moral themes and this has been the focus of the extracts. What struck me was her constant creation of boundaries as a safe haven for herself within her collective identity. Her primary need appears to be connection since she is alone. People who share the same moral code are all part of her collective identity. She appears to have a sense of absolute sameness with them (Jenkins 1996). That is to say, their moral views are perceived as identical. Put simply, she seeks to connect with them because she thinks they share her moral beliefs. This was also the main theme in the data from the other interviewees. Therefore, the data from Hettie serves as an ideal type for the data as a whole. In this instance the analysis reveals the way she deals with her particular circumstances of loss and bereavement, including her active efforts to maintain 'continuing bonds' with her deceased relatives (Moss and Moss 1996).

Even in the face of all of her crises, Hettie actively highlights the positive. As much as it can be held that aging can help a person clarify their sense of identity (Williams 1990), Hettie's pain and suffering has meant that she works constantly at her idea of virtue as a means of coping. In a society where the idea of autonomy is dominant, aging represents a loss of control over the performance of routine activities, and the desire for independence, especially in very late life (Seale 1996: 76). Thus pursuing virtue allows Hettie to highlight the positive. She wants to feel connected or achieve a sense of belonging, as many older adults do (Mehta 1997: 254). It is within this context, therefore, that an orientation towards the collective or relational, and the ideal of interdependence proffered by older men and women needs to be considered. Faced with the facts of her own aging, the analysis has shown how Hettie's beliefs represent a sense of a sovereign and morally virtuous identity. More research on beliefs in the final stage of life, or the 'last frontier' is needed (Fontana 1977). This needs to place beliefs into the context of the relationship between the fourth age and society.

For Hettie, the pursuit of virtue was achieved on a number of levels. Her collective sense of identification with people whom she looks upon as morally virtuous, such as in her memories of family members, was sustained by *thinking* and *doing* as she thinks they would have done. Alternatively, her agency reveals her perception of how she thinks her relatives, especially her dead partner, would have wanted her to conduct herself. Famous and good people from literature and TV also appear to be role models. As do people from the past, who are portrayed as being much kinder and willing to help each other than people in the present. Hettie associates herself with people from the past because, as she puts it, she is 'too old for the times in which we live'. The spiritual maturation that she emphasizes can also be considered to represent her movement through the social time of the lifecourse. By implication, she is simultaneously, distancing herself from others she regards as less virtuous, by her association of aging and longevity with spiritual maturity, and her sense of moral outrage towards those she regards as impure. The high value she places upon independence is also another example of Hettie's pursuit of virtue. It is within these terms that Hettie's beliefs can be understood to represent an expression of agency through her constant and active pursuit of virtue.

As noted earlier, a case study approach has been used here because the circumstances described in Hettie's talk are much more adverse and disempowering than those described by the other interviewees. On the face of it, her agency would appear to be severely constrained. However, despite her loss and bereavement, and her failing health, her pursuit of virtue far exceeded that of the other interviewees. The moral sense of social identity that Hettie constructs provides her with sets of precepts and practices for 'goodness' or community. These help her feel needed, connected, protected and independent. Her beliefs are therefore fundamentally moral to her, and they also help her face crises and loneliness. In doing so, and to paraphrase the moral economy arguments cited at the beginning of this chapter, Hettie's beliefs help her to constitute a system of reciprocal social relations. Thus, in a micro-political sense, the beliefs examined in this chapter reflect the macro-political arguments of the advocates of moral economy.

## CONCLUSION

In conclusion to a review of critical perspectives on health and aging, Estes and Linkins (2000: 168) write:

> Attention must be given to re-balancing studies of the individual aspects of health and aging with the 'social', including the examination of the political, economic and cultural processes underlying public policy . . . The historic and relative disciplinary funding advantage of psychology, biology and economics over sociology has diminished the prevalence of more critical studies while producing the knowledge structure of the field through the funding of positivistic research approaches that are perceived as more 'scientific'.

Coping with aging in terms of the beliefs examined here goes beyond the comprehension of biology, psychology or economics. The above analysis has hopefully demonstrated the merits of a critical and sociological understanding of the interplay of agency/structure within the context of bereavement and loss. Indeed, further scrutiny could be given to what Estes and Linkins call the 'social'. For instance, the beliefs could be examined as an example of 'governmentality' (Foucault 1991), where 'self-subjection' is linked with 'societal regulation' (Turner 1997: xv). In particular, Hettie's self-subjection involves the government of her own identity through the attainment of what she understands as the socially appropriate category of independence. However, her ability to be the independent ethical citizen that neo-liberalism demands is very tenuous, she is bereaved and is alone. Thus she identifies herself most strongly with her view of the past, were communities and interdependence allowed people to lead virtuous lives.

In other words, power does not simply reside within society or individuals. Instead, it is determined in social relations and interactions between person and society. As Foucault has pointed out in an often neglected phrase, '...where there is power there is resistance' (Armstrong 1987). In the critical social policy literature what has been gleaned from Foucault's concept of governmentality is the notion of the disciplining and regulation of populations from a distance, and how individuals govern themselves within the loci of social relations (Dean 1999). Indeed, ideas about governmentality have been applied to later life by the editor of this book (Tulle and Mooney 2002). Drawing upon the current understanding of governmentality what needs to be emphasized here is that Hettie's beliefs reveal two things.

Firstly, how her agency reflects the intertwining of agency/structure. Thus her pursuit of virtue and the way she associates this with the past, is her way of resisting the hostile environment of the 'times in which we live.' Therefore and secondly, her agency comes into being, and is acted upon, within the context of social relations between the person and society. She is alone and bereaved but the past offers her the security to face up to the present. Hettie positions herself as a virtuous person by harking back to a view of the past where communities and interdependence allowed people to lead 'moral' lives. She does this in relation to her own circumstances. She has created community and interdependence in her continuing bonds with the past. Therefore her beliefs can be understood as an example of thinking and doing moral economy.

What this chapter has shown is that more interpretive work on the interplay of agency/structure within the lives of older people is needed. If we are to recognize their agency and also contest the fostering of dependency, a more 'bottom-up' understanding is needed.

Also, this chapter has begun to illustrate that aging into the fourth age is a complicated social process. Older adults may express highly moral or virtuous beliefs about their aging and sense of social identity, and these are shaped and constrained by powerful social forces within particular life histories. As noted, Gubrium and Wallace (1990) have suggested there are parallels between the theorizing of older adults and gerontologists. Critical gerontologists have argued for a moral economy of aging as a means of changing the social status and economic position of older people. What this chapter suggests is that more space should be devoted to the micro-politics of the experiences of older adults. Hopefully, this may serve as interpretive evidence for a moral economy of aging.

# REFERENCES

Arber, S. and Ginn, J. 1991a. *Gender and Later Life*, London: Sage.

Arber, S. and Ginn, J. 1991b. "The Invisibility of Age: Gender and Class Relations in Later Life." *Sociological Review* 39: 260-91.

Armstrong, D. 1987. "Bodies of Knowledge: Foucault and the Problem of Human Anatomy." pp. 59-76 in *Sociological Theory and Medical Sociology*, edited by G. Scambler. London: Tavistock.

Bertaux, D. (ed). 1981. *Biography and Society: The Life History Approach in the Social Sciences*. London: Sage.

Bond, J. and Coleman, P. (editors). 1990. *Aging in Society: An Introduction to Social Gerontology*. London: Sage.

Britten, N., Jones, R., Murphy, E. and Stacy, R. 1995. "Qualitative Research Methods in General Practice." *Family Practice* 12: 104-114.

Conway, S. 2003. "Ageing and Imagined Community: Some Cultural Constructions and Reconstructions." *Sociological Research Online*. 8(2), http://www.socresonline/8/2/html.

Conway, S. and Hockey, J.L. 1998. "Resisting the Mask of Old Age? The Social Meaning of Lay Health Beliefs in Later Life." *Aging and Society* 18: 469-494.

Dant, T. and Gearing, B. 1990. "Doing Biographical Research." pp. 143-159 in *Researching Social Gerontology: Concepts, Methods and Issues,* edited by S.M. Peace. London: Sage.

Dean, M. 1999. *Governmentality: Power and Rule in Modern Society*. London: Sage.

Douglas, M. 1995. [1966] *Purity and Danger: An Analysis of Concepts of Pollution and Taboo*. Harmondsworth: Penguin Books.

Durkheim, E. 1984. [1893] *The Division of Labour in Society*. London: Macmillan.

Ekerdt, D.J. 1986. "The Busy Ethic: Moral Continuity Between Work and Retirement." *Gerontologist* 26: 239-244.

Estes, C.L and Binney, E.A. 1991. "The Biomedicalization of Aging: Dangers and Dilemmas." pp. 116-138 in *Critical Perspectives on Aging: The Political and Moral Economy of Growing,* edited by.M. Minkler and C.L. Estes. Amityville, New York: Baywood.

Estes, C.L. and Linkins, K.W. 2000. "Critical Perspectives on Health and Aging." pp. 154-172 in *Handbook of Social Studies in Health and Medicine*, edited by G.L. Albrecht, R. Fitzpatrick and S.C. Scrimshaw. London: Sage.

Evans, M. 1993. "Reading Lives: How the Personal might be Social." *Sociology* (27)1: 5-14.

Featherstone, M. 1992. "The Heroic Life and Everyday Life." *Theory, Culture and Society* 9: 159-182.

Fennell, G., Phillipson, C. and Evers, H. 1988. *The Sociology of Old Age*. Milton Keynes: Open University Press.

Finch, J. 1987. "Family Obligations and the Lifecourse." pp. 155-169 in *Rethinking the Life Cycle*, edited by A. Bryman, B. Bytheway, P. Allat and T. Keil. Basingstoke: Macmillan.

Fontana, A. 1977. *The Last Frontier: The Social Meaning of Growing Old*. Beverley Hills, Ca.: Sage.

Foucault, M. 1988. "The Dangerous Individual." pp. 125-151 in *Michel Foucault: Politics, Philosophy, Culture*, edited by L.D. Kritzman. New York: Routledge.

Foucault, M. 1991. "Governmentality." pp. 87-104 in *The Foucault Effect: Studies in Governmentality*, edited by G. Burchell, C. Gordon, and P. Miller. Chicago: University of Chicago Press.

Goffman, E. 1968a. *Asylums: Essays on the Social Situation of Mental Patients and Other Inmates*. Harmondsworth: Penguin.

Goffman, E. 1968b. *Stigma: Notes on The Management of Spoiled Identity*. Harmondsworth: Penguin.

Gubrium, J. and Wallace, B. 1990. Who Theorises Age? *Aging and Society* 10: 131-150.

Hammersley, M. 1992. *What's Wrong With Ethnography*? London: Routledge.

Hepworth, M. 1995. "Positive Aging: What is the Message? pp. 176-190 in *The Sociology of Health Promotion: A Critical Analysis of Consumption, Lifestyle and Risk,* edited by R. Bunton, R. Burrows and S. Nettleton. London: Routledge.

Holstein, M. and Minkler, M. 1991 "The Short Life and Painful Death of the Medicare Catastrophic Coverage Act." pp. 93-115 in *Critical Perspectives on Aging: The Political and Moral Economy of Growing Old,* edited by M. Minkler and C.L. Estes. Amityville, New York: Baywood.

Jenkins, R. 1996. *Social Identity*. London: Routledge.

Jerrome, D. 1992. *Good Company: An Anthropological Study of People in Groups*. Edinburgh: Edinburgh University Press.

Jerrome, D. 1994. "Time, Change and Continuity in Family Life. *Ageing and Society* 14: 1-27.

Johnson, M.L. 1995. "Interdependency and the General Compact." *Ageing and Society* 15: 243-265.

Katz, S. 1996. *Disciplining Old Age: The Formation of Gerontological Knowledge.* Charlottesville: University Press of Virginia.

Kirk, H. 1992 "Geriatric Medicine and the Categorisation of Old Age." *Ageing and Society* 12: 483-497.

Kohli, M. 1991. "Retirement and the Moral Economy: An Historical Interpretation of the German Case." pp. 273-292 in *Critical Perspectives on Aging: The Political and Moral Economy of Growing Old,* edited by M. Minkler, and C.L. Estes. New York: Baywood Amityville.

Laslett, P. 1987. "The Emergence of the Third Age." *Ageing and Society* 7: 113-160.

Laslett, P. 1989. *A Fresh Map of Life: The Emergence of The Third Age.* London: Weidenfield and Nicholson.

Lyotard, J.F 1984. *The Post-Modern Condition: A Report on Knowledge.* Manchester: Manchester University Press

Mannheim, K. 1952. "The Problem of Generations." pp. 276-320 in *Essays on the Sociology of Knowledge,* edited by K. Mannheim, and D. Kecskemeti. London: Routledge and Kegan Paul.

Mason, J. 1996. *Qualitative Researching.* London: Sage.

Mehta, K. 1997. "Cultural Scripts and the Social Integration of Older People." *Ageing and Society* 17: 253-275.

Mills, C.W. (1940) "Situated Action and Vocabularies of Motive." *American Sociological Review* 5: 904-913.

Minkler, M. 1991. "Generational Equity and the New Victim Blaming." pp. 139-61 in *Critical Perspectives on Aging: The Political and Moral Economy of Growing Old,* edited by M. Minkler and C.L. Estes. Amityville, New York: Baywood.

Minkler, M. and Cole, T. 1991. "Political and Moral Economy: Not Such Strange Bedfellows." pp. 37-49 in *Critical Perspectives on Aging: The Political and Moral Economy of Growing Old,* edited by M. Minkler and C.L. Estes. Amityville, New York: Baywood.

Minkler, M. and Estes, C.L. (editors). 1991. *Critical Perspectives on Aging: The Political and Moral Economy of Growing Old.* Amityville, New York: Baywood.

Moss, N. and Moss, S.Z 1996. "Remarriage of Widowed Persons". pp. 163-178 in *Continuing Bonds: A New Understanding of Grief,* edited by D. Klass, P.R. Silverman **and S.L. Nickman.** London: Taylor and Francis.

Phillipson, C. 1982. *Capitalism and the Construction of Old Age.* London: Macmillan.

Phillipson, C. 1998. *Reconstructing Old Age: New Agendas in Social Theory and Practice.* London: Macmillan.

Robertson, A. 1997. "Beyond Apocalyptic Demography: Towards a Moral Economy of Interdependence." *Ageing and Society* 17: 425-446.

Rose, N. 1993. "Government, Authority and Expertise in Advanced Liberalism." *Economy and Society* 22: 283-298.

Seale, C. 1996. "Living Alone Towards the End of Life." *Ageing and Society,* 16:75-91.

Sontag, S. 1978. *Illness as Metaphor.* New York: Vintage.

Thompson, P., Itzin, C. and Abendstern M. 1992. "I don't feel Old: Subjective Aging and the Search for Meaning in Later Life." *Ageing and Society* 12: 23-47.

Thompson, P., Itzin, C. and Abendstern, M. 1990. *I Don't Feel Old: The Experience Of Later Life.* Oxford: Open University Press.

Tulle, E. and Mooney E. 2002. "Moving to Age-Appropriate Housing: Government and Self in Later Life." *Sociology* 336(3): 685-702.

Turner, B.S. 1997. "From Governmentality to Risk: Some Reflections on Foucault's Contribution to Medical Sociology." pp. ix-xxi in *Foucault, Health and Medicine*, edited by **A. Petersen and R. Bunton.** London: Routledge.

Vincent, J.A. 1995. *Inequality and Old Age*, London: UCL Press.

Vincent, J.A. 1996. "Who's Afraid of an Aging Population? Nationalism, the Free Market, and the Construction of Old Age as an Issue." *Critical Social Policy* 47: 3-26.

Williams, G. 1993. "Chronic Illness and the Pursuit of Virtue in Everyday Life." pp. 92-108 in *Worlds of Illness: Biographical and Cultural Perspectives on Health and Disease* edited by A. Radley. London: Routledge.

Williams, G. 1996. "The Genesis of Chronic Illness: Narrative Reconstruction." pp. 244-270 in *Perspectives in Medical Sociology*, edited by P. Brown. Belmont: Wadsworth.

Williams, R. 1990. *A Protestant Legacy: Attitudes to Death and Illness Among Older Aberdonians*. Oxford: Clarendon Press.

*Chapter 7*

# EMBODIED SELFHOOD: REDEFINING AGENCY IN ALZHEIMER'S DISEASE

## *Pia C. Kontos*

## ABSTRACT

Implicit in the prevailing paradigm of Alzheimer's disease is the assumption that memory impairment caused by cognitive deficiencies leads to a steady loss of the self. Underpinning this assumption is the Western representation of personhood that emphasizes cognitive orientation such that a sense of self-worth is achieved through the display and nurturance of cognitive or intellectual abilities. The insistence that selfhood is dependent upon cognition has its origins in the modern Western philosophical tradition that separates the mind, where human meaning and intelligence is said to reside, from the body, which is reduced to inert matter. Underlying this understanding is the belief that the body is fundamentally passive, rendering the lived materiality of the body silent and inconsequential. I explore how a notion of embodiment, one that acknowledges that capacities, senses, and experiences of bodies are central to the exercise of human agency, challenges the idea of an inevitable erosion of selfhood in Alzheimer's. I propose to integrate Merleau-Ponty's radical philosophical reconceptualization of perception and Bourdieu's sociological exploration of the logic of practice, yielding a theoretical framework that advocates the irreducibly embodied nature of human agency. The controversy surrounding the late paintings of Abstract Expressionist Willem de Kooning as well as the self-portraits of figurative painter William Utermohlen will be drawn upon in order to elucidate the perspective advanced here.

## INTRODUCTION

The purpose of this chapter is to contribute to critical gerontology by developing a notion of embodiment and exploring how this perspective constitutes a challenge to the presumed loss of agency in Alzheimer's disease. Much of the literature on Alzheimer's promotes the view that individuals with dementia experience a steady erosion of selfhood to the point at which no person remains (Kitwood and Benson 1995). The self is thought to be increasingly devoid of content, a process that has been referred to as "unbecoming" a self (Fontana and Smith 1989), and a "drifting towards the threshold of unbeing" (Kitwood and Bredin

1992:285). Thus, while Alzheimer's and its kindred dementias are usually described and analyzed in terms of the cognitive dysfunction they produce, there is as well, an assumed existential outcome: The loss of self with the concomitant erosion of individual agency (Herskovitz 1995; Ronch 1996).

This presumed loss of agency implicit in the current Alzheimer's construct is a product of the Western assumption that memory and cognition are the guarantors of personhood. Under the influence of English empirical philosophy (Locke 1700/1975) and the extreme individualism that has dominated Western society, personhood is framed by cognition and is reduced to consciousness, memory, and rationality. This representation of personhood is itself the legacy of Western philosophy's tendency to split mind from body, and position the former in hierarchical superiority over the latter. In contrast to the Cartesian mind/body dualism, where human meaning and intelligence are attributed to the mind, I propose to integrate Merleau-Ponty's radical philosophical reconceptualization of perception (1962) and Bourdieu's sociological exploration of the logic of practice (1977, 1990), yielding a theoretical framework that captures the existential immediacy of the body as well as its interrelationship with culture and history.

It is the central aim of this chapter to explore how this alternative perspective on the body brings a new and critical dimension to the challenge of the presumed loss of agency in Alzheimer's, and, more broadly, the implicit assumption that personhood depends exclusively upon memory and cognition. To do so, I will analyze from the perspective of embodiment that I advocate here, the controversy surrounding the late paintings of Abstract Expressionist, Willem de Kooning (Kontos 2003), paintings that were produced in the face of his progressing Alzheimer's disease, as well as a series of self-portraits produced by figurative painter, William Utermohlen, created over the course of his battle against Alzheimer's. I have chosen the cases of de Kooning and Utermohlen for they raise crucial questions about agency and intentionality, which form the focus of my analysis.

## DE KOONING'S COGNITIVE DISORDER

Willem de Kooning, who in 1997 died at the age of 92, is regarded as one of the greatest American artists of the twentieth century. He was a major exponent of Abstract Expressionism whose art has been the subject of numerous museum exhibitions. However, only one of these exhibitions has thoroughly examined the final body of de Kooning's work[1], namely his paintings from the 1980s. While these late works represent a distinguishable period in his career, controversy nonetheless surrounds their appraisal since they were produced while, by all accounts, de Kooning was losing his mind to Alzheimer's disease.

In 1979, following nearly a decade of struggle with amnesia, de Kooning began a slow recovery from twenty-five years of alcoholism, leading to a period of depression. His health was breaking down by perceptible degrees and his prognosis was dismal. At this point, de Kooning was encouraged by family and friends to seek therapy at Alcoholics Anonymous, and studio assistants were hired to help him stay sober. The alcohol-withdrawal process lasted

---

[1] The exhibition "Willem de Kooning: The Late Paintings, The 1980s" was organized collaboratively by the San Francisco Museum of Modern Art and the Walker Art Center, Minneapolis. The exhibition was conceived by Gary Garrels, former senior curator at the Walker, and Elise Haas, chief curator and curator of painting and sculpture at San Francisco Museum of Modern Art.

nearly two years, during which time he hardly painted at all (Tomkins 1997). A sort of deathwatch had settled over the art world as it mourned the loss of one of the greatest painters of this century for it looked as if his then most recent works would be his last (Espinel 1996).

De Kooning slowly regained his strength and began painting again in earnest, producing a substantial body of work in a style that departed radically from anything he had done before (Tomkins 1997; Worth 1997). The late paintings have an airy lightness and a lyricism for which there is no precedent in a half century of the artist's work (Garrels 1995; Tomkins 1997). The dense, tactile markings of heavy paint of the nineteen-seventies abstractions were gone; instead, the rough surfaces became serene with the paint in these new canvases scraped down and sometimes rubbed with sandpaper, yielding a flat even surface. The usual pigment trio of red, yellow and blue that had a rough edge to them gave way to the exotic colours of orange, green and violet set against and within large smooth areas of white. As a result, compared with his paintings of the previous decade, "which pull the viewer right into a vortex of agitated and highly physical activity, the new work exists in a separate space, a more contemplative arena with less drama and cleaner air" (Tomkins 1997:76).

De Kooning's faltering memory, disorientation, vagueness and uncommunicativeness progressively worsened. He was diagnosed with Alzheimer's disease in 1989 (Crutch, Isaacs, and Rossor 2001). Because of his progressing dementia he was unable to identify friends or participate in conversation. When asked a factual question, de Kooning was helpless, ignorant of the date, of where he lived. Yet with respect to his own work his memory was vivid. At his easel, or sitting in his rocker studying a work underway, he was alert and decisive. In the production of his final works, with each brush stroke de Kooning selected the colour, swirl, thickness, touch, and shadow (Espinel 1996). Though he would often confuse his wife with his sister, he would choose from among an infinite number of possible lines, curves, shapes, and colours. De Kooning the artist was alive, producing an exuberant, carefree art, full of life. For the near part of a decade, long after he had lost the ability to sign his own name, de Kooning would continue to paint (Worth 1997).

## WILLIAM UTERMOHLEN: A PORTRAIT OF ALZHEIMER'S

In 1996, William Utermohlen, a figurative painter who is best known for his portraits and murals, learned he had Alzheimer's disease. He was 60 at the time and had just finished a self-portrait. Over the next five years, as the disease progressed, he continued creating self-portraits until he became too weak to put his brush to canvas. A number of these self-portraits were brought together in an exhibition both in Paris and London, causing a tremendous stir in both the artistic and medical world. Doctors monitoring Utermohlen's condition selected five of these self-portraits as the basis of an academic paper published in the British medical journal *The Lancet* (Crutch et al. 2001). The authors treat the portraits as a window into the impact and rapid progression of dementia, a chronicle of the artist's loss of cognitive skills such as visual perception, spatial functions, and concentration. They argue that the portraits chart the objective deterioration in the quality of Utermohlen's artwork, deterioration that is commensurate and consistent with the decline in the artist's cognitive state. The authors also note that there is evidence of a decline in Utermohlen's ability to represent proportion and perspective in that facial features appear either blurred together or disjointed, and in the last few self-portraits, only the fundamental components of the face are recognizable.

Although many of the changes in Utermohlen's style are said to be the direct result of declining co-ordination and spatial awareness, Patricia Utermohlen, William's wife, herself an art historian, noted that some of the distortions in the self-portraits were intentional (Derbyshire 2001). She notes for example that her husband's hearing problems are reflected in the enlarged ears of one of the self-portraits, a distortion that Crutch et al. (2001) refer to as evidence of the artist's decline in ability to represent proportion. Ms. Utermohlen also attributes much of the blurring and disjointed effects in the self-portraits to her husband's tendency to rub out sections of the paintings with which he was displeased. Commenting on one of the self-portraits in which the facial features are extremely distorted, Ms. Utermohlen said "the sad thing about this picture is that at one stage when it was more complete than this it was really very good despite its complete mismanagement of space, and then he got distressed about it and just rubbed it out" (Derbyshire 2001).

With his coordination and memory steadily and rapidly failing, Utermohlen, who is now 66 years of age, has difficulty with the simplest of daily activities, such as fastening his belt. He puts his shoes on the wrong feet and can't figure out the heel from the toe of his socks (Driscoll 2001). The artist's cognitive decline is treated as of primary importance in accounting for the observed artistic change in the series of self-portraits. However, despite the effects of dementia, Utermohlen showed a persistent desire and ability, albeit impaired, to paint. As Crutch et al. (2001) themselves note, all five of the portraits were self-motivated and represent original attempts at self-portrayal rather than copying of previous efforts.

## ARTISTIC INTENTION: CONSCIOUS WILL, UNCONSCIOUS INTUITION OR NEITHER?

De Kooning's revolutionary change in style from his earlier work coupled with what is known about the artist's mental decline during these years, have led some critics to suggest that someone other than de Kooning actually painted his late works. Others, while accepting that de Kooning himself produced the "eighties paintings", nonetheless question their value since they do not emulate the signature style of de Kooning, lacking the "...coarse and disturbing beauty that was at the core of his art" (Tomkins 1997:77). To such critics, de Kooning's late paintings are of interest only inasmuch as they were from the hand of de Kooning and, as such, are "important for the historical record but... [cannot] stand on their own as fully realized works of art" (Garrels 1995:33). Some go as far as to reduce his final body of work to the "...senile doodlings of a once great artist whose reputation is being damaged for the sake of commercial exploitation" (Tomkins 1997:74) whilst others "think they document an old man still young in his art" (Worth 1997:2). There is greater consensus regarding the evaluation of the series of self-portraits created by Utermohlen, with critics suggesting that they evidence progressive deterioration of the artist's constructional abilities (Crutch et al. 2001; Derbyshire 2001). There is widespread agreement that the self-portraits reveal a marked decline from "refined realism to a style that more closely resembles primitive abstraction" (Gerlin 2001:2). That his self-portraits became less coherent, organized, and recognizable is widely held to be an inevitable consequence of Alzheimer's disease.

The participants to the debate around de Kooning's late works are not confined to art critics, but also include those in the medical world. Yet the medical authorities are as divided as the art critics in their approach to understanding de Kooning's state of mind and his final works. As Storr notes (1995:50), there is "little agreement on the medical etiology of the disease", as well as to "how its development would affect a person of de Kooning's special talents". Some neurologists maintain that Alzheimer's leads to a global loss of mental capacity, from which no particular areas are spared. Thus, if de Kooning continued to paint "as well as ever", as some maintain, it is asserted that "either the diagnosis is wrong or there is something rotten in the studio of de Kooning" (Klawans 1992:84). Clearly, the implication being that if de Kooning did in fact have Alzheimer's disease, then his assistants surely were doing the painting for him.

Medical expert opinion is sharply divided on the issue of the development of Alzheimer's disease with other specialists maintaining that "…[Alzheimer's disease] touches several different areas of intellectual function, but not all areas. We know Alzheimer's affects declarative memory – memory that you are consciously aware of. But it spares procedural memory: the ability to perform complex motor acts. Procedural memory is preserved throughout most of the illness" (quoted in Larson 1994:42). Crutch et al. (2001), in their analysis of Utermohlen's artistic creativity in the face of neurological impairment, similarly suggest that the skills required to implement artistic intention may be unequally affected by neurological impairment. Thus, both de Kooning's and Utermohlen's ability to paint can be explained by the sparing of a crucial area of their mental capacity.

Despite the fact that medical explanations of Alzheimer's disease and the late works of artists de Kooning and Utermohlen belie different assumptions regarding the nature and extent of this disease, common to all is inherent resistance to the possibility that these artists went on to create *despite* their dementia. There is either disbelief that creativity can withstand the ravages of Alzheimer's, or, it is accepted that artistic drive persists but only because right hemisphere structures of the brain are spared by the disease (Crutch et al. 2001:2132). The cases of de Kooning and Utermohlen are of interest only to the extent that they may shed light on where in the brain creativity is based. On the issue of de Kooning's ability to paint while suffering from Alzheimer's disease, it has been speculated more recently that his paintings were possible only because his artistic engagement with color and form played a role in what is believed must have been de Kooning's recovery from Alzheimer's disease. Here the suggestion is that color and form, through the stimulation of sensory pathways, heal (Espinel 1996). The common thread running through all of these positions is resistance to the notion that creativity and inventiveness could persist *in the presence* of cognitive impairment – that artistic intention persists, not because cognitive operation is spared or even healed, but perhaps because artistic intention is not the exclusive privilege of cognition.

I attribute this resistance to the biomedical commitment (of medical authorities) to link inseparably intention and mental capacity. Amongst art critics too, it appears that the degree to which de Kooning was thought to exercise intentionality either invokes or deflects positive appraisal of his late works. However, here the debate is more complex as the role of non-conscious intuition is introduced as an alternative to conscious will in explaining de Kooning's creative talent that persisted in the face of his progressing Alzheimer's disease. It is speculated that in the absence of a coherent mind, it was non-conscious intuition that led de Kooning's final works to fruition (Fraser 1998).

This raises the issue of what precisely constitutes "the active presence" (Fraser 1998:6) of the artist. Sacks, whose case studies of neurological anomalies underscore essential characteristics of the imagination, argues that style, neurologically, is the deepest part of one's being, and thus persists even in advanced stages of dementing diseases such as

Alzheimer's (referred to in Storr 1995:51). Sacks' interpretation suggests that artistic style is literally inscribed onto the brain of the artist, allowing creativity to persist despite cognitive impairment. Hess introduces a metaphorical argument that could be said to extend Sacks' insight about style and creativity to the body itself. Hess states "perhaps it is the brain in the wrist - a highly developed, self-critical center of physical actions, which works faster than the brain in the head can predict - that takes over" (quoted in Storr 1995:69). Hess seems to be privileging the hand as a body part that possesses a will of its own in his assertion that "there is a brain in the hand which, while drawing, will criticize, improvise, invent, erase - think new thoughts" (quoted in Storr 1995:69).

While Storr acknowledges that there is truth in this idea of a brain in the wrist, he concludes with skepticism: "What remains to be resolved is how focused intuition defines the larger ambition that triggers or restrains that 'brain in the hand'" (1995:9). Implicit here is the notion that there is something larger than intuition, specifically, the "brain in the head", that controls the "brain in the hand". As a result, the focus of inquiry becomes that of assessing the distinction between instinct and intent (the unconscious versus conscious will), a dichotomy that does not allow for the possibility that intention could actually reside in the body. In other words, intention to Storr is dependent upon cognition, and it is this relationship of dependence that implicitly denies that there could be intention in the face of cognitive impairment or that the body itself could be a source of intention. Hess similarly associates intention with cognition by insisting on portraying the body's intelligibility in reference to a brain. It is my contention that what Hess and Storr are both overlooking is that the body can be a source of inventiveness and creativity, inviting us to understand the body as active, that is, imbued with a life-force which has its own intentionality. This vitality should, as I maintain, be attributed to the domain of the body itself and not to what Hess and Storr attribute exclusively to cognition.

This distinction between conscious will and non-conscious intuition, as well as the implicit assumption that with the loss of the mind there is a corresponding loss of agency, can be read as a legacy of Western philosophy's tendency to separate the mind, where human meaning and intelligence is said to reside, from the body, which is reduced to inert matter. In both the medical and artistic context, the commentaries surrounding de Kooning's and Utermohlen's later works unwittingly raise the issue of the subordination of body to mind, and the associated dominance of cognitive rationalization. Underlying this understanding is the belief that the body is fundamentally passive. I have argued elsewhere (Kontos 1999) that there is an absence of the body in gerontological explorations of the experience of old age, an argument that is equally germane to the discourse on Alzheimer's disease. The body has yet to be incorporated into explorations of the subjective experience of Alzheimer's disease, as well as to the increasing dialogue between diverse representations of the nature of the self. The discourse on Alzheimer's disease must embrace the facticity of our embodiment, and, in seeking to bring the body into this discourse, I turn to scholarship on the body in social theory.

## BRINGING IN THE BODY: A PERSPECTIVE ON EMBODIMENT

The past two decades have marked an enormous upsurge of interest in the body. Scholarship in the social sciences and humanities has challenged in a substantial way theories of the body which rest on dichotomies such as mind/body, subject/object, and biology/culture, thus rendering the body "an entirely problematic notion" (Csordas 1994:1). While perspectives on the body are united in their attempt to break down Western dualist legacies, there is less consensus regarding the precise relation between the body as a material entity and the body as culturally located. The problem of the body, argues Turner (1996), lies at the juncture of the major issues of sociological theory; the epistemological problems of sociology center on the membership of the human species in both nature and culture. That is, "the human body is subject to processes of birth, decay and death which result from its placement in the natural world, but these processes are also 'meaningful' events located in a world of cultural beliefs, symbols and practices" (Turner 1996:82).

Social theorists, in their efforts to capture the complex nature of the body, have stimulated intellectual rigour by advocating stronger ties to feminism, cultural studies, and the humanities. Studies emerging from this interdisciplinary endeavor have challenged previous dualist approaches and have addressed the politics of the production and reproduction of the body (Benhabib 1992; Butler 1993; Featherstone, Hepworth, and Turner 1991; Grosz 1994; Haraway 1991; Shilling 1993; Turner 1996). However, much of social theory of the body suffers from limitations as a consequence of giving primacy to representational (i.e. social constructionist) rather than experiential (i.e. existential/ phenomenological) issues. As Williams and Bendelow so aptly argue (1998:126), "bodies...[have] become elusive, de-materialized, incorporeal entities through a postmodern bracketing of ontological questions (i.e. the search for underlying 'essences') and a prioritization instead of a relativist epistemological stance".

Numerous scholars have proposed that the absence of "voices" from bodies themselves can be corrected by bringing into focus the body as an animate organism (Csordas 1994; Nettleton and Watson 1998; Turner 1996). This calls for an alternative formulation of the body as a source of subjectivity, with a focus on "lived experience" and the body's existential immediacy. This more sensate and dynamic perspective has increasingly supplanted the very expression "the body" with the term "embodiment" (Weiss and Haber 1999). What appears to distinguish a sociology of the body that is grounded in the notion of embodiment from the various forms taken by social theory of the body, is that the "lived body" is treated as the "personal ground of culture, structure, and behaviour" (Watson et al. 1996). Focus, therefore, is placed on lay accounts of lived experiences of the body since they are upheld as holding the key to our understanding of the extraordinarily complex engagement between biology, individual sentience, culture, and history.

The paradigm of embodiment, despite its proclaimed interest in the modality of being-in-the-world, a term taken from the phenomenological tradition, has not for the most part taken seriously the notion of "bodily intentionality" as advanced by Merleau-Ponty (1962). Featherstone and Hepworth speak of embodiment as a process by which "bodily and biological conditions enter human life through the interpretations that are made of them in different cultures and during varying periods of human history" (1998:156). Much of the embodiment literature adopts this perspective, and, consequently, in its treatment of "the body", assumes the pragmatic and epistemological primacy of objective structure/culture, which leads away from attending to the physical body as a site of origination.[2] Featherstone and Hepworth's perspective on embodiment reveals such a bias in favour of the symbolic and cultural dimensions of the body, overlooking the significance of the *phenomenal body* and thus rendering silent what Lock and Scheper-Hughes have referred to as "the language of the organs" (1990:71). Analyses of phenomenological experiences are thus limited to the way in which social and historical structures become embodied. Consequently, while the paradigm of embodiment has emerged with increasing sophistication and insight, scholars inadvertently perpetuate the limitation inherent in prevailing social theory of the body: Objectifying the body as a material substrate on which culture operates which excludes the body from primordial participation in the domain of culture.

The tendency to overlook embodied consciousness (Merleau-Ponty 1962) in studies of embodiment is surprising given that Merleau-Ponty's principle of the potentiality of the body, widely regarded as critical to an appreciation of embodiment (Crossley 1995; Csordas 1999; Nettleton and Watson 1998), states that the physical body itself possesses a dynamic life-force emanating from a *primordial* unity of consciousness and the body. In other words, Merleau-Ponty privileges the phenomenal body as the *original* source of intentional processes of perception; perception consists in a meaningful configuration of sensations (Merleau-Ponty 1962:52, 235) and these sensations belong to the body as a sentient being, which refers to the body's basic property of being embodied or incarnated in the world.

The significance of the primary perceptual level that Merleau-Ponty speaks of has yet to be brought into the problematic of embodiment because the very categories of perception and appreciation are deemed socially and historically constituted (Bourdieu 1977, 1990). The challenge that faces the paradigm of embodiment is a serious consideration of the pre-objective, primordial relationship we have to our bodies and the world and, further, the exploration of the interrelationship between the phenomenal body, culture, and social/historical contexts. In order to bring the paradigm of embodiment to its full fruition, a theoretical framework is required that respects the existential immediacy of the body with the pre-objective reservoir of meaning implied therein, without rendering the socio-cultural, -historical and -political environments peripheral.

With an interest in developing such a framework, I propose to draw upon Merleau-Ponty's philosophy of embodiment and Bourdieu's sociology of embodiment. More specifically, I intend to extract the fundamentals of Merleau-Ponty's radical reconceptualization of perception in order to capture the phenomenal body and Bourdieu's notion of habitus in order to capture the social/historical body.[3] It goes beyond the scope of this paper to explore the possibility of a full integration of the whole of Merleau-Ponty's and Bourdieu's approaches to embodiment, and to consider the implications such an integration would have for their respective approaches. It is my claim that for the purposes of this chapter Merleau-Ponty's principle of the potentiality of the body, and Bourdieu's account of the formation and acquisition of the generative structures that constitute habitus, can be brought

---

[2] Williams and Bendelow (1998:126) are an exception in their effort to theorize the relationship between "the immediate embodiment of disease as brute materiality and its meaning-laden character as human experience" through their analysis of pain.

[3] Crossley (2001) similarly argues for the beneficial integration of the thought of Bourdieu and Merleau-Ponty. While Crossley's purpose is to advance a theoretical enrichment of Bourdieu's notion of habitus in order to resolve dualisms prevalent in contemporary sociological theory, my purpose in drawing upon both Merleau Ponty's phenomenology and Bourdieu's sociology, is to develop a notion of embodiment that achieves an integrated and critical perspective on the body.

together in such a way as to illuminate a richer concept of embodiment. Bourdieu correctly emphasizes and provides a comprehensive analysis of the social and historical dimensions of the body. However, Bourdieu's understanding of the social can be complemented and enriched by drawing upon Merleau-Ponty's reference to a more existential understanding of agency, precisely what Bourdieu ignores.

## MERLEAU-PONTY'S RECONCEPTUALIZATION OF PERCEPTION

Merleau-Ponty's existential phenomenology takes as its starting point an extended critique of two schools of thought, empiricism and intellectualism. For Merleau-Ponty both are positivist philosophies since they favor objective thought, accounting only for the objective world (Merleau-Ponty 1962:23). Empiricism reduces all experience and behavior of an organism to a series of basic elements such as sensations or sense-data, or basic responses such as reflexes. As a result, innovation, creativity and/or improvisation in behavior cannot be accounted for by this perspective because behavior is viewed as intelligible only in terms of response to given stimuli. Consequently, Merleau-Ponty argues that empiricism is unsuitable to understanding the human world as it reduces everything to simple causal and physiological mechanisms (1962:23).

In contrast to the empiricist view of the world as a collection of externally related facts, intellectualism takes the world to be the result of processes of consciousness (Merleau-Ponty 1962:39). It is the mind that gives meaning to the world, and its mode of operation can be grasped in the state of pure reflection. Merleau-Ponty's specific objections to intellectualism are directed against intellectualism's understanding of reflection and consciousness:

> The world is there before any possible analysis of mine...Analytical reflection believes that it can trace back the course followed by a prior constituting act and arrive, in the 'inner man' - to use St. Augustine's expression - at a constituting power which has always been identical with that inner self. Thus reflection itself is carried away and transplanted in an impregnable subjectivity, as yet untouched by being and time. But this is very ingenuous, or at least it is an incomplete form of reflection which loses sight of its own beginning (1962:x).

In contrast to intellectualism which insulates consciousness from the world, Merleau-Ponty insists that human beings exist *in-the-world* and only in the world do we know ourselves (Merleau-Ponty 1962:xi, 27). He reiterates this point again by stating that "reflection is not absolutely transparent for itself, it is always given to itself in an *experience...*" (1962:42, emphasis in original).

Merleau-Ponty's proposed solution to the inadequacies of empiricism and intellectualism is to transcend both in terms of a phenomenology of existence. Central to his philosophical program is a radical redefinition of perception; in contrast to both empiricism and intellectualism, Merleau-Ponty argues that perceptual experience is neither purely physiological and automatic, nor purely psychological and reflective (Merleau-Ponty 1962:204). For Merleau-Ponty, perception is a *pre-reflective* intercourse with the world. Of paramount importance to this radical reconceptualization of perceptual experience is that it is not a handmaid of cognitive consciousness (1962:204). Existential understanding is prior to and independent of reflective thought. It is not a proposition of the form "I think that", but rather a practical form of "I know how", which is in no way dependent upon language.

Practical consciousness represents that inarticulate but fundamental attunement to things, which is our being-in-the-world (1962:79).

Merleau-Ponty argues that the pre-reflective body is itself intentional in the sense that it is directed towards the world without allowing for a reflective understanding of the manner in which it is directed (Merleau-Ponty 1962:213, 233). He gives an example of a person waving to a friend in the street (1962:111) – the friend waves back without first thinking or planning to do so, without having to wonder where the hand is or how it should be moved. The coordination of all movements involved in the waving is achieved without reflective thought. Moreover, the waving is the bearer or manifestation of the intention to wave. In other words, the intention to wave is not affected prior to the act; intention and the waving are simultaneously constituted. Thus intentionality is not a thought in that "it does not come into being through the transparency of any consciousness, but takes for granted all the latent knowledge of itself that...[our] body possesses" (Merleau-Ponty 1962:233). This latent knowledge is a field of possible actions and movements, a kind of inner map of possible movements the body "knows" how to perform. Because of the apparent synthesis between intention and the body, Merleau-Ponty concludes that the relationship between the former and the latter is, in movement, "magic" (1962:94).

The body possesses, according to Merleau-Ponty, a coordinating power in relation to itself that is prior to any explicit act of intellection on our part. An example he provides to illustrate the pre-reflective nature of the coordination of visual, tactile, and motor aspects of our body is the following:

> If I am sitting at my table and I want to reach the telephone, the movement of my hand towards it, the straightening of the upper part of the body, the tautening of the leg muscles are super-imposed on each other. I desire a certain result and the relevant tasks are spontaneously distributed amongst the appropriate segments
> *(1962:149).*

Merleau-Ponty argues that no aspect of this existential knowledge of coordination is reflective or discursive (i.e. learnt). Hence, as Merleau-Ponty notes, in their first attempts at reaching for an object, children look not at their hand but at the object. The implication being that the various parts of the body are known to us through their functionality, with their co-ordination never having to be learnt (Merleau-Ponty 1962:149).

Merleau-Ponty affirms the primacy of practical over theoretical or abstract ways of being-in-the-world (Merleau-Ponty 1962:137). Our primary relation to our environment consists in practical competence. We do not relate to our bodies as we do to an external object in that we do not reflect upon the hows, what and wheres of our bodily movement. To understand, in this sense, consists in competent bodily action. To understand is to experience the harmony between what we aim at and what is given, between the intention and the performance (1962:144). Bodily movement is not a cognitive operation; it is not intellection infused throughout the body, but rather is a kind of knowledge that does not derive from or rely upon cognition.

Merleau-Ponty does not incorporate the social and historical dimensions of the body into his philosophical program; his focus on perceptual experience renders the social and political environment peripheral. As Turner so powerfully asserts, while it may be true that phenomenologically individuals have direct government over their bodies, this is never true socially in the sense that the social reproduction of populations is subject to institutional regulation, power, ideology, and economics (1996:82). It is because of this crucial sociological point that I turn to Bourdieu's structural theory of practice that connects the body to culture and to social structure and power.[4]

## HABITUS

According to Bourdieu, when analyzing theoretically the structure of ongoing human existence (practices), the "ruinous" opposition between objectivism and subjectivism must be overcome since both these modes of knowledge are equally indispensable to a science of the social world (Bourdieu 1990:25). Bourdieu asserts that a genuine science of human practice must account for both structures of the social world and the perceptual and evaluative schemata that agents invest in their everyday life. What establishes the originality and importance of Bourdieu's work, precisely what constitutes the foundational hypothesis that anchors his sociology, is his exploration of where these schemata come from and what the precise correspondence is between them and the external structures of society. What Bourdieu seeks to describe are the principles of practical logic responsible for social and cultural practices regarding human behavior (1990:26, 91). Bourdieu analyses the structure of this logic, the internalized principles of the habitus, from which agents produce regulated practices.

Bourdieu argues that the conditionings associated with membership in a particular social class tend, through the relationship to one's own body, to shape the dispositions constituting social identity. Bourdieu defines a disposition as "a way of being, a habitual state...a tendency, propensity, or inclination" (Bourdieu 1977:214n1). Dispositions are corporeal in that they are embodied in real human beings and converted into motor schemes and body automatisms, which, in practice, materialize as postures, gestures, and movements (Bourdieu 1977:93-94, 1990:69). The process of socialization through a cumulative exposure to certain social conditions instills in individuals dispositions and generative schemes for being and perceiving. Bodily expressions (e.g. the way we walk, the way we eat) stress the durability of the effects of socialization.

Of paramount importance to the concept of habitus is the notion that an individual's actions are the product of a *modus operandi* of which the individual is not the sole producer and, for the most part, has no conscious mastery (Bourdieu 1977:72-73, 79-80). "Le sense practique" is a form of knowledge that is learnt by the body but cannot be explicitly articulated. It is a form of knowledge that does not pass through consciousness for it is enacted at a pre-reflective level. This is aptly captured in the following:

---

[4] It is not my intention to engage in a comprehensive review of Bourdieu's sociology or a point-by-point exegesis of its conceptual structure. What is of relevance to my argument here is Bourdieu's notion of the unconscious character of bodily knowledge, the internalized principles of habitus, from which agents produce regulated practices.

...habitus...function[s]...as principles which generate and organize practices and representations that can be objectively adapted to their outcomes without presupposing a conscious aiming at ends or an express mastery of the operations necessary in order to attain them. Objectively 'regulated' and 'regular' without being in any way the product of obedience to rules, they can be collectively orchestrated without being the product of the organizing action of a conductor
*(Bourdieu 1990:53).*

Bourdieu's reference to the unconscious character of practical logic and dispositions raises the crucial issue of the actual manifestation of social structure in practice, or how habitus actually operates. The actual genesis of the socialized biological individual, that is, of the social conditions of formation and acquisition of the generative structures that constitute habitus as the social embodied, is an extremely complex process. Bourdieu argues that structural principles of the social world and bodily schemata are structurally homologous because they are *physiologically linked* rendering the latter nothing other than the embodiment of the former. The direct correspondence between the body and the social world results from cumulative exposure to social conditions, which instills in individuals an ensemble of dispositions, and internalizes the necessities of the social environment, "inscribing inside the organism the...constraints of external reality" (Bourdieu and Wacquant 1992:13). Turning to Bourdieu's ethnographic research in the North African society of Kabyle will provide an example of the internalization of the constraints of a social system.

Bourdieu's ethnographic research shows how masculine domination assumes a natural status through its inscription in the objective structure of the social world, which is then incorporated into and reproduced in the habitus of individuals (Bourdieu 1990:70-72). Gender inequality, Bourdieu argues, is invoked through the inscription of a system of sexualized oppositions in the structuring of social space and the division of labour, which, for the most part, confines women to circumscribed domestic, pastoral, and market locations as opposed to the masculine sites of the public sphere. Bourdieu argues that the social determinations attached to one's social position shape the dispositions constituting social identity (ways of standing, speaking, walking, etc.) (1990:71). Bourdieu observes, for example, that in Kabyle "the opposition between male and female *is realized in posture, in the gestures and movements of the body*, in the form of the opposition between the straight and the bent, between firmness, uprightness and directness...and restraint, reserve and flexibility" (1990:70, emphasis added). Thus, the submissiveness of Kabylian women is actually embodied in the curvature of their spines towards the ground; restraint and reserve orient the whole female body downwards.

Bourdieu's example of the binary opposition between male and female in Kabyle illustrates his argument that implicit in the techniques of the body is the hidden persuasion of a whole social system of values. As McNay points out in discussing habitus (1999:100), "hierarchical gender relations are embedded in bodily *hexis*, that is to say arbitrary power relations are inculcated upon the body in the naturalized form of gender identity". Bourdieu states that "arms and legs are full of numb imperatives" which seem perfectly "natural" but are, according to Bourdieu, an embodied "political mythology" (1990:69-70). The unconscious bodily expressions of the social *hexis* stress the durability of socialization whereby the most fundamental material conditions of existence and the practice of structured actions become instilled in the primary experiences of the body.

## RETHINKING THE CASES OF DE KOONING AND UTERMOHLEN: EMBODIED SELFHOOD

The perspective on embodiment advanced here, in contrast to the distinction between conscious will and non-conscious intuition implicit in commentaries on de Kooning's and Utermohlen's late works, accepts as a guiding premise that the body is a source of agency. The body, from this perspective, is understood as a realm where intention, as will that is not dependent upon cognition, persists *despite* cognitive impairment. It is my contention that this more sensate and dynamic perspective on the body has the potential to move us beyond the simple distinction between conscious will and non-conscious intuition, thereby leading to new and more critical interpretations of de Kooning's and Utermohlen's ability to paint while suffering from Alzheimer's disease. Thinking of the body as a source of inventiveness and intention that does not necessarily emerge from a conscious form of knowledge is significant because of its potential implications. Even if Alzheimer's had robbed these artists of their conscious will, it was their hands, "intrinsically painterly", that allowed their creativity to persist nonetheless (Fraser 1998:7). It would therefore be more accurate to say that artistic creativity and intention are literally held in the hand rather than speaking of a "brain in the wrist" (quoted in Storr 1995:69).

The seeming tension between cognitive impairment and the coherent expression of creative talent raises the crucial issue of the process by which the hand becomes "intrinsically painterly". The actual genesis of such bodily intentionality is an extremely complex process, one that I maintain has its origins in what Merleau-Ponty understands to be the primordial body. The primordial becomes intertwined with the bodily dispositions and generative schemes which are the essence of the habitus. It is a relationship whereby the primordial subtends habitus, providing the foundation for social and cultural dispositions. It goes beyond the scope of this chapter to explore the complexity of the interrelationship between the primordial and the social. However, of utmost significance here is that the primordial origins of creative talent as well as the effects of cultural conditioning are grounded in the preobjective level of experience. Indeed, the power of such embodiment derives from the fact that movement and practice are not dependent upon cognition. Hence the reason for the resilience of manifestations of selfhood in painting that is apparent in the cases of de Kooning and Utermohlen is that primordial existence and socio-cultural bodily dispositions are remote and distinct from the self-transparent activities of a reflective subject.

By locating selfhood in the body and not in the mind as distinct and separate from the body, Utermohlen's self-portraits can be seen for their creativity, aesthetic feeling, and intention rather than exclusively as a chronicle of the artist's loss of cognitive skills. Figurative drawing for Utermohlen is an embodied talent, not necessarily requiring self-consciousness or self-reflexivity. It is precisely this creative impulse that results in a behavior that is "an intentional-action rather than an action added to or caused by an intention" (Crossley 2001:101). As such, the impulse to draw is driven not by reflective knowledge but rather by bodily knowledge. The cases of de Kooning and Utermohlen suggest a notion of creativity that displaces the primacy of cognitive consciousness and underscores the significance of bodily or embodied consciousness.

Precisely because of de Kooning's and Uthermohlen's cognitive impairment, their artistic creations cannot be persuasively explained by reference to reflective deliberation. It is, however, wholly consistent with the perspective on embodiment advanced here, that despite their cognitive impairment, their "active presence" as artists remained intact. This is because, as Merleau-Ponty argues, our primary relation to our world is not, in the first instance, a matter of reflective thought, but rather of practical involvement. De Kooning's late paintings and Utermohlen's self-portraits illustrate *the primacy of practical over reflective forms of being,* and indicate that corporeality is the ground of agency, and that selfhood, and not just artistic creativity, inheres "deep within".

## CONCLUSION

The presumed loss of selfhood implicit in the literature on Alzheimer's is a product of the assumption that only the mind relates us to the world and gives it meaning, rendering the lived materiality of the body silent and inconsequential. Central to this assumption is a concept of personhood that hinges on cognition ignoring the primacy of perception and the significance of habitus. Following the perspective on embodiment advocated here, these existential and social aspects of the body are indispensable for the articulation of selfhood. Thus, thinking of selfhood as embodied, formed and reproduced non-discursively through our practical action in the world, invites a rethinking of the implications of dementia. Namely, that dementia sufferers must be understood as retaining personhood and agency, despite cognitive impairment.

The cases of de Kooning and Utermohlen invite a rethinking of conventional notions of personhood. These cases of Alzheimer's disease call for the understanding of intention not only as the exclusive privilege of the sphere of conscious will but also emanating from our corporeal depths. It entails a shift in the current preoccupation with assessing the extent to which agency is a product of reflex or reflective thought, to treating the body as itself having creative and intentional capacity. Taken together, Merleau-Ponty and Bourdieu show that there is agency that is always and already anchored in the body, thus confirming, as I have argued, the personhood of those who suffer from cognitive impairment. This is not to suggest that with Merleau-Ponty and Bourdieu we have found a substitute for the mind in the notion of embodied selfhood. If, however, there is truth, as I maintain, to the claims of Merleau-Ponty and Bourdieu about the body, then clearly by not paying attention to these aspects of human behavior, in the case of Alzheimer's disease, we ignore this vital source of personhood that is present in the sufferer.

It has been said that "...[de Kooning's] resurgence is a testimony to the potential of the human mind" (Espinel 1996:1098). However, as my argument suggests, the continued implementation of his artistic intention in the face of neurological impairment is a testimony to the *body's* potentiality for innovation and creative action. Putting aside the differing opinions regarding the success or failure of de Kooning's and Utermohlen's paintings, their art is a powerful reminder that the pre-reflective intentional body is essential to our existence. Crutch et al. (2001) assert that Utermohlen's continued artistic endeavor at a stage when Alzheimer's disease affected his constructional abilities, offers a testament to the resilience of human creativity. I would add that it also offers a testament to the resilience of "primary consciousness", "perceptual synthesis", "pre-reflective intercourse with the world", "intentionality", and "internalized principles of the habitus". These aspects of our being are embodied and amount to a pre-reflective mastery that agents have of their world by way of immersion within it.

The notion of embodiment, more precisely embodied selfhood, sets an important agenda for critical gerontological inquiry into the complex phenomenon of Alzheimer's disease. It is not intended to resolve the debate about the self in Alzheimer's disease but rather to provide new insight and direction for future investigation. Thinking of selfhood as embodied not only adds a new dimension to this debate but, in a broader sense, challenges traditional notions of personhood and informs a new understanding of the nature of human agency, selfhood and embodiment. It is a critical approach to the body that invites a carefully contextualized discussion and exploration of the localized symbiosis of pre-reflective intentionality and structures of the social world. It is a symbiosis that is "enacted at every instant in the movement of existence" (Merleau-Ponty 1962:89) rendering the animated, living, experiential body of paramount importance for sociological enquiry.

Of further significance is the enrichment that a notion of embodied selfhood could bring to clinical research. While biomedical research has made enormous advances in the generation of knowledge about Alzheimer's, the biomedical construction of the disease has the consequence of treating the person with Alzheimer's as an object of study, reduced to cognitive deficits. As a result there is almost no sociological literature on the experiences of dementia sufferers, apart from the representations offered by caregivers, which often tell us more about the experiences of the caregivers than those of their patients. Changing our view of the person with dementia from an object of study to a subject whose perspective can enrich our understanding of the complexity of Alzheimer's will encourage researchers to include explorations of the lived experience of the illness into their research agendas.

Relationships and care environments that recognize and support the personhood of those who suffer cognitive impairment have important implications for treatment and care. Recognition of the larger human dimension of individuals with Alzheimer's disease could lead to significant improvements in their functioning and quality of life. Kitwood's research supports this, and he goes as far as to argue that person-centred care can offset neurological impairment and even promote some degree of structural regeneration in the neurons that remain (Kitwood 1997). It is crucial for practitioners and care providers to recognize that even when the ravages inflicted by neuropathology are severe, the personhood of the sufferer persists as an embodied dimension of human existence and, as such, must be embraced in dementia care.

## ACKNOWLEDGMENTS

I wish to thank Ann Robertson for her incisive comments on an earlier draft of this chapter.

## REFERENCES

Benhabib, S. 1992. *Situating the Self: Gender, Community and Postmodernism in Contemporary Ethics*. New York: Routledge.

Bourdieu, P. 1977. *Outline of a Theory of Practice*. Translated by R. Nice. Cambridge: Cambridge University Press.

—. 1990. *The Logic of Practice*. Translated by R. Nice. Cambridge: Polity Press.

Bourdieu, P. and L.J.D. Wacquant. 1992. "The Purpose of Reflexive Sociology (The Chicago Workshop)." pp. 62-215 in *An Invitation to Reflexive Sociology*, edited by P. Bourdieu and L. J. D. Wacquant. Chicago: University of Chicago Press.

Butler, J. 1993. *Bodies That Matter: On the Discursive Limits of 'Sex'*. New York: Routledge.

Crossley, N. 1995. "Merleau-Ponty, the Elusive Body and Carnal Sociology." *Body & Society* 1:43-63.

—. 2001. "The Phenomenological Habitus and its Construction." *Theory and Society* 30:81-120.

Crutch, S., R. Isaacs, and M. Rossor. 2001. "Some Workmen Can Blame their Tools: Artistic Change in an Individual with Alzheimer's Disease." *The Lancet* 357:2129-2133.

Csordas, T.J. 1994. "Introduction: The Body as Representation and Being-in-the-World." pp. 1-24 in *Embodiment and Experience: The Existential Ground of Culture and Self*, edited by T. J. Csordas. Cambridge: Cambridge University Press.

—. 1999. "Embodiment and Cultural Phenomenology." pp. 143-162 in *Perspectives on Embodiment: The Intersections of Nature and Culture*, edited by G. Weiss and H. F. Haber. New York: Routledge.

Derbyshire, D. 2001. "Self-Portrait of Dementia in Progress." pp. A3 in *National Post*, July 3.

Driscoll, M. 2001. "Artist Paints His Alzheimer's." pp. F2 in *Toronto Star*, July 29.

Espinel, C.H. 1996. "De Kooning's Late Colours and Forms: Dementia, Creativity, and the Healing Power of Art." *The Lancet* 347:1096-1098.

Featherstone, M. and M. Hepworth. 1998. "Ageing, the Lifecourse and the Sociology of Embodiment." pp. 147-175 in *Modernity, Medicine and Health: Medical Sociology Towards 2000*, edited by G. Scambler and P. Higgs. London: Routledge.

Featherstone, M., M. Hepworth, and B.S. Turner. 1991. *The Body: Social Process and Cultural Theory*. London: Sage.

Fontana, A. and R.W. Smith. 1989. "Alzheimer's Disease Victims: The 'Unbecoming' of Self and the Normalization of Competence." *Sociological Perspectives* 32:35-46.

Fraser, M. 1998. "'The Face-Off Between Will and Fate': Artistic Identity and Neurological Style in de Kooning's Late Works." *Body & Society* 4:1-22.

Garrels, G. 1995. "Three Toads in the Garden: Line, Color, and Form." pp. 9-37 in *Willem de Kooning: The Late Paintings, The 1980s*, edited by J. Jenkins. Minneapolis: Walker Art Center and San Francisco Museum of Modern Art.

Gerlin, A. 2001. "Artist Paints a Self-Portrait of Alzheimer's Disease." *Beacon Journal* [Online] Available: *http://www.ohio.com/bj/features/2001/August/28/docs/016578.htm*.

Grosz, E. 1994. *Volatile Bodies: Toward a Corporeal Feminism*. Bloomington: Indiana University Press.

Haraway, D.J. 1991. *Simians, Cyborgs, and Women: The Reinvention of Nature*. New York: Routledge.

Herskovitz, E. 1995. "Struggling over Subjectivity: Debates about the 'Self' and Alzheimer's Disease." *Medical Anthropology Quarterly* 9:146-164.

Kitwood, T. 1997. *Dementia Reconsidered: The Person Comes First*. Buckingham: Open University Press.

Kitwood, T. and S. Benson. 1995. *The New Culture of Dementia Care*. London: Hawker.

Kitwood, T. and K. Bredin. 1992. "Towards a Theory of Dementia Care: Personhood and Well-being." *Ageing and Society* 12:269-287.

Klawans, H.L. 1992. *Life, Death, and In Between*. New York: Paragon House.

Kontos, P. 1999. "Local Biology: Bodies of Difference in Ageing Studies." *Ageing and Society* 19:677-689.

—. 2003. "'The Painterly Hand': Embodied Consciousness and Alzheimer's Disease." *Journal of Aging Studies* 17: 151-170.

Larson, K. 1994. "Alzheimer's Expressionism: The Conundrum of de Kooning's Last Paintings." *Village Voice*, May 31.

Lock, M. and N. Scheper-Hughes. 1990. "A Critical-Interpretive Approach in Medical Anthropology: Rituals and Routines of Discipline and Dissent." pp. 47-72 in *Medical Anthropology: Contemporary Theory and Method*, edited by T. M. Johnson and C. G. Sargent. New York: Praeger.

Locke, J. 1700/1975. "Of Identity and Diversity." pp. 328-348 in *An Essay Concerning Human Understanding*, edited by P. H. Nidditch. Oxford: Clarendon Press.

McNay, L. 1999. "Gender, Habitus and the Field: Pierre Bourdieu and the Limits of Reflexivity." *Theory, Culture & Society* 16:95-117.

Merleau-Ponty, M. 1962. *Phenomenology of Perception*. Translated by C. Smith. London: Routledge & Kegan Paul.

Nettleton, S. and J. Watson. 1998. *The Body in Everyday Life*. London: Routledge.

Ronch, J. 1996. "Mourning and Grief in Late Life Alzheimer's Dementia: Revisiting the Vanishing Self." *American Journal of Alzheimer's Disease* 11:25-28.

Shilling, C. 1993. *The Body and Social Theory*. London: Sage.

Storr, R. 1995. "'At Last Light'." pp. 39-79 in *Willem de Kooning: The Late Paintings, The 1980s*, edited by J. Jenkins. Minneapolis: Walker Art Center and San Francisco Museum of Modern Art.

Tomkins, C. 1997. "De Kooning as Melodrama: What do the Late Paintings Really Reveal?" *The New Yorker*, February 10: 74-77.

Turner, B.S. 1996. *The Body & Society*. London: Sage.

Watson, J., S. Cunningham-Burley, N. Watson, and K. Milburn. 1996. "Lay Theorizing About 'the Body' and Implications for Health Promotion." *Health Education Research* 11:161-172.

Weiss, G. and H.F. Haber. 1999. "Introduction." pp. xiii-xvii in *Perspectives on Embodiment: The Intersections of Nature and Culture*, edited by G. Weiss and H. F. Haber. New York: Routledge.

Williams, S. and G. Bendelow. 1998. "In Search of the 'Missing Body': Pain, Suffering and the (Post)modern Condition." pp. 125-146 in *Modernity, Medicine and Health: Medical Sociology Towards 2000*, edited by G. Scambler and P. Higgs. London: Routledge.

Worth, A. 1997. "Brushed Off: Why Willem de Kooning's Late Works Shouldn't Be." *Slate Magazine* [On-line] Available: *http://slate.msn.com/?id=2912*.

# PART 4.
# THE INTERNAL EXPERIENCE OF AGENCY

# Chapter 8

# EMBODIED AGENCY, DECLINE AND THE MASKS OF AGING

## *Mike Hepworth*

### ABSTRACT

This chapter is a critical discussion of the problematic issue of embodied agency in later life. Arguably, embodied agency requires physical competencies of the body through which the self is socially expressed. A prominent theme amongst sociologists of the body is the importance of bringing the body back into sociological analysis and what interests me in contemporary efforts to reconstruct the processes of human aging is that everyone has great difficulty in keeping the body out. This dilemma arises from the unresolved tension between concepts of embodied agency (body and self as essentially interdependent) and experiences of the aging self as disembodied. I therefore examine recent discussions in social science of the boundaries between the biological body and the socially constructed body through a comparison of the recent work of Gilleard and Higgs, and Hallam, Hockey and Howarth. Secondly I revisit the concept of the mask of aging as culturally constructed in contemporary western society. The basic proposition of the mask of aging is that there are considerable and ambiguous variations in the experience of embodied agency as individuals grow older. The mask of aging is a range of complex and subtle interactive processes which have been oversimplified by critics as a dualistic separation of body and self. This chapter concludes, therefore, with a discussion of the mask (or more appropriately *masks*) of aging as the experience of continuities and discontinuities in embodied agency. In other words, there are variations in later life in the capacity of the biological body to act as an expressive agent of the personal and social self which in a wider context reflect the essential ambiguity of attitudes towards aging in contemporary western culture.

## INTRODUCTION

The sociological concept of agency refers to the perennial problem of the tension between freedom and constraint in individual action. Human action has for a long time been defined by sociologists as essentially reflexive and interpretive; motivated by the meanings which individuals attribute to the social context within which the 'lived body' is experienced. Although human beings are seen as conscious, reflective actors, they are not considered totally free to act outside the historical social context within which they live. In contemporary society the high value placed on the independent active and 'mature' individual inevitably influences social attitudes to human agency and in particular towards aging and individual experiences of the aging process. In this context the role of the biological body as an enabler of, or constraint on, individual agency inevitably has become a contentious issue in the sociology of aging.

One of the most influential sociologists in this regard is Norbert Elias, with his unrivalled sociological analysis of the problem of the aging body in contemporary 'civilized' societies. Elias puts the control of the body and the emotions at the centre of his theory of the civilizing process and the capacity of the body to act as an agent of action is given a high value in contemporary western culture. Biological aging may erode the power of the body to act as an agent of expression of the 'civilized' human. This concept of civilized 'normality' is deliberately used by Elias to explain the source of the social difference of old age: 'the view that 'people grow different in old age is often involuntarily seen as a deviation from the social norm. The others, the normal age groups, often have difficulty in empathizing with older people in their experience of aging – understandably. For most younger people have no basis in their experience for imagining how it feels when muscle tissue gradually hardens and perhaps becomes fatty, when connective tissue multiplies and cell renewal slows down...' (1985: 69) The problems of empathy are not surprising to Elias – the control of the aging body has an effect on the human imagination so that 'identification with the aging body...understandably poses special difficulties for people of other age groups.' (1985: 69) 'Now that I myself am old I know, as it were, from the other side how difficult it is for people, young or middle-aged, to understand the situation and the experiences of older people.' (1985: 70) The problem according to Elias is the shift in the balance of power between younger and older people which aging brings. As far as the biological body is concerned one of the problems with aging into old age and death is that these are conditions for which science has as yet no remedy. Old age and death indicate in western culture that the 'the increase in human control of nature can have limits.' (1985: 78)

This analysis may at first sight seem to confirm biologistic stereotypes of aging as decline and give comfort to ageism but the good news is that Elias does not regard these attitudes as necessarily unalterable: they are 'peculiarities of societies at a particular stage of development and so with a particular structure.' (1985: 84-85) As such the balances of power between younger and older people may change with developments in the social configurations of which they are an essential part.

The possibility for future change in negative attitudes towards aging can be traced to the view held by Elias and many more recent critics of biological essentialism (see for example Kontos 1999) that biology, society and culture are inseparable and closely integrated processes. Empirical research findings at first sight support the argument that biological aging is far less significant as a factor in the ability to act as an active social agent than are socially constructed beliefs that biological change as such inevitably results in personal and social decline. In their research in the North of England Conway and Hockey show how the personal experience of aging involves a process of self-labelling whereby older people internalise social beliefs that in later life illness and increasing dependency are inevitable. Ros, for example, is quoted as saying: 'As you get older, your body gets older, and you look older. But if you had no mirrors and no clocks you would never know that you are getting older, because the inside of your brain is exactly the same…You think exactly as you thought…fifty years ago.' (1998: 480).

In American research into nursing homes Gubrium and Holstein argue the nursing home is a special site for interpreting the biological body as a site of decline: 'Staff, residents, and family members inspect and, in turn, are incited to describe bodies …in the language of decay, decrepitude, or surprising fitness.' (1999: 533) The aging body is a social construct because we age bodily 'as much because our bodies are discursively anchored by a particular institution as because our bodies grow old.' (1999: 537) The meaning of the body – and in particular, its future – is shaped by the presence of people who are certainly more frail and dependent than some of their contemporaries but there is also an increased intensity of scrutiny and surveillance of the body which has the effect of concentrating and reaffirming negative conceptions of ageing. Moreover this process is one which the authors see as extending to the private domestic home and interaction between carers and those for whom they care. This process involves a subtle inteplay between wider cultural concepts of aging and local cultures of embodiment resulting in a 'multilayered' categorisation of the aging body. This means that at the local level there is scope to negotiate the meanings of aging, a process described as 'discursive embodiment'. (1999: 533) A crucial distinction, for example, is made in the nursing home between 'vegetables' who are non-persons requiring only bodywork and those who are still regarded as mentally competent individual persons.

The aging body is therefore increasingly the focus of social surveillance in the search of signs of competent agency. Essentially the social surveillance of later life is a matter of scrutinizing processes of interaction between the body, self and society as they relate to the ability to act independently as a person in a highly individualized society. But the problem of the biologically aging body, as described by Elias, still remains unresolved. In the words of Gilleard and Higgs the question is 'how the biological nature of ageing might place limits on the social and cultural expression of ageing' (2000: 148). And conclusive answers to this question, I suggest, may well prove to be more elusive than sociologists of aging would like to believe.

## AGENCY, EMBODIMENT AND THE AMBIGUITY OF AGING

As previously suggested, a constructionist critique of biological essentialism is crucial to the anti-ageist project. The current position has been cogently summarized by Hockey and James who write: in social contructionism the body 'is not seen, in and of itself, to initiate or construct the aging process. Rather, the aging of the body is regarded as a continuous process which takes place outside such structures, occurring too slowly for us to catch it in motion – no matter how watchful we might be in front of the bathroom mirror. Age has therefore to be stamped on the body by society, in order for us to "know" or "experience" it through the symbolic marking out of differences between "then" and "now".' (2003: 46-47)

The role of the body in this subtle interpretation is problematic because the biological changes that occur as individuals grow older are often imperceptible and have therefore to be given personal and social significance through social interaction. When the body ages 'normally' through biological changes (as distinct from the dramatic onset of disease) decline becomes elusive and the unambiguous markers of old age difficult to identify. Hence the frequent and sometimes poignant question: 'How do I know I'm growing old?' Empirical research shows that the boundaries between middle and old age are by no means clearly defined by biological markers and older people are often engaged in exploring with friends and contemporaries ways of giving individual and social meaning to changes in their bodies and their lives (Jerrome 1992). What I want to do now, therefore, is explore this tension through a comparative review of the sociological perspectives adopted in the recent work of Gilleard and Higgs (2000), and Hallam, Hockey and Howarth (1999).

## Gilleard and Higgs: Cultures of Ageing

In Gilleard and Higgs' analysis of the contribution of postmodern culture to the aging process the problem of reconciling biology and sociology is clearly displayed. The majority of the book is an unambiguous rejection of biological essentialism and championing of a postmodern sociology of aging where the focus is on the positive value of asserting the possibility of diversity and multiplicity of roles and agency in later life. They rightly argue that the biological model of aging is reductionist because the 'physical changes that most people experience as ageing' do not necessarily 'serve as defining moments in individuals' post-work lives.' (2000: 202) Health consciousness, for example, is not a defining feature of later life and occurs right across the life course. The issue facing old people is the creation of a narrative of the self and continuous engagement with the question: 'how shall I live?' (2000: 38), including the obligation to fight decline. They argue for the arrival of the ageless society and the 'agentically constructed later life' (200: 39); a new age for older people of self-invention and the 'declared freedom to define one's identity' (2000: 61).

Gilleard and Higgs ground their argument for a critique of the biological decline model of aging in the sociology of postmodern culture and castigate gerontologists for their preoccupation with 'documenting physical and mental dependency' (2000: 16). Contemporary gerontologists should now regard aging not as a biological but a 'cultural process' - a shift from the conceptualisation of aging as 'something that happens to people' towards the view that it is 'something individuals have to engage with'. (2000: 13) The transition is from grand narratives of biological causality to 'individual narrative and difference'. (2000: 12)

They argue therefore for the 'unfinished body' thesis: the boundaries between the biological and the cultural are increasingly blurred as biotechnology manipulates what was once believed to be fixed as 'natural'. Furthermore, 'In the absence of an inner logic to ageing, the play of signification that is involved in choosing how and when to age offers a wide scope for the marketing of desire.' (2000: 132)

In this analysis biological definitions of aging are the product of pre-modern and modern forms of social organisation or master meta-narratives. 'Senility', for example, is denoted as a 'pre-modern term' to be replaced with a positive postmodern reconstruction of old age 'as a compendium of risky but potentially avoidable medical conditions.'(2000: 171). Diversification apparently is evident in the proliferation of cultures of aging and a consequent increase in the range of individual personal experiences of aging. The postmodern liberation of the older person as an active individualised social agent is a major force for anti-ageism. An increasing individualisation of aging will follow from an increase in the number of social agents 'acting within the complex structures that currently shape the experience of "ageing"' (2000: 84)

This optimistic vision is, of course, a welcome critical alternative to the grim biological determinism predicting uniform decline but at the end of the line, as in all constructionist analysis, the problem of the biological body in which mental and physical competencies have declined remains unresolved. Whilst the postmodern project of the unfinished body is progressively reducing the 'natural' element in aging, biological decline is not totally erased nor is there any prospect of this being achieved. In effect biological decline and its personal and social consequences are displaced from the third to the fourth age. It is during the third age, the active, potentially creative, period of later life as defined by Laslett (1989), that an anxious concern about confusion, dementia and physical dependency takes place and in the fourth age that a struggle takes place to separate 'normal' aging from 'abnormal' aging. Dementia, they say, has little 'exchange value' (2000: 180). And if ' there should be limits to human agency, the morbidity of the mind may prove the most instrumental in setting those limits and…the most unyielding to any attempt to blur or redefine them.' (2000: 188)

At the conclusion of the book Gilleard and Higgs summarise the criticisms they anticipate readers might make of their argument and critique. Significantly these include the final problem of the biological body equated at the end of life with reduced function: 'the physical reality of ageing and the inevitable age determination of disability and frailty…(will undermine)…any cultural capital that contemporary retired people may have acquired.' (2000: 200). Age as biological decline has therefore not finally been deconstructed, merely delayed in an extended phase of postmodern agency. Perhaps it is necessary to wait for science to conquer biological aging, frailty, illness and death – those problems for contemporary society which Elias detected as a major factor determining negative attitudes towards old age and death. In the end the processes of biological aging are described as 'age-associated functional decline and death' (200: 148) and 'the body remains problematic, occupying a complex and contradictory position in relation to ageing and its cultural possibilities.' (2000: 142) To establish that people are 'happy to age but not be aged, is a necessary step in establishing a cultural and political agenda to combat ageism', and yet this is a kind of 'personal aesthetic' with an 'inherent contradiction…namely that one day we must fail.' (2000: 143)

The problem of failure is painfully detailed in Lawton's (1998) research in an inpatient hospice in the South of England into the personal and social problems surrounding the body when it is afflicted by certain illnesses which produce irreversible deterioration. She draws on Elias' theory of the civilizing process and on Douglas' conception of dirt as matter out of place (1984) to explore ethnographically the reasons why 'the disintegrating, decaying body appears to have become such a marked feature of the contemporary West…' (1998: 123) Following Elias, the contemporary body is at the end of a long process of 'civilization', 'a body with clearly defined boundaries, isolated, alone, and fenced off from other bodies.' (1998: 135) As a 'closed' body. (1998: 137) the modern body is 'central to constructions of selfhood and identity within the contemporary Western context.' (1998: 138) The unbounded body is a source of 'dirt' or matter out of place, which results in the loss of individual control over the self and recognition as a full person. However Lawton cautions that not all dying patients should be lumped together in this single category but it is important to discriminate between variations in the body and bodily processes. 'Dirty dying' is different in this respect from other preferred ways of ending one's life: as with old age not all terminal illness results in 'dirty dying'.

Such a 'dirty' death represents the extreme example of biological decline and its deleterious effects on the persona and social self of the sufferer. The decaying body is one where the contained or 'boundedness' of the body breaks down and internal bodily secretions can no longer be contained within but leak out to contaminate the self of the sufferer and those around. If it is possible to control leaking fluids with, for example, bandages then some boundaries can be restored to the body making restoration of 'normal' personhood and agency possible. But with other forms of illness boundaries are impossible to restore. In this situation certain patients disengage from full social interaction with family and friends. And Lawton distinguishes between temporary disengagement or the fragmentation of the self that may be experienced for example in acute illness from 'the severely and irreversibly "unbounded" hospice patients whom I observed.' (1998: 130) In these latter cases the self has not temporarily been masked or disguised by illness but 'appears to have "gone" altogether leaving little, if anything, but the empty" body.' She adds that it is 'reasonable to suggest that "mental shut down" expresses, and reflects, a total loss of selfhood if one accepts Giddens' argument that the contemporary Western "self" is an eminently social and relational entity, reflexively constituted through processes connecting the "personal" to the "social". (1998: 130)

## Hallam, Hockey and Howarth: Beyond The Body

Working from a critical perspective informed by anthropology, Hallam, Hockey and Howarth offer a provocative analysis of the aging and dying body which aims to break down the boundaries between embodiment and disembodiment in terms of the symbolic influence disembodied people have on everyday social life. Whilst Gilleard and Higgs stay resolutely in the observable material world, Hallam et al argue for an alternative epistemology which establishes close interconnections between visible and invisible, symbolically conceived, worlds.

Their point of departure is a critique of what they consider to be the predominant reading in contemporary sociological theories of the body, namely the 'ethos within which the body is imaged as the finite container of a self defined primarily in terms of its separation from other bodies. This we argue is a highly localised reading of the body and its role in identity construction' (1999: 11). Their interpretation of agency therefore rejects the view that individuality is dependent on the material existence of the body and 'the death of the body means that the individual has ceased to be.' (1999: 8). The popular notion of agency as embodied in this respect imposes serious limitations on cultural resources for developing concepts of positive aging. For the authors the 'body-as-knowledge-source is but one among many constructions or readings of the flesh' (1999: 204). They offer an alternative model to the model of agency which assumes that 'individual, intentional and embodied action (are) a prerequisite for social being' (1999: 146) and this is a perspective on aging and the body informed by 'an examination of human embodiment which situates itself at and beyond the body's boundaries' and takes into account 'situations which involve the dislocation of bodily and social being.' (1999: x). It is an approach which refuses to 'privilege the individual's agency, their ability to manage the body in particular ways in face-to-face interactions.' (1999: 7)

The conventional materialist conception of embodied agency 'cannot easily account for the embodied experience of those whose bodies have become extremely frail and/or brain function has diminished' (1999: 7). Questioning the assumption that selves 'necessarily reside within discrete bounded bodies' (1999: 2), the central concern of the authors is with the theorisation of the 'deteriorating, dying and dead body' (1999: x) through a series of studies of a local authority residential homes for older people, field research into the work of coroners, an ethnographic study of funeral directors in the East End of London, observations of the work of a Church of England exorcist, and data from women who practised as clairvoyants in the English Midlands. Their critique of the privileging of embodied agency is grounded in research showing the persistence of self-identity when the body has made the transition to 'social death' (a situation described, for example in Lawton's research) or physically ceased to exist. Social death is therefore defined as the point at which a person is no longer treated as an active agent in the social world.

As far as aging is concerned, the concept of embodied agency 'marginalises those members of society who may be physically alive yet socially dead, and those biologically deceased who nevertheless retain an influential social presence in the lives of others' (1999: ix). A preferable conception requires a relational or collective conception of embodiment where embodied experience is influenced by the situation of the self in a relational matrix and an interpretation of the boundary between self and others as flexible and fluid. Identify is seen as intersubjective and cannot be explained solely in terms of the mind or the body. The Giddens view of the 'post-traditional project of self-reconstruction' can 'be seen merely as the individual resisting the body's constraints and limitations in a spurious attempt to deflect awareness of its inevitable mortal nature.' (1999: 18) Whilst all bodies are biologically aging and dying, not all 'are synonymous with a self and not all selves have an embodied corporeal presence.' (1999: 1).

In this analysis the relationship between the aging body and the self 'remains elusive' (1999: 207). The authors would agree with Gilleard and Higgs that social death is 'an imposed condition.' (1999: 49) but they also believe that older bodies have a 'symbolic potency' which tends to be disregarded by sociologists. (1999:50) Much current work on the body 'neglects the older body and in so doings fails to provide an account of its symbolic power, its phenomenology, and its agency.' (1999: 51)

There is therefore evidence of forms of resistance around the aging body: one is found in the ways in which residents of a local authority home in the North of England exploited the tendency of staff to treat them as dependent infants. In this situation the deteriorating body is treated as a resource which may be 'subversively deployed': older people were observed flaunting 'the breaching of their bodies (sic) boundaries' (1999: 54), through such derisive activities as refusing to use the toilets for defecation and urination, thus creating more work for the staff who had to clean up after them. They would refuse to stay in their rooms and make bids for freedom outside the institution. Possibly as a form of the 'playful masking' referred to below, some would pretend, for example, that they were hard of hearing and would shout in a style of communication associated with the deaf.

The old body is therefore not an inactive body and is capable of social disruption through deviant activity. Such disruptive activity threatens the balance of power which is often assumed to be tipped in favour of the institutional staff. Social being thus continues in forms of embodied agency which are regarded as 'disgusting' and socially deviant.

An important aspect of Hallam et al's critical engagement with the embodiment issue is their discussion of the experience of 'disembodiment' amongst older people. Even after death, they argue, the disposal of the body may not bring social interaction and being to an end: 'Older widows and widowers, for example, may continue to enjoy significant social relationships with their "dead" spouse.' (1999: 143) Here the authors offer a model of disembodied agency which goes beyond the belief that the dead only survive socially as 'memories locked within the imaginations of others.' (146) Social life can thus continue without the living biological presence of significant persons. 'The extent to which the dead make themselves felt by the living depends in part on the degree to which the living invite them to do so.' (1999: 149) Objects, clothing and photographs perform this function. The existence of the self after the death of the body is made possible by the intersubjectivity of human relationships. When a significant person dies, 'In relationships that extend beyond biological death, the body of the widow is intimately connected with the self of the dead husband' (1999: 151) and these relationships do not merely operate on the symbolic level but generate physical sensations and responses. It is also important to emphasise that in the authors' view order of experience cannot be classified as a psychological phenomenon because 'sensations are experienced through the living body and its senses. Although (in the case of a widow) the physical body of the dead partner is absent, his presence is experienced though and within the body of the widow, via feelings and senses such as sight, sound, smell, touch. The senses link individuals to the external world and facilitate contact with it.' (1999: 151).

## THE MASK OF AGING

In the light of the previous discussion of variations in the experience of embodied agency, and reported experiences of disembodied agency, it is not surprising that the mask of aging has become a convenient term for referring to the interactive processes that interrelate the biological body with self, culture and society. As interest in the mask idea has gradually grown, the trend is towards greater subtlety of interpretation in the light of theoretical developments and empirical research. Hepworth (1995), for example, describes three variations in the mask of aging: the older mask concealing the younger self; the mask of youth concealing the older self; and the playful mask.

In a discussing of the tendency to ignore the body in the sociology of aging Peter Öberg argues that the dualistic tradition in western thought of separating the soul (mind) from the body has resulted in the experience of the mask of aging as a self divorced from the body. He quotes the words of a 79 year-old Finnish woman: 'I see an old withered woman...A toothless mouth, when my good, beautiful teeth fell out because of the calcium deficiency. *My picture is ugly, but my soul here inside is not ugly...*' (1996: 712) Öberg's data were derived from interviews with 37 Finns aged between 73 and 83 who were seen in their own homes. The aim of the research was to find out how these people gave meaning to aging in the context of their life stories. At one point in the interviews they were given a mirror and asked to comment on what they saw.

From this research Öberg concludes that the experience of aging as a mask - a distance between the self and the body - can be differentiated in terms of two kinds of aging: successful and unsuccessful aging. Öberg defines successful aging as the 'The Sweet Life', a feeling of being at home in one's body and therefore not a youthful self imprisoned somehow in an alien aging body. In these examples individuals have adapted to the changes taking place in their bodies and tend to experience a sense of harmony between body and self. As one woman aged 75 put it: 'Of course, I'm not as strong...both muscles and various senses. But in some way it's as though you get healthier when you get older. You don't have the same needs; you don't have to accomplish so terribly much.' (1996: 713)

In contrast unsuccessful aging is experienced as a mask or dissociation of self from body. Öberg describes this as 'The Bitter Life' or 'dysfunctional ageing' (1996: 711). Whilst the 'The Sweet Life' is a story of how a good old age follows on from a good childhood and adult life, 'The Bitter Life' is, a noted above, one of suffering and loss: an aging process filled with problems.

Öberg argues that the negative mask is mostly used in the process of self-labelling of aging by a relative minority of older people who have a problem-filled aging and are experiencing bodily dysfunctions such as ill health and disability. Whilst those who are aging successfully may experience some sense of distance between the self and the body they do not dissociate themselves from their bodies entirely and may feel harmoniously embodied.

The basic idea of the mask relates to a continuum of experiences of continuity and discontinuity between the body and the self during later life. As originally formulated (Featherstone and Hepworth 1989) it was not intended to be an argument in favour of an essentialist dualistic separation of body from self as critics have sometimes suggested (Andrews 1999; Öberg 1996). It was theorised as a reflection on problematic aspects of the concept of embodied selfhood as celebrated in contemporary postmodern consumer culture. As the above discussion shows, the experience of a disjunction between the body and the self in later life implicit in the image of the mask is not necessarily universal but certainly an issue for those whose aging is problematic (Öberg 1996; Öberg and Tornstam 1999) or those individuals with bodies which are sorely afflicted by erosive terminal illness (Lawton 1998). Nor is the experience simply a disjunction between a younger 'ageless' self and an older body; it exhibits much wider variations which include, as previously suggested, the 'youthful mask' (the experience of an older self in a younger body and the 'playful mask' (where an older person manipulates masks in a performance of both youth and old age) (Hepworth 1995).

In his Jungian analysis of the mask of aging Simon Biggs (1999) shares the view of most students of aging that a central preoccupation for any older individual is to maintain a coherent sense of personal identity. And he also shares the view discussed specifically in the review of the work of Gilleard and Higgs, that these efforts are taking place in a rapidly changing world where traditional roles for older people appear to be breaking down and social expectations of older people seem to be undergoing an unprecedented fluidity of change. In this context he offers what he considers to be a more positive view of the mask as 'persona' or social mask derived from the task that Jung associated with the second half of life: namely individuation or 'the process by which persons become themselves' (1999: 40). This process makes it possible for the aging individual to extend his/her repertoire of personae and thus to compensate for any physical deficiencies through the manipulation of a variety of social masks. According to this interpretation one of the advantages of 'maturity' over preceding phases of psychological development such as childhood and youth is an expansion in the range of masks or 'personae' the aging individual can actively deploy in maintaining a balance between self-consciousness as a unique individual and the demands of other people. The mask of aging need not therefore indicate the existence of a state of conflict between the body and the self, which seems to be derived from the superficial concentration of consumer culture on the surface appearance of the body, but has the potential of becoming a positive process of maturity: a multilayered subjectivity which is grounded in an acceptance of the aging body and thus a more authentic engagement with the wider world.

In this sense the mask and the masquerade indicates the existence of free spaces in later life to maintain the integrity of the self amidst the constraints originating in the biological body and also exerted by the expectations of other people. The mask/s become a form of protective wear which is a sign of positive aging in an unpredictable and highly changeable world.

## CONCLUSION

From their different perspectives these interpretations of the mask/masks in effect expand and enrich the sociological concept of embodied agency in later life. The image of the mask supports the widely held belief in the sociology of aging that the cultural resources currently available to describe the experience of aging display only a limited reflection of the wide variations in the lived experience of aging. As Hallam et al (1999) indicate, it is possible that a large number of older people experience some form of disembodied agency which has generally been ignored by sociologists whose analysis is confined to a limited definition of embodied agency. Relationships between younger and older people and between older people themselves are reduced in their potential when human interaction does not develop beyond the impressions conveyed by the surface appearance of the body and, indeed, the internal symptoms of biological dysfunction. These variations in the experience of the body/self relationship also have a significant though often ignored emotional dimension (Hepworth 1998). In addition to being a biological process, aging is, as Dorothy Jerrome has written, 'a state of feeling and behaving' (1992: 130).

At the same time, a clear contradiction persists in a great deal of sociological analysis of human aging. The belief that aging is simply a biological or medical problem which can be cured at some blessed point in the future by advances in bio-medical science is implicit in the concept of embodied agency. The dilemma of the self imprisoned in the body so cogently discussed by Elias (1985) is addressed in everyday social life by countless individuals whose experiences of aging have yet to be explored. And yet, the problem of the body is, as Elias indicated, unresolved at the current period of social development. As long as the self continues to be expressed through bodily and emotional control then any decline in biological functions is inevitably subjectively, socially and sociologically problematic.

Finally, critics of the concept of the mask as essentially dualistic or empirically suspect often fail to engage with the concept of the mask as it has developed in western culture at least since the emergence of theatrical performance in classical antiquity. Since that time the historical meaning of the mask in western culture has continued to be ambiguous; the function of the mask both in the theatre and everyday life has two functions: to *conceal* and to *reveal* the identity of the wearer. Thus, as noted above, the aging body may be regarded by one person as an authentic expression of the inner self whilst for another it may be regarded as a disguise either deliberately chosen or externally imposed by biology or cruel fate. In any case the biologically changing body, like the sculptured mask assumed by the actor in classical drama, continues to set certain limits to the performance an audience may witness and an actor may display.

# REFERENCES

Andrews, M. 1999. "The Seductiveness of Agelessness". *Ageing and Society* 19: 301-318.

Biggs, S. 1999. *The Mature Imagination: Dynamics of Identity in Midlife and Beyond.* Buckingham: Open University Press.

Conway, S. and Hockey, J. 1998. "Resisting the 'Mask' of Old Age?: The Social Meaning of Lay Health Beliefs in Later Life." *Ageing and Society* 18: 469-494.

Douglas, M. 1984. *Purity and Danger: An Analysis of The Concepts of Pollutionand Taboo.* London: Ark

Elias, N. 1985. *The Loneliness of The Dying.* Oxford: Basil Blackwell.

Featherstone, M. and Hepworth, M. 1989. "Ageing and Old Age: Reflections on The Postmodern Life Course." Pp 143- 157 in *Becoming and Being Old: Sociological Approaches to Later Life*, edited by B.Bytheway et al. London: Sage.

Gilleard, C. and Higgs, P. 2000. *Cultures of Ageing: Self, Citizen and The Body.* London: Prentice Hall.

Gubrium, J.F. and Holstein, J.A. 1999. "The Nursing Home as A Discursive Anchor for The Ageing Body." *Ageing and Society* 19: 519-538.

Hallam, E., Hockey, J. and Howarth, G. 1999. *Beyond The Body: Death and Social Identity.* London and New York: Routledge.

Hepworth, M. 1995. "Images of Old Age." pp. 5-37 in *Handbook of Communication and Ageing Research*, edited by J.F.Nussbaum and J.Coupland. Mahwah, NJ and Hove, UK: Lawrence Erlbaum Asociates.

Hepworth, M. 1998. "Ageing and The Emotions." Pp 173-189 in *Emotions in Social Life: Critical Themes and Contemporary Issues*, edited by G.Bendelow and S.J.Williams. London and New York: Routledge.

Hockey, J. and James, A. 2003. *Social Identities Across The Life Course.* Basingstoke: Palgrave Macmillan.

Jerrome, D. 1992. *Good Company : An Anthropological Study of Old People in Groups.* Edinburgh: Edinburgh University Press.

Kontos, P. 1999. "Local Biology: Bodies of Difference in Ageing Studies." *Ageing and Society* 19: 677-689.

Laslett, P. 1989. *A Fresh Map of Life: The Emergence of The Third Age.* London: Weidenfeld and Nicolson.

Lawton, J. 1998. "Contemporary Hospice Care: The Sequestration of The Unbounded Body and 'Dirty Dying.' *Sociology of Health and Illness* 20: 121-143.

Öberg, P. 1996 "The Absent Body - A Social Gerontological Paradox." *Ageing and Society* 16: 701-719.

Öberg, P. and Tornstam, L. 1999. "Body Images Among men and Women of Different Ages." *Ageing and Society* 19: 629-644.

# Chapter 9

# IN PURSUIT OF SUCCESSFUL IDENTITIES AND AUTHENTIC AGING

## *Simon Biggs*

## ABSTRACT

Contemporary thinking about success in aging has centered around a number of imperatives, each holding a different vision of agency and authenticity in later life. This chapter critically examines the metaphor of masquerade as a means of making sense of the often contradictory demands to age successfully. Masquerade, and indeed any form of social masking strategy, suggests the existence of surface and hidden elements in identity performance. We each, in other words, maintain ourselves as social beings through dialogue between an internal and an external logic with the former referring to an inner world of self and the latter to social expectation. This distinction between depth and surface also raises the question of whether some aspects of identity are more core, key or authentic than others. Nobody likes to think of themselves as lacking depth. However, the idea that these hidden and deeper aspects of identity may also be in some way more agentic as a source of greater authenticity is difficult for many social scientists to accept. Various candidates are examined to explore what might exist behind the mask, which arise from contemporary developments in social gerontology. These include a sense of personal continuity and integration, emotional content and existential issues arising from one's position in the lifecourse. The argument is seen to turn on the consideration of age as a determining factor in the maintenance of adult identity and agency. Finally, possibilities of creating the conditions of dialogue both between different parts of the self and between self and others will be discussed.

## INTRODUCTION

This chapter critically examines the interplay between different attempts to specify 'success' as adults age and the metaphor of masquerade as a means of making sense of agency in later life. Masquerade, and indeed any form of social masking strategy, suggests the existence of surface and hidden elements in identity performance. We each, in other words, maintain our agency as social beings through dialogue between an internal and an external logic, with the former referring to an inner world of self and the latter to outer social expectation. This distinction between depth and surface also raises the question of whether some aspects of identity are more core or key, and thus validate aspects of personal agency as being more authentic than others. It is a predicament that challenges some of the most deeply held beliefs of gerontology and about the ways in which social scientists investigate and theorise old age. As such, I will approach the question of agency, not primarily as a form of action upon the outside world, but rather as the agentic self-organisation of the inner world of self, which is related and key to examining the authenticity of action, but is by no means the same thing.

Nobody likes to think of themselves as lacking depth. However, the idea that these hidden and deeper aspects of identity may also be in some way more genuine or a source of greater authenticity is difficult for many social scientists to accept. This is perhaps because of a contemporary infatuation with the notion of multiple selves as a means of avoiding limits or fixity, in a mistaken belief that a carousel of surface appearances in some way confers agency. However, one of the most important challenges arising from an aging identity is the emerging recognition of one's inability to choose not to grow old. Agency, therefore takes on a deeper aspect, in so far as it is associated with increased personal integration and the ability to express oneself in circumstances not of one's own choosing, both of which occur as part of the process of adult aging. Agency in later life has to take a position in relation to bodily challenges, social prejudice and the fact that life is finite.

It is possible to read a debate around what constitutes 'success' in terms of aging as a way in which social gerontology has responded to questions of authenticity in agency as outlined above. This paper critically assesses two aspects of age-identity in this light.

First, we all like to be thought of as successful. Indeed, active, successful and productive aging have taken on a normative significance that mediates our everyday understanding of what it is to age well. However, when compared to a dynamic understanding of interior aging and the existential priorities of the second half of life, these notions of success appear limiting and socially conforming.

Second, we generally prefer authenticity to superficiality. One of the ways that individuals negotiate the contradictions of contemporary aging is through the submersion of elements of self-experience that cannot be expressed directly and be socially accepted. These elements are hidden from social view, protected in an interior world, such that social connection and conformity are separated psychologically from an inner world of self. It is within this imaginative realm, beyond the masquerade, that personal development and integration may take place. Agency therefore takes on an aspect of interiority, which may not be so prominent during earlier life-phases.

Various candidates will be examined to explore what might exist behind the masquerade and help to elaborate what a deeper, more authentic form of adult aging might entail. These include a sense of personal continuity and integration, emotional content and existential issues arising from one's position in the lifecourse. The argument is seen to turn on the consideration of age as a determining factor in the maintenance of adult identity and agency.

Finally, possibilities of creating the conditions of dialogue both between different parts of the self and between self and others will be discussed. It is suggested that we may be able to begin to critically evaluate statements about success and other spaces created for aging individuals, in terms of the degree of harmony allowed to exist between these inner and outer realities.

## SUCCESS AND CONTEMPORARY AGING

It is often assumed that we know what aging is and what 'success' in terms of adult aging might look like. But when interrogated further these assumptions are often based on the absence of something else, mostly illness or infirmity; or in comparison to one's peers; or to social expectations, carving the lifecourse up into age-specific tasks. It would be easy to conclude from this that when we interrogate aging we come up with something that is relative, something contingent and at root something to be avoided. This makes agency very difficult to articulate, other than in terms of what one should not be doing. In its extreme form this line of thought leads us to believe that the experience of aging, like many other elements of contemporary society, lacks substance. It is of little intrinsic value and with the right lifestyle and consumption of the right technology may be abolished without much mourning. Given the opportunity, most aging adults, most of the time, one suspects, would be happy to settle for choosing not to grow old.

Perhaps, then, aging is simply a case of youthful selves trapped in aging bodies and the proper study of gerontology should be the search for the key with which to unlock them. This position has been suggested by Featherstone and Hepworth (1991), who have proposed not only that contemporary society affords a blurring of human characteristics traditionally associated with age, but that advances in bio-technology, virtual and internet identity-building plus the consumption of multiple lifestyle options, may abolish aging altogether. The implications of such thinking can be seen in a broad band of activities: including retirement communities (Laws, 1997, Biggs et al 2000), consumer lifestyles (Gilleard and Higgs, 2000), and a preoccupation with longevity and medico/technical innovation (Katz, 1996; Moody, 1998).

Often these initiatives consist of an appeal to agelessness as a basis for identity (Andrews, 1999) and are at root an attempted denial of aging. It is perhaps a paradox that these activities have become constitutive of old age, or at least the personal expectation and social criterion by which aging should be judged.

Consideration of the past, memory and of experience that goes beyond the here and now becomes particularly problematic once aging has been subsumed under the logic of lifestyle and the happy shopper. Once an alternative is sought to the self-disgust latent in a desire for agelessness, one becomes aware of a striking absence of curiosity about aging identity, its dynamic and the forms it might take. Indeed, a preoccupation with surface, with consumer choices available from which to pick-and-mix an aging identity, appears to side-step questions of authenticity and the freedom of expression that on first inspection it so confidently promises. Rather than a series of surface appearances, a second line of inquiry suggests that aging consists of a layering of the mature self, the use of agency in deciding how and what should be presented for social connection and what requires protection. Ultimately this strategic presentation of the aging self promises greater freedom than an understanding of multiplicity alone. This is because it is not based on selection from an existing menu of consumer identities, rather it opens a critical distance between surface appearance and personal desire. And it is within this space that agency takes place.

# CONTEMPORARY AGING IDENTITIES

A starting point, when considering the possibilities for authentic expression, is that contemporary adult aging takes place in circumstances that are variable in their acceptance of an aging identity. This is in part due to the privileging of younger adulthood in advanced capitalist societies, both as producers and as consumers (Phillipson and Biggs, 1998). Whilst it can be argued (Gilleard and Higgs, 2000) that consuming in the 'grey market' allows a new freedom for older adults, such trends interact with an enduring aesthetic of commodified youth and beauty. This variability, more often than not skewed toward negative associations with adult aging, leads to the need for strategies that protect personal identity from social stereotyping. On the one hand, protection is required to safeguard the self from relatively fixed social-cultural stereotyping that may deny or restrict possibilities for personal growth and social inclusion. On the other, uncertainties arising from the increased fluidity of external supports to identity may make a sense of personal coherence difficult to maintain. If this argument is accepted, then an aging identity has to protect itself from both an excess of structure on the one hand and an excess of flux on the other.

Under such conditions, identity needs to be negotiated, and circumstances will vary depending on the degree of genuine personal expression they afford. There will be a need to both protect identity and connect with the wider social world, through forms of impression management and masquerade. In the process the self becomes layered, with some aspects finding expression and others having to be suppressed.

Thinking about the maintenance of an aging identity in this way raises a number of interesting questions for personal agency, including:

- The definitions of success made available by the social world.
- The nature of an inner logic, existing beneath the surface forms and elisions that masking suggests.
- The circumstances that affect the likelihood of more authentic aspects of an aging identity being expressed.
- The expression of agency in later life and whether there are age-specific aspects to the deployment of agency itself.

# FINDING AUTHENTICITY THROUGH ACTIVE, SUCCESSFUL AND PRODUCTIVE AGING

One way in which contemporary gerontological thinking has approached questions of authenticity is through an attempt to identify forms of active, successful or productive aging. Such positions recognise that there are growing numbers of relatively fit older adults and that medical advances have made many of the decrements previously associated with old age modifiable and in some cases reversible (Rowe and Kahn, 1987). Debates over active, successful and productive aging go to the heart of aging studies, and have formed the core of disciplinary development within contemporary social gerontology. This is largely because they suggest a means of countering negative stereotyping of older people and increasing their social inclusion. It also raises the question of how far success in terms of aging should be critical of wider ideological structures and how far to age successfully requires that older people fit into them.

The phrases, active, successful and productive aging are often used interchangeably, even though each implies a particular moral as well as a material basis on which to grow old authentically. It is therefore important to critically interrogate the uses made of these different descriptions, before going on to look at the tension between masquerade and authentic agency in more detail.

## Activity

Lynott and Lynott (1996) have claimed that a debate over activity and disengagement, as alternative goals in later life, marked the beginnings of modern theorising in gerontology. Activity theory (Havighurst and Albrecht, 1958) provided a better fit with the 'problem solving' approach adopted by the new discipline, which has been described by Butler and Schechter (1995) as an alliance between advocacy and scientific advance. The theory provided a clear series of objectives that were easy to measure, making it attractive to social workers, nurses and physicians alike. According to this approach, older people needed to maintain their existing activities for as long as possible and replace activities that they had lost with new ones. Whilst much has been made of the differences between this and disengagement, which suggested that older people should progressively withdraw from social engagement, Marshall (1999) points out that both positions arose from the same Kansas Study. Both disengagement and activity theories are a response to the problematisation of older people as non-productive, with one seeing the solution to be withdrawal from society, and the other to keep doing things for as long as possible. Indeed, the latter has been satirised by Ekerdt (1986) as 'the busy ethic' as little attention has been paid to the purpose of the techniques involved. Regardless of its limitations, Activity theory has gained widespread acceptance in professional circles and amongst older people themselves as an antidote to aging (Gubrium and Wallace, 1990; Biggs et al 2000). It allows the active body to colonise the sense of self, which is then quantifiable and can be turned into measures and regimes, dividing the world into active elders and those described as 'potentially active'.

## Successful Aging

Baltes and Baltes, (1990) have suggested that successful aging, rather than arising from externally imposed regimes and activities, should be grounded in the approaches spontaneously arising in elder behaviour. Their approach sidesteps the issue of prescribing objectives and contents by engaging with social-psychological processes, and moves the question of authenticity away from the 'what' of aging to the 'how' (Baltes and Carstensen, 1996). Thus the Successful Aging approach is based upon a counter-intuitive observation that older people are by and large satisfied with their lives in spite of increasing disability or hardship (Rowe and Kahn, 1987). Baltes and Baltes (1990) suggest that by adopting a strategy of selective optimisation with compensation, or SOC, older people are able to negotiate the gains and the losses that arise through age with psychological success. Older people, it is argued, are satisfied because they have found strategies to minimise the losses and maximise the gains and therefore age well even in the face of bodily and social adversity. Baltes and Carstensen (1996) also point out that to discover how an individual manages to age successfully, it is important to 'know the domains of functioning and goals that the individual considers important, personally meaningful and in which he or she feels competent' (1996:399). Success, then, depends on circumstances and may be context specific. According to Carstersen (1993), this understanding of aging relies on mastering the challenges of aging, whilst allowing wide variety in the ways mastery can be achieved. It is difficult, however, to identify what purpose successful aging achieves beyond a form of survivorship (Moody, 2001). To be successful is to have life satisfaction for as long as possible. Once satisfaction ends, Moody observes, the next strategy available is euthanasia.

## Productive Aging

Successful Aging avoids issues of authenticity by focussing on non-judgemental and individualised strategies and a concentration on process rather than content. By contrast, advocates of Productive Aging raise the problem head-on, by examining the question of aging through the lens of economic usefulness. Thus, Hinterlong et al (2001) argue that 'society simply cannot afford to continue to overlook the potential of the older population to serve as a resource for social change and economic growth' (2001:4).

The prospect of continued productivity in later life is premised on the observation that rather than a steady slide into increasing incapacity, most people are healthy and active for most of the adult lifecourse and then decline very quickly before death, a phenomenon described as a compression of morbidity (Fries 1980). Further, there are many advantages for employers hiring older workers, including reliability, prior investment in skills and know-how and company loyalty (Schultz 2001). It is assumed that there is a basic connection between continued health and productivity, because 'engagement in productive behaviour requires a certain level of physical, cognitive and emotional functioning' (Butler et al 1990). A number of authors have attempted definitions of productive aging including activity by an older individual that 'contributes to producing goods and services or develops the capacity to produce them' (Caro, Bass and Chen 1993), 'anything that produces goods and services' (Morgan, 1986) and 'to serve in the paid workforce, to serve in volunteer activities, to assist in the family, and to maintain himself or herself as independently as possible' (Butler and Schechter 1995). Bass and Caro (2001) rule out pursuits done simply for personal gain or self-enhancement, such as meditation, excursions, carrying on correspondence, worship or visiting with family and friends, leaving productive aging unashamedly economic in its foundation and using efficiency as its core argument. The purpose of aging is, accordingly, to be economically useful, either directly, or as some revisionist definitions imply, indirectly.

## A DESIRE FOR CONTINUITY

A common thread that exists between the three models for 'success' in aging outlined above lies in the sense of continuity, or the need to maintain continuity of identity for as long as is possible. It is perhaps unsurprising, then, that a closely related approach to aging and authenticity can be found in continuity theory. Atchley (1989, 1999) maintains that continuity of identity supplies a robust framework of ideas that neutralise disadvantage, insulate the self from the effects of social ageism and for maintaining one's identity in the face of a changing social environment. Continuity theory 'presumes that most people learn continuously from their life experiences and continue to grow and evolve in directions of their own choosing' (1999:i). The logic of continuity of identity as a source of positive value in later life, is reflected in therapeutic approaches such as life story and reminiscence (Coleman 1996) plus as an aid to coping with transitions most notably around institutional care (Tobin 1989). Whilst Atchley (1999) maintains that adult development is relatively continuous, citing empirical findings from a longitudinal study, spanning some 20 years, these findings were, however, collected in a stable 'college town'. It is observed that this environment was 'relatively free of urban problems' and contained a 'full range of retirement activities, health and social care programs' (Atchley, 1999 preface xi). It could be argued that this is a population relatively unchallenged by uncertainty and socio-economic disruption of chosen life-trajectories. Continuity is nevertheless presented as both empirically valid and as an effective strategy with which to sustain identity as adults age.

Whilst a mechanism for protecting identity is proposed in continuity theory, it lacks a critical perspective. It is essentially an 'investment' model of identity that works by building up certain continuities of adult identity over time. There appear to be few crises occasioned by economic uncertainty or existential doubt as it is assumed that identities from the 'productive' part of life can be unproblematically maintained into old age. There is thus an absence of consideration of existential questions arising for identity arising because aging processes are themselves taking place (Cole 1992; Biggs 1999). The assumptions underlying the continuity approach to aging allow this, productive and other forms of 'success' in aging to merge seamlessly one into another.

When assessed in view of the points raised in the preceding section, these theories shed little light on the key theoretical problems arising from contemporary critiques of identity and aging. In terms of the form that a masquerade might take, there is little recognition of a need to protect identity from a potentially hostile environment, nor as a connective bridge to wider social realities. Rather, where problems do arise their solutions are assumed to lie in personal adaptation, with some recognition that ageism may lead to biases that assume older people are not up to the job. The problem is posed in terms of others wanting older adults to behave differently from the rest. Not, then, that there is anything special or valuable about aging itself that requires agency in its protection. This leads to a particularly one-dimensional perspective on aging. Without a distinction between the inner logic of personal desire and outer logic of social conformity these explanations lack any depth or complexity. So, whilst there is some recognition of the circumstances that affect the likelihood of more genuine aspects of an aging identity being expressed, these always fold back into a conformist identity, slavishly and often unsuccessfully trying to 'fit in'.

## MASQUERADE

So what is this masquerade associated with aging and how can it lead us to a deeper examination of the vexing question of authenticity?

The question of masquerade and hidden identity is increasingly being used in gerontological literature to examine the relationship between social and personal potential in later life (Featherstone and Hepworth 1989, 1995; Woodward 1991, 1995; Biggs 1993, 1999). A mask motif has been employed to interpret the management of an aging self in an uncertain world. The nature of this uncertainty, brought about, in part, by the erosion of traditional role expectations and the advent of a consumerist culture, contains elements that are both threatening and encouraging to experiments with identity in later life. Aging individuals simultaneously encounter two possibilities. Increased lifestyle choice and bodily malleability hold out the promise of a flexible and ageless identity. This coexists with the discovery of greater personal potential that might need to be protected from an often hostile and fragmentary social environment. Under such conditions, identity can become a balancing act between these possibilities through which an aging self might find expression.

There are at least two interpretations of masquerade in later life. The 'mask of aging' position (Featherstone and Hepworth 1989, 1995) holds that the aging body becomes a cage from which a younger self-identity cannot escape. Here, the mask motif and the problem of aging is couched in terms of a tension between the aging body and a youthful 'inner' self. The body, whilst it is malleable, can still provide access to a variety of consumer identities. However, as aging gathers pace, it becomes increasingly difficult to 're-cycle' the body and it becomes a cage, which both entraps and denies access to that world of choice. An endgame emerges with older people being at war with themselves, an internalised battle between a desire to express oneself and the aging body. Aging, as a mask, thus becomes a nightmare for the consumer dream as aging reverses its libertarian possibilities. The mask emerges as a contradiction between the fixedness of the body and the fluidity of social images.

Elsewhere it is suggested that a masquerade can be deployed to protect a mature identity in the context of an increasingly ambiguous external environment (Woodward 1991, 1995; Biggs 1993, 1999).

Here, masquerade consists of language games, body language and forms of personal adornment which contribute to performances of particular versions of the self. Masquerade is of particular interest because it occurs at the meeting point of both the personal-social axis and that of surface appearances and the inner worlds of identity. It is, in this sense, an arbitrator between inner and outer logics concerning the apprehension of selfhood.

Deploying social masking is seen as a means of negotiating identity between people of different ages as well as age peers. Rather like the persona in Jungian psychology (Hopcke 1995), masking becomes a bridge between internal psychological and external social realities. An element of social protection occurs for parts of the self that cannot be expressed without transgressing contemporary expectations around age. This perspective emphasises the increased possibilities for self-actualisation that come with age. The experience of a long life and the existential questions that aging brings with it are conceived as provoking an expanded and more grounded sense of self. This new and evolving self-discovery, which can be called maturity, or the 'Mature Imagination' (Biggs, 1999) still exists, however within a predominantly ageist society. In such circumstances, masquerade is seen as a source of inauthenticity, a means of protecting this mature self from external attack, which is nevertheless a vehicle for self-expression. Accordingly, relationships underscored by age provoke a masquerade which holds a more positive and protective nuance than Featherstone and Hepworth's reading would suggest, but also is seen to involve a more 'Machiavellian' use of masking phenomena. That is to say, masquerade is actively used to deceive others and protect the self in potentially threatening interactions. Whereas the 'mask of aging' is seen as an increasingly fixed and oppressive physical cage, masquerade, as an essentially social phenomenon, becomes part of a coping strategy to maintain identity. Rather than being the sum of attributes through which a sense of otherness can be deduced, masquerade is simply a device through which an active agent looks out at and negotiates with the world.

Masquerade is largely a result, then, of an irony of later life: that a withdrawal of psychological inhibition and an increase in negative social coercion are experienced simultaneously by many mature adults. The problem of an aging identity is located both in a struggle between body and self, and between self and other. In terms of agency, social masking is self-constructed and is intimately related to issues of generational power. Of course, masquerade may take place at any age. It is argued, however, that the form it takes - most notably in the inversions characteristic of depth and appearance, the contents that are expressed or hidden, and the degree of control social agents have to deploy this strategy - are related to age. Older people may be much more experienced and in much more control of their masquerade. They may deploy it or say 'what the hell' and just throw it away, depending upon the circumstances they find themselves in.

## THE INNER LOGIC OF GENUINENESS AND AUTHENTICITY

Metaphors of masquerade raise as problematic the question of genuineness in terms of a criterion for 'successful' adult aging. The possibility of a more authentic sense of identity lies in an agentic tension between inner and outer logic and how this finds expression. The relationship between what remains hidden and what is expressed, will have implications for the degree of genuineness tapped by empirical investigation of an essentially layered and contingent set of responses.

The possibility of a more authentic or genuine basis for aging identity, or at least criteria that allow the possibility of discriminating between alternative notions of 'success' in aging, is a difficult and dangerous question to ask. It engages with two distinct, but related notions of agency. Here, authenticity of agency denotes a degree of self-integrity, genuineness of agency, a manifestation in terms of communication to others, including researchers. It problematises the easy relativism of consumer choice, whilst raising the now unbuckable problem of the intrinsic value of aging itself. It includes the possibility of exploring core elements of the aging experience, and thereby moving beyond an examination of the barriers to some improved state that is often poorly defined. It raises the possibility of naming existential projects specifically arising from the experience of aging and how likely it is that this can form the basis of genuine social agency.

Three qualities that might contribute to layers of identity beyond masquerade, yet contribute to it, are coherence, depth and emotional resonance. There is no guarantee however, that any one, or even combination of these qualities will provide 'success' in terms of agency. Rather, they constitute a sort of internal topography, which may be expressed in terms of more or less coherence, depth or emotional resonance. They are qualities that can exist behind the masquerade, which in an optimal form might allow a genuine or authentic basis for action and agency. The masquerade might equally disguise a state of incoherence, absence of any significant depth or emotional confusion. The point here is to begin to explore whether each of these qualities reflect, in later life, a basis for that topography, rather than the form it might take.

## Coherence

One way of approaching the challenges raised by the above would be to examine the personal coherence that deeper layers of the self may hold. How, in other words, does the self 'make sense' of itself and how does it hold together as a believable narrative?

Coherence addresses both issues of personal and social identity plus the notion of depth and surface. Within the fractured world of masquerade and hidden identity, coherence would entail continuity with the personal and social past and cohesion in the present. It must 'make sense', then, at two levels, one in relation to past remembered experience and another in a way that fits together convincingly under current circumstances. As such, the task of coherence is more complicated than interpreting the past from the perspective of the present because it recognises that both past and present 'have a life of their own'. This gives us some idea of what the hidden or protected elements might be, and also some of the implications of bridging to an external surface.

For cohesion to free aging from the extreme contingency of dependence on immediate surfaces alone, however, a wider horizon needs to be envisaged, one that includes longer-term existential projects: an issue of what is meant when people say 'now' (Amery, 1968). When somebody says that they are doing this 'now' or that they 'now' hold certain views or aims these imply a particular time horizon, a plan and a commitment. They rarely mean exclusively an immediate preoccupation. Rather, 'nowness' implies a time horizon by which identity is placed within a longer-term framework, drawing on past experience and on future projection.

So part of what is being protected, even within an immediate sense of cohesion, is a sense of personal continuity. One is put in touch with oneself as embodying the latest point in time of a trail through past experience, consisting of collected personal and social-historical events, experiences and imaginings. Deeper components of identity, such as remembered experience, can form a platform for engagement with future projects. This becomes part of a self that coheres, makes sense in immediate social situations and forms the basis of a stance toward external events. It becomes the 'ground' for performing identity, an amalgam of constituents, shaped into a personal project, but also experienced as solid and extending beyond the self. As such it supplies a foundation upon which inner and outer worlds can interact.

The importance of re-introducing questions of continuity at this point should not be underestimated. It underpins assumptions that one is the same person over time, can be held responsible for one's actions, learn from history, predict the consequences of action with a degree of certainty and a variety of other factors key to ontological security.

We have seen already that continuity, as a source of genuine selfhood, has a significant history in social gerontological thinking, as evidenced by continuity theory (Atchley, 1999). Here, it is argued that continuity is less concerned with external conformity and most concerned with the connective depth within the psyche itself. Less work has been done on the degree to which an internal sense of continuity can find expression, the nature of that expression and how it is negotiated. It is perhaps in the intermediate territory, the temporal horizon for action, the 'now', that some merger and reconciliation of the two forms of personal coherence, cohesion and continuity, can come together. The aging self can thereby be thought of as a continuing (but not necessarily continuous) trajectory in relation to a past which allows aging to take place with, rather than in, or by denying, the past.

## Depth

It is in the nature of masquerade that it assumes different levels of disclosure of self, of visibility, as inner intention encounters outsider perception. It therefore raises the issues of depth, and of the degree of overlap between what an observer sees and what the performer intends them to see. There is an implication in all of this that the greater the depth of personal material that can be expressed, the greater the authenticity of the inner logic being tapped. This understanding of authenticity and genuineness is reflected closely in everyday language. Phrases such as 'depth of feeling' indicate how strongly a position is held, how central is it to that person's values, how key to their personality. Someone having 'depth' indicates how profound rather than superficial, how 'thought-through', how convincing they appear. There is something to what they say, there is substance to it. Equally, one can't always see to the bottom, there may be 'hidden depth', beyond the surface impression. Depth, then, is in some way anchoring, or at least more slow moving than appearances. It prevents, by degrees, unintended movement.

Depth is a key notion associated with psychodynamic theory, explaining where memories and phantasies are retained when not in consciousness (Stevens 1999), and being a home for the life-forces which motivate behaviour (Burman 1996). These aspects of the self vary in their accessibility to conscious awareness, but also draw attention to internal psychic space, which Craib (1998) has argued, allows freedom from everyday conformity and social control. Indeed it is possible to read the history of psychodynamic thinking as a progressive differentiation of that internal world. Within Freud's own lifetime, for example, an original distinction between conscious and unconscious became a matter of degree, allowing the recognition of ' preconscious' psychological material. This material had not been repressed and was amenable to consciousness under certain conditions, being neither irretrievably unconscious nor fully amenable to consciousness (Freud, 1915). More recently, psychoanalysis has been used to highlight pre-verbal bodily awareness, the liberating and constraining effects of language and a decentred self (Elliot and Spezzano 2000). Decentring is itself a radical shift attributed to psychoanalysis (Frosh 1991) which ensured that individuals could no longer cling to an entirely rational and transparent identity because perceptions of self and others were driven by forces that were not necessarily visible to the actor or an observer.

These subtle gradations of self have rarely been explored directly in relation to adult aging. Jung (CW 9, 1934), an exception in this regard, proposed archetypal images, psychological templates that took the form of particular people within the imagination. They inhabited the psyche, influencing everyday behaviour and took the form of person's of different ages. More recently Knight (1986) has suggested that therapists who work with older people should be aware that a variety of transference phenomena and identifications might be brought into play. In other words, older clients may elicit emotional resonance from other relationships from a wide variety of significant others, from across the lifecourse.

Key to such psychodynamic understandings of the relationship between depth, identity and adult aging is the idea that with age comes increasing integration of the self. Parts of the personality that have here-to-fore been submerged or projected onto others are acknowledged by the aging individual. The aging adult is, given the right circumstances, more likely to become 'individuated', Jung's own term for a progressive self- recognition and recovery of previously unconscious personal material. According to this view, success in aging would require a process whereby individuals would gain greater conscious awareness of themselves in the round, an ability to accept positive and negative personal attributes and live with pleasurable and disturbing experience. More of one's personal history has become available. There is more data, more options and more integration such that identity makes sense in a way that is relatively detached from social contexts. However, as Labouvie-Vief (2000) has pointed out, all this does not necessarily correlate with a corresponding increase in contentedness. Well-being and personal integration may not be coterminous.

## Emotion

A third candidate for the apperception of aging beyond the mask lies in emotional resonance, the degree to which experiences and memories are invested with psychological energy. Emotions can be 'primitive' in the psychodynamic sense of being deep because they have been held for a long time and have formed the foundation on which subsequent experience has been built. They are often linked with early experience that is itself assumed to be closer to raw and 'uncultured' responses to sensation. The emotional force residing in a particular belief often confers a sense of realness. Experiences with emotional content appear to be more convincing, they evidence, perhaps, significant personal investment. However, emotions can also be fleeting, contingent and insufficiently stable to form the ground for an enduring sense of selfhood.

Intensity of emotional resonance seems to offer a means of calibrating connections between inner and outer worlds. Emotions are intensely personal, yet are a common coin that can apparently cut through social differences. However, emotionality appears to have been invested with qualities of the ephemeral and the profound that make it difficult to locate.

The end of the twentieth century saw a renewed interest in emotional aspects of aging. Gullette (1998) has suggested the 'peak and slide', which the dominant culture teaches western adults to associate with adult aging, has led to a preoccupation with nostalgia. Nostalgia contains a perception of the fleeting, a longing for past experiences, as sort of sustained emotional reflexivity which makes it attractive to a certain view of adult aging.

Hepworth (1998) cites, with approval, Davis' (1979) observation that nostalgia is a convenient emotion in which to immerse age because it endorses a pre-existing social construction of that stage of life. Nostalgia confirms the otherness of later life as well as the superiority of earlier stages. Hepworth contrasts this with the commonly observed statement that aging adults rarely admit to 'feeling old'. Emotions, he argues, are timeless experiences that defy age-classification, even though there may be social rules specifying the appropriateness of certain emotions to be expressed at certain periods of the lifecourse. In Hepworth's hands emotions become a means of making connections across an age-segregated lifecourse, they are another means of recognising the 'youthful' self that is hidden within.

In contrast to this view, writers such as Jaques (1965), Kastenbaum (1992) and Labouvie-Vief (2000) have noted that there appears to be changes in emotional resonance across the lifecourse, particularly evidenced in the quality of creative activity. The creative production of older adults is more likely to reflect sustained, reflective and by degrees melancholic emotional content than that of younger adults, which is much more subject to the will, personal success and agency. Lebouvie-Vief indicates that older individuals may generally exhibit well-being, emotional adjustment and an ability to regulate emotional behaviour, although whether these are lifecourse or cohort effects is presently difficult to ascertain.

Whilst recent writing has tended not to follow Erikson (1962) in specifying emotional life tasks associated with stages throughout the human life-cycle, there is a widespread tendency to associate success in aging with an accumulation of emotional wisdom (Kivnick 1993). This is, of course, only a partial reading of the Eriksonian insight into emotionality in later life. It says little about coming to terms with elements of despair, wisdom's doppelganger, which perhaps forms a link between the personal integration suggested by a depth perspective and the reflective emotions cited here. Both would need to be taken into account as aspects of a successful maintenance of identity and are important elements in encounters between internal and external worlds.

## LIFECOURSE, CIRCUMSTANCE AND OPPORTUNITY

Each of the elements outlined above, coherence, depth and emotional resonance, vary in the likelihood of their expression. Whilst they are subject to gradations of self-knowledge and may form by degrees, a basis for authentic self-expression, they are contingent on particular circumstances facilitating genuine communication beyond masquerade.

Circumstances refer here to an external ground that arises from the more general social context in which aging takes place. When these circumstances contribute to an increased likelihood of harmony between internal and external aspects of identity, they would be permissive of self-expression. Here, depth would refer to an inner, vertical dimension, to personal identity. Coherence refers to the 'now' created by elements of cohesion and continuity, provoked by the specific situation aging adults find themselves in. For current purposes, this could be thought of as a horizontal dimension to identity. Emotional resonance helps fill out identity as it emerges. Flexibility afforded self-expression would depend upon the variety of social contexts available, in which identity might be performed. This configuration of aging identity allows for a certain harmony between the social and the personal and also the depth and surface elements when the circumstances are right. As such it begins to discover elements that may help us discriminate between 'successes' in aging that are likely in differing social contexts. When there is harmony between inner (personal/ depth) and outer (social/surface), conditions are right for the dropping of the protective aspects of masquerade.

But it doesn't really help with the problem of whether this co-terminosity of inner and outer worlds facilitates authenticity. It is possible to achieve harmony at any level within such a model, and one can gain harmony just as easily at a relatively superficial level or at a level of profound understanding. This is similar to problems that arise if one relies on exclusively social theories of the self. From this point of view, sociological explanations based on impression management, social constructionism and the postmodern celebration of social surfaces all fail to engage with the question of depth and genuineness. It is interesting, here, to return to Labouvie-Vief's distinction between well-being and self-understanding. Harmony, as described above, appears to allow for the feeling of well-being, as an absence of tension between inner and outer aspects of self-identity. It does not however take into account the depth, emotional resonance or internal continuity of the maturing imagination.

It would appear that to avoid a shallow sense of well-being in later life, the depth element of personal integration must be taken into account as a key factor in the relative authenticity of successful aging. However it is also possible to be 'deep', in the sense of having an internally coherent, emotionally sustained self-identity that is related to the past and to be profoundly out of touch with social reality. Paranoid reactions are a case in point here, as a cast iron and deeply held conviction can be held, which rarely conforms to everyday understandings of day-to-day experience. The internal and the external worlds do not, at least at first, match. An excessive focus on inner realities also has created theoretical difficulties of psychodynamic thinking in general. This is because key mechanisms such as the 'return of projections', identification and even the collective unconscious offer internal coherence, which folds back into an internal world for its justification and tends to exclude external and social terms of reference.

Whilst defensive aspects of the masquerade may dissolve as a result of harmonious identity, then, there is still a need to bridge the inner and the outer. This suggests that bridging itself may need continued grounding in both internal and external frames of reference.

For a specifically aging identity, grounding might be found in the experience of aging itself. If this argument is accepted, it becomes important to ask whether there is a particular sense of 'nowness' that is characteristic of particular phases of the human lifecourse. And specifically, whether there are existential issues that are particular to adult aging.

## FINITUDE AND POSTMODERNITY

In the case of adult aging a number of writers have drawn attention to the importance of the finite nature of the lifecourse, and the human capacity to reflect on one's own condition as key elements, allowing the location of aging identity. Jung (1934) has observed that during the first half of adult life, for example, individuals look back to childhood as a defining identity that has to be escaped, whilst the rest of life appears to be endless. In the second half, however, there is a tendency to define oneself in terms of looking forward to the time that is left before life ends. Unsurprisingly, life's priorities change accordingly, as position on the reasonably expected lifecourse becomes an important existential marker. Yalom (1980) and Frankl (1952) have also maintained that the apperception of finitude makes sense of life. Without death, it is argued, there would be no reason to do anything today - one could always put things off till tomorrow. The urgency that a finite lifespan provides, the need to make sense of aging, and through this, personal identity are grounded in an existential truth, however unpalatable.

From this perspective, the postmodern contention that technological fixes may remove the 'barrier' of an aging body, simply adds another layer of uncertainty and potential source of inequity to aging identity. One may achieve well being, perhaps, but not integrity, if a preoccupation with longevity rules out a need to encounter finitude and its implications for the human condition. Grounding aging within the context of a limited and democratic lifecourse also raises a number of important questions about the desirability of ecologically greedy extensions to the lifecourse for the few that can afford it. The notion that salvation lies in indefinite extension of longevity for a 'lucky' elite, is a very different future for aging than one based in the dissolution of age prejudice, requiring social commitment and combining emotional force with personal integration.

Notions of an 'expected life-span' may be one way of grounding aging identity in something that is firmer than the shifting sands of social expectation, yet more connected than an exclusively inward-looking self-integration. It is certainly not unproblematic. The development of such a grounding would need to avoid the conclusion that a 'normal life-span' might be used to ration services for those who exceed it, as has been suggested by Callahan (1987) and Daniels (1988). Rather, it would need to imply that later life is part of the human condition to be experienced and that older citizens should be given the resources to do so. Also, some resolution would need to be found for the identification of age-intrinsic tasks arising from the lifecourse without sliding back into fixed stages, which, more often than not turn out to be socially and historically contingent. An answer, here, may lie in a concentration on process, rather than the content of age-priorities. Such is already nascent in the work of Jung (1932), Baltes and Baltes (1990), Cole (1991) and Tornstam (1998). Whilst process may ultimately prove to be historically contingent, it leaves much more room to manoeuvre than a focus on the oughts of content alone. A full exploration of these issues, however, would be the job of another paper.

## CONCLUSION

I began this chapter by outlining some of the key issues that the study of age and identity might properly consider, in an attempt to see whether this helps us interrogate questions of what an agentic and authentic late life experience might be like. These issues included the form that a masquerade might take, the nature of an inner logic, existing beneath the surface conformities and the circumstances that affect the likelihood of more genuine aspects of an aging identity being expressed.

If there is an answer to these questions, I believe that it may lie in the twin issues of likelihood and lifecourse. Likelihood refers to the degree to which particular social spaces facilitate the expression of depth and surface elements of self-identity. The attraction of lifecourse lies in its ability to ground aging in a common human experience and a universal encounter with finitude. Both of these observations point us toward a consideration of process rather than content as a means of exploring success, authenticity and agency in later life. So, to live authentically in later life would mean an ability to express deeper and thus more integrated aspects of oneself that arise with maturity, and to anchor this experience in a recognition of the tasks and issues arising from a certain position upon an ultimately biologically determined life-trajectory.

There may, in other words, be something unique that aging gives us. If we work toward some understanding of what this might be, it may allow 'success' to be based on aging itself, within its own terms of reference. An understanding of the special nature of aging would also be an important justification of social gerontology as a discipline. Key to this question, at least in terms of the study of identity, would be what lies behind appearances in aging and whether there are reasons for attributing more importance to this than to the appearances themselves.

If the arguments above are accepted, there are some important questions emerging for aging studies. These would include whether it is possible to work out which level of identity research picks up. Certain methods may pick up different layers of identity, depending on generational and other power relations between researcher and respondent. It may be possible to work toward environments that increase the likelihood that deeper, and perhaps less superficial, elements of the aging experience are expressed. Contemporary efforts to define what successful aging might look like should, according to this logic, allow space for an examination of the processes that present one series of contents as normative at one socio-historical juncture and another at another. At a personal level it has been suggested that understanding the processes and inversions of masquerade might help in this regard, as this is a key factor in the expression of agency itself.

The aim, then, may not be to supply another model for success in aging, although some element of the judgmental is perhaps unavoidable in such territory. Rather, we need to work toward processes that help critically map out the relative strengths and emphases of particular assertions. The notion of success in aging should itself be interrogated as to its cultural importance as we become clear about the ways that discriminating judgements might be made about models of aging and their implications. As gerontologists we have no lack of models, that describe withdrawal, activity, transcendence or social inclusion to be the proper aim of successful aging, after all.

It follows that gerontological theorising and interpretation of empirical findings must take into account the probability that the performance of an aging identity is inevitably layered. Some older adults may have had the opportunity over a long life to achieve a greater integration and clarity of self-expression and thus more genuine agency. They may require suitably facilitative environments in which to express it. The degree to which researchers, policymakers and helping professionals can establish a rapport with more authentic expressions of the aging experience, and eventually the achievement of greater well being within an aging society, will depend on the development of methods of inquiry sensitised to the complexity of the mature imagination.

## REFERENCES

Amery, J. 1968. *On Aging: Revolt And Resignation*. Bloomington: Indiana University Press.

Andrews, M. 1999. "The Seductiveness Of Agelessness." *Ageing and Society* 19: 301-318.

Atchley, R. 1989. "A Continuity Theory Of Normal Aging." *The Gerontologist* 29: 183-190.

Atchley, R. 1999. *Continuity And Adaptation In Aging*. Baltimore: Johns Hopkins.

Baltes, P. and Baltes, M. 1990. *Successful Aging: Perspectives From The Behavioral Sciences*. New York: Cambridge.

Baltes, M. And Carstensen, L. 1996. "The Process Of Successful Aging". *Ageing and Society* 16:397-442.

Bass, S. And Caro, F. 2001. "Productive Aging: A Conceptual Framework." in *Productive Aging: Concepts And Challenges* edited by Morrow-Howell, N., Hinterlong, J. and Sherraden, M. Baltimore: Johns Hopkins.

Biggs, S. 1993. *Understanding Ageing: Images Attitudes and Professional Practice*. Buckingham: Open University Press.

Biggs, S. 1997. "Choosing Not To Be Old? Masks, Bodies and Identity Management in Later Life." *Ageing and Society* 17, 553 - 570.

Biggs, S. 1999. *The Mature Imagination Dynamics of Identity in Midlife and Beyond*. Buckingham: Open University Press.

Biggs, S. 2001. "Toward Critical Narrativity: Stories Of Aging In Contemporoary Social Policy." *Journal Of Aging Studies* 15: 1-14.

Biggs, S., Bernard, M, Kingston, P. And Nettleton, H. 2000. "Lifestyles Of Belief: Narrative And Culture In A Retirement Community." *Ageing and Society* 20:649-672.

Burman, E. 1996. "False Memories, True Hopes And The Angelic." *New Formations* 30:122-134.

Butler, J. 1996. "Gender As Performance." in *A Critical Sense,* edited by Osbourne, P. London: Routledge.

Butler, R. 1963. *Why Survive? Being Old In America.* San Francisco. Harper and Row.

Butler, R And Schechter, M. 1995. "Productive Aging." in *The Encyclopaedia Of Aging* edited by Maddox, G. (Ed). New York: Springer.

Callahan, D. 1987. "Setting Limits." in *A Good Old Age?* edited by Homer,P. and Holstein, M. New York: Simon and Schuster.

Caro, F., Bass, S. And Chen, Y. 1993. *Achieving A Productive Aging Society.* Westport: Auburn House.

Carstensen, L. 1993. "Motivation For Social Contact Across The Lifespan." in *Nebraska Symposium On Motivation* edited by Jacobs, J. Lincoln: Nabraska University Press.

Cole, T. 1992. *The Journey Of Life.* New York: Springer.

Cole, T., Kastenbaum, R. And Ray, R. 2000. *Handbook Of The Humanities And Aging.* New York: Springer.

Coleman, P. 1994. "Issues In The Therapeutic Use Of Reminiscence With Elderly People". in *Psychological Therapies For The Elderly, edited by* Hanley, I and Gilhooly, M.. London: Croom Helm.

Craib, I. 1998. *Experiencing Identity.* London: Sage.

Daniels, N. 1989. *Am I My Parents Keeper?* New York: Oxford.

Davis, F. 1979. *Yearning For Yesterday.* New York: Free Press.

Elliot, A. And Spezzano, C. 2000. *Psychoanalysis At Its Limits.* London: Free Association Books.

Erikson, E. 1962. *Childhood And Society.* New York: Norton.

Ekerdt, D. 1986. "Busy Ethic: Moral Continuity Between Work And Retirement." *The Gerontologist* 26: 239-244.

Featherstone, M. And M. Hepworth. 1995. "The Mask Of Aging And The Postmodern Lifecourse." pp. 371-398 In *The Body: Social Process And Cultural Theory*, edited By M. Featherstone, M. Hepworth, And B. Turner. Thousand Oaks, CA: Sage.

Featherstone, M. And Hepworth, M. 1989. "Ageing And Old Age: Reflections On The Postmodern Lifecourse." in *Becoming And Being Old,* edited by Bytheway, B. London: Sage.

Featherstone, M. And Hepworth, M. 1995. "Images Of Positive Aging." in *Images Of Aging*, edited by Featherstone, M. and Wernick, A. London: Routledge.

Frankl, V. 1958. *The Doctor And The Soul.* London: Penguin.

Freud, S. 1915(1963). *Collected Works.* London: Routledge and Kegan Paul.

Fries, J. 1980. "Aging, Natural Death And The Compression Of Morbidity." *New England Journal Of Medicine* 303:130-135.

Frosh, S. 1991. *Identity Crisis: Modernity, Psychoanalysis And The Self.* London: Macmillan.

Gilleard, C. And Higgs, P. 2000. *Cultures Of Ageing: Self, Citizen And The Body.* London: Prentice-Hall.

Gubrium, J. And Wallace, J. 1990. "Who Theorises Age?" *Ageing and Society* 10: 131-49.

Gullette, M. 1998. "Midlife Discourses In Twentieth Century United States." isn *Welcome To Middle Age, edited by* Shweder, R. Chicago: University Of Chicago Press.

Havighurst , R. And Albrecht, R. 1958. *Older People.* New York: Longmans.

Hepworth, M. 1998. "Aging And The Emotions." in *Emotions In Social Life,* edited by Bendelow, G. and Williams, S. London: Routledge.

Hinterlong, J., Morrow-Howell, N. And Sherraden, M. 2001. "Productive Aging: Principles And Perspectives." in *Productive Aging Concepts And Challenges,* edited by Morrow-Howell, N., Hinterlong, J. and Sherraden, M. Baltimore: Johns Hopkins.

Holstein, J. And Gubrium, J. 2000. *The Self We Live By.* New York: Oxford.

Hopcke, R. 1995. *Persona.* Boston: Shambhala.

Jaques, E. 1965. "Death And The Midlife Crisis." *International Journal Of Psychoanalysis* 46:507-514.

Jung, C. 1934(1967). *Collected Works.* Vol. 7. London: Routledge.

Kastenbaum, R. 1992. "Encrusted Elders." in *Voices And Visions Of Aging,* edited by Cole, T. Charlottesville: Virginia University Press.

Katz, S. 1999. "Fashioning Agehood: Lifestyle Imagery And The Commercial Spirit Of Seniors Culture." in *Childhood And Old Age,* edited by Povlsen, J. Odense: Odense University Press.

Katz, S. 1996. *Disciplining Old Age.* Charlottesville: Virginia University Press.

Kivnick, H. 1993. "Everyday Mental Health." in *Mental Health And Aging*, edited by Symer, M. (Ed) New York: Springer.

Knight, T.1986. *Psychotherapy With Older Adults*. Beverley Hills: Sage

Laws, G. 1997. "Spatiality And Age Relations." in *Critical Approaches To Ageing And Later Life*, edited by Jamieson, A., Harper, S. And Victor, C. Buckingham: Open University Press.

Labouvie-Vief, G. 2000. "Emotions In Adulthood." in *Handbook Of Theories Of Aging,* edited by Bengtson,V. And Schaie, K. New York: Springer.

Lynott, R. And Lynott, P. 1996. "Tracing The Course Of Theoretical Development In The Sociology Of Aging." *The Gerontologist* 36:749-760.

Marshall,V. 1999. "Analysing Social Theories Of Aging". in Bengtson, V. and Schaie, K. (Eds) *Handbook Of Theories Of Aging.* New York: Springer.

Minkler, M. And Estes, C. 1999. *Critical Gerontology.* New York: Baywood.

Moody, H. 1998. *Aging: Concepts And Controversies.* Thousand Oaks: Pine Forge.

Moody, H. 2001. "Productive Aging And The Ideology Of Old Age". in *Productive Aging: Concepts And Challenges*, edited by Morrow-Howell, N., Hinterlong, J. and Sherraden, M. Baltimore: Johns Hopkins.

Morgan 1988. "The Relationship Of Housing And Living Arrangements To The Productivity Of Older People". In *Committee On An Aging Society.* Washington, D.C.: National Academy Press.

Phillipson, C. 1998. *Reconstructing Old Age: New Agendas In Social Theory And Practice.* London: Sage.

Phillipson, C. And Biggs, S. 1998. "Modernity And Identity: Themes And Perspectives In The Study Of Older Adults". *Journal Of Aging And Identity.* 3: 11-23.

Polikva, J. 2000. "Postmodern Aging And The Loss Of Meaning". *Journal Of Aging And Identity* 5: 225-35.

Rowe, J. And Kahn, R. 1998 *Successful Aging*. New York: Pantheon.

Schultz,J. 2001. "Productive Aging: An Economist's View". in *Productive Aging Concepts And Challenge,* edited by Morrow-Howell, N., Hinterlong, J. And Sherraden, M. Baltimore: Johns Hopkins.

Stevens, A. 1999. *On Jung.* London: Penguin.

Thane, P. 2000. "The History Of Aging In The West". in *Handbook Of Humanities And Aging,* edited by Cole, T., Kastenbaum, R. And Ray, R. New York: Springer.

Tobin, S. 1989. "The Effects Of Institutionalisation". in *Aging, Stress And Health.,* edited by Markides, K. and Cooper, C. New York: Wiley.

Tornstam, L. 1996. "Gerotranscendence: A Theory About Maturing Into Old Age". *Journal Of Aging And Identity* 1: 37-50.

Woodward, K. 1991. *Aging And Its Discontents.* Indiana: Indiana University Press.

Woodward, K. 1995 "Tribute To The Older Woman". in *Images Of Aging,* edited by Featherstone, M. And Wernick, A. London: Routledge.

Yalom, I. 1980. *Existential Psychotherapy.* New York: Basic Books.

# Chapter 10

# HOW DO WE KNOW THAT WE ARE AGING? EMBODIMENT, AGENCY AND LATER LIFE

## *Jenny Hockey and Allison James*

## ABSTRACT

This chapter grounds its approach to aging within the contemporary literature on identity – and in particular in the notion of *identification*; the negotiated, unfinished processes of becoming. Revisiting structuralist sociological and anthropological approaches to aging, it identifies their theoretical inadequacy when it comes to understanding how the individual experiences time's passage and the process we know as 'aging'. In their place, the chapter sets out an approach which emphasises the importance of the body as a site at which discourses of aging are animated, reproduced or resisted. Whilst paying attention to postmodernist arguments which privilege the individual's scope for transcending bodily deterioration, the chapter argues that consumerist strategies in effect underscore the body's centrality within the aging process by making it the focus of exercise regimes and other forms of body modification. The agency implied in this self-as-project approach is nonetheless salient, one part of a broader range of strategies through which particular trajectories of aging are negotiated and achieved. In the examples of the twenty-first century grandmother whose contemporary identity – being without obvious precedent – requires active learning and negotiation; and the re-alignment of child/parent identities during periods of illness or disability, we investigate the everyday agency of individuals as they appropriate and experience changing age-based identities. Our conclusion centres around the practice of remembering as a way, not just of ordering one's past, but also of developing a relationship with the aging bodies that we have and are, an activity through which the processes of both present and indeed future identification come to take place. In sum, our chapter represents a critical re-working of agency-focussed theories of later life which calls attention to the centrality of embodiment as a social process which enables aging to be both experienced and actively engaged with.

# INTRODUCTION

This chapter aims to provide a way of understanding how we know that we are aging which approximates more closely to the lived experiences of peoples' everyday lives. We argue that at different points in the life course people engage in or are made subject to different processes of identification as aged persons. Some of these are welcomed, others rejected, some are open to negotiation while others are heavily constraining of individual choice. We therefore view aging across the life course as a fundamental feature of social identity, a fact which, hitherto, has largely escaped the attention of identity theorists. In charting this path this chapter represents aging as a fundamentally embodied process and explores how this bodily condition of life is - or is not - managed and negotiated by individuals in different ways, by employing different resources and strategies, at different points in the life course with different consequences and effects. Thus, for example, while children may seek to 'grow up' by adopting the behaviours of older teenagers, adults themselves may be relatively silent on the topic of their chronological age, and older adults may draw on resources ranging from the body modifications offered by cosmetic surgery to resistance to the infantilisation strategies of younger adults (Hockey and James 1993).

To this end we draw on social theory and small-scale empirical studies, alongside newspaper articles, advertisements, novels and biographical writings. In so doing, we show that the separate disciplines of sociology, anthropology, history, social policy, geography, health and gender studies all have a contribution to make in helping unpack the complexity of factors which together shape the ways in which we come to know that we are aging.

# IDENTITY, AGING AND THE LIFE COURSE

In seeking to define 'social identity' Jenkins argues for the significance of its temporal framing. He says:

> identity can only be understood as process. As ' being' or ' becoming'. One's social identity - indeed one's social identities, for who we are is always singular and plural - is never a final or settled matter.
> *(1996: 4)*

This focus on time and temporality, we argue, can help us understand how identities come to be formed and are made 'real' in people's everyday biographical experiences. As Roseneil and Seymour (1999:3) argue, contemporary work on identity can be divided into two main strands. The first asks about the conditions surrounding an individual's emerging consciousness of the self, whereby we learn to see ourselves by the way others see us (Mead 1934). The second, linked to poststructuralist cultural theory, is focused more on the politics of identity and cultural difference, highlighting the role of power in the construction of identity through discourses of difference - I know what I am by what I am not. *Both* theoretical strands reject 'the Enlightenment philosophical tradition which conceives of identity as essential, unitary, fixed and unchanging' (Roseneil and Seymour 1999:3). Rather than a notion that specific social identities can be stamped upon the 'plastic' individual across the life course, contemporary work highlights the importance of agency for an understanding of how identity comes into being and how the individual, in this sense, authors themselves in the course of everyday life experiences.

## THEORISING AGING ACROSS THE LIFE COURSE

We begin by reviewing theories of age and aging which argue that it must be seen as a social – or socially constructed, process, not an unmediated biological trajectory. Working with a social constructionist perspective, Van Gennep saw the transience of the individual, a transience which age itself accomplishes, as a form of social disturbance: 'Such changes of condition do not occur without disturbing the life of society and the individual, and it is the function of rites of passage to reduce their harmful effects' (Van Gennep [1908]1960:13). In his view, that individuals age was at best a social inconvenience, at worst a severe disruption.

However, as Baxter and Almagor note, 'age-grading whether formally marked by a rite of passage or merely tacitly recognised, is probably universal, and gives the process of ageing a social impress' (1978: 2). The concept of rites of passage is therefore one among other accounts of forms of social organisation studied by anthropologists - age-sets and age grades - all of which show how the relationship between ageing, identity and power comes to be articulated in societies. However, these concepts are focussed not so much on the boundaries of age-based identities and their active negotiation by individuals, as on the structural relationships established between the age categories through which the order of society is reproduced. As a result individual agency fails to be addressed. Significantly, like Van Gennep's schema of the rites of passage ([1908]1960) Radcliffe-Brown's study of age-sets (1929) represents them, for example, as classificatory devices, and as not necessarily grounded in the biological reality of the aging process. Indeed as Baxter and Almagor point out, biology and the relentless flow of time frequently disrupts such cognitive ordering systems, by throwing up anomalies, whereby 'the biological facts of birth and death ... slide out of alignment with the social order with which they should conform'(1978:5). Thus, although age-sets essentially stratify the society along generational lines, often leading to the establishment of gerontocratic control, this "gerontocracy" may be grounded less in the materiality of age than in its social construction.

Notwithstanding more recent accounts (cf. Stamp 1999), what perspectives such as these demonstrate is a concern with social structure and the structuring of identities across the life course. The agency and the experience of the individual who is taking on a changed, age-based social identity has received comparatively little attention. This may be because aging is a process which is imperceptible to the self. It takes place behind our backs, creeps up on us and is not , therefore, easily amenable to self-articulation. Thus, social science literature often attests to the individual's own personal experience of transition and changed identity only in discussions of the transition to other kinds of non-aged based identities, such as the move into chronic illness or the process of bereavement.

If it is the case, therefore, that aging creeps up on us, largely unnoticed, then we need to understand how we come to recognise it – for we do recognise that we are aging! Here Lakoff and Johnson (1980) usefully highlight the central role of metaphor in making such human experiences possible. They argue that '[t]he essence of metaphor is understanding and experiencing one thing in terms of another' and that, for example, the experience of one's body in space, and the materiality of its immediate environment provide a basis for metaphorical concepts which allow us to access more abstract or inchoate dimensions of human experience (1980:5). In rites of passage, therefore, it could be argued that it is the ritual use of *space* which allows individuals to engage directly with the *temporal* distance between two statuses or identities by actively experiencing the process of leaving one location and entering another.

When Victor Turner (1967), for example, develops his account of the rite of passage experiences of Ndembu initiands, he suggests that they are pivoted away from profane time and space and into an ambiguous, liminal threshold between what came before and what is to follow. While some anthropologists have stressed the *conservative* function of this liminal period, Turner argues that the experience of liminality is not just about repetition and reinforcement. It contains within it the seeds of change, a later elaboration of the concept of rites of passage which helps us to better understand how our identities might change across the life course. However, this account remains focused on the *structure* of experience, rather than on the experience itself.

In such socially constructed accounts, the body itself is not seen to *initiate* the aging process. Rather the aging of the body is regarded as a continuous process taking place outwith such structures, occurring too slowly for us to catch it in motion - no matter how watchful we might be in front of the bathroom mirror. Age has therefore to be stamped upon the body by society, in order for us to 'know' or 'experience' it through the symbolic marking out of differences between 'then' and 'now', through for example, ritual practices of circumcision or female genital mutilation (Talle 1993).

Classic accounts of aging therefore represent it as a cultural rather than a simply biological phenomenon. Indeed they suggest that our notion of 'biological aging' itself needs to be recognised as something which is socially constructed. However, social constructionist theorising which simply privileges structural explanations of change, cannot offer an adequate insight into the experience which often dramatic and powerful rites of passage represent for the individual (Talle 1993). Nor indeed can such approaches shed much light on the more mundane experience which we all share, of our bodies changing as they begin to show the signs of aging, be it the onset of menstruation and growth of body hair at puberty, or the wrinkles and grey hair of old age. Without paying attention to how the individual *animates* the social repertoire of aged life course positions and processes, we cannot begin to articulate the ways in which these bodily changes come to constitute that which we experience as 'aging'.

Some initial clues as to how a more agency centred perspective on aging might be developed can be found in the work of Erving Goffman (1961) who, drawing on G.H.Mead, explores the way individuals who encounter sickness, physical or mental impairment, a break with the law, the ravages of war or the assumption of a religious vocation, may undergo changes in their social identity. Intent upon a micro-sociology rooted in the specificities of individual interaction, the autobiographical accounts which Goffman draws on again and again cite the body as a source of, and for the experience of changed and changing identities. And, as in the rites of passage model, Goffman is concerned with the spatialisation of identity, be it front stage, back stage or behind the walls of a total institution (1971, 1968) However, despite this, as Craib (1998) observes, Goffman's engagement with agency and embodiment, gets us no nearer to the experiencing self, for Goffman's overarching concern remains with the identification of a 'similarity of form' within different organisational settings. He does not relate these to the way an individual may make sense of this in terms of their own life experiences.

Bryan Turner (1995), however, moves beyond a view of the person as passively moulded by society, to highlight the importance of embodiment. Describing his body as 'a walking memory' (1995:250), he suggests that while bodily aging may be inaccessible to direct experience, the body *does* evidence for us that aging is taking place. Indeed, in Turner's view, human beings are haunted by their own mortality. Photographs of the body, for example, represent for us images of our own aging, rather as scarring might after a rite of initiation. Both juxtapose 'then' and 'now', 'before' and ' after' in the single moment, the Western imaged body and lived body set literally alongside one another, like the imaginative juxtaposing of the unscarred and the scarred body of the Massai child. However, though Turner suggests that in this way the body can provide us with a sense of the past - and by implication, the future – this is not directly experiential.

Zonabend, however, moves us further forward when she notes that the life course is constructed around key embodied moments: '[b]irth, first communion, marriage and death make up the points of reference around which the individual constructs his time' (1984 : 197). The body is in this sense both a source of memories and a catalyst for change. Moreover, such embodied experiences also provide the reference points through which external historical events are recorded: 'When I made my first communion, it was war time' (1984:198). Laurie Lees's autobiographical novel offers a comparable example when he describes leaving home at nineteen , an age-based turning point , as a primarily embodied experience:

> The stooping figure of my mother, waist-deep in the grass and caught there like a piece of sheep's wool, was the last I saw of my country home as I left to discover the world. She stood old and bent at the top of the bank, silently watching me go, one gnarled hand raised in farewell and blessing, not questioning why I went. At the bend of the road I looked back again and saw the gold light die behind her: then I turned the corner, passed the village school, and closed that part of my life for ever.
> *(Lee 1969:11)*

## IDENTIFYING WITH THE AGING PROCESS

Bryan Turner's description of the body as 'a walking memory' (1995:250) – which we could conceptualise as the memoried body - can usefully be aligned with Hall's (2000) work on cultural identity. Together they help explain how it is that we know we are aging. Hall argues that identity cannot be seen as a fixed or enduring aspect of the self but, rather, as something which emerges, for a period, out of what it is not, or that which it lacks. The Other, therefore, crucially constitutes the self and in consequence the identities we produce are never complete. Instead, we experience a lack of fit with what we think we are or should be - or with what others project upon us, or the self we remember ourselves to have been. This is particularly evident for those hidden by the 'mask of ageing' (Featherstone and Hepworth 1991), a concept which describes the common experience of a mismatch between the self we think we are 'inside' and the much older self which others read off from the exterior of our visibly aging bodies.

However, in that our identities are always conditional, or as Hall says, 'lodged in contingency', they contain within them scope for fluidity, for combining or moving between identities (2000:17). This means that categories such as 'elderly' are umbrella terms which can include 'chronically sick patient', 'gardener', 'great granny', 'charity worker', 'community carer' and 'little old lady'. Any one eighty-year-old woman may move between all these identities, many of them defined by what they are not - 'chronically ill' and 'worker', for example, being seen as mutually exclusive categories As Hall (2000) reminds us, the fit with any one identity is likely, therefore, to be only approximate.

This links with his second important point: that identity emerges more out of difference than sameness: '[t]hroughout their careers, identities can function as points of identification and attachment only *because* of their capacity to exclude, to leave out, to render "outside", abjected' (Hall 2000:18). In the case of age-based categories, these unravel by the day. In adulthood, therefore, one's age no longer constitutes an aspect of social identity in the same way as it did whilst 'growing up', nor as it will once 'grown old' (Hockey and James 1993). Thus childhood and old age are mutually defining, being constituted either through their lack of 'age' or through their excess, as the marked halves of the twin hierarchies of child/adult and adult/elderly.

And while, in the privacy of family birthdays and on tax forms adults may disclose their age, albeit reluctantly, within many other social interactions the aging process in later life is not something readily enquired about, referred to or declared. For as Laclau argues, the apparent objectivity of dominant categories or identities is affirmed 'only by repressing that which threatens it' (cited in Hall 2000:18). Once achieved, adulthood is constantly under threat from old age, a threat which is intensified in relation to the extent to which it is abjected. Sontag, for example, highlights the particular losses which women suffer in old age (1978), their sexual and reproductive roles being both core to their social identity and seen as transitory. Men by contrast draw more on their work-based identities and, once retired, are less harshly judged in terms of their looks. Reproductively they suffer no evident cut-off point to their capacities. For women, therefore, their 'adult' bodies are likely to be monitored for signs of 'old age' almost as soon as they have made the transition from 'youth'.

## AGING AS LIFESTYLE AND STRATEGY?

Writing about aging in the late twentieth century Featherstone and Hepworth (1991) identify two important drivers. The first is the state, which promotes an ideology of personal responsibility in the areas of health and welfare, health promotion strategies enjoining individuals of all ages to develop a 'healthy lifestyle', the benefits of which will reduce the burden of an aging population on central funds, both now and in the future. Secondly, they point to the cultural sphere which promotes the possibility of designing one's own life through patterns of consumption which stray well beyond buying extra vegetables, into the more creative and exploratory realms of theme parks and post-tourism where new vistas and alternative identities are imaged. Echoing this view, the social geography of aging describes post modernism as 'an approach ... concerned to deconstruct categories, to celebrate diversity rather than seek universal laws and to explore other than dominant meta-narratives' (Harper and Laws 1995:212). Contrasting with the rigid stages of the modern life cycle, this fluid postmodern life course perspective opens up the possibilities of multiple lifestyles and identities which can be combined or exchanged across time and space. Giddens (1991) argues, for example, that self concern or reflexivity has become a core feature of high modernity and he is not persuaded that people aging during other eras engaged in comparable practices of self-reflection. Thus he refers to 'a process of "finding oneself" which the social conditions of modernity enforce on all of us. This process is one of active intervention and transformation' (1991:12).

Giddens' vision of personal agency and indeed empowerment against a backdrop of structural change has, however, been challenged. Featherstone and Hepworth (1991), for example, argue that, with respect to aging, this process is one largely confined to middle class sections of the population, members of the post-Second World War baby boomer generation, who grew up during an era of political radicalism and consumer growth. This experience left them empowered with the vision and the resources to redesign successive life course phases as they age, reinforcing the argument that historical time has to be taken into account when exploring individual biographical trajectories of the life course. Blaikie agrees:

> better health statuses and higher life expectancy may allow a sharper gradient to emerge between the fit and active ('use it or lose it') majority and a minority group sans teeth, sans eyes, increasingly sans NHS, but most older people are neither affluent nor infirm: they are both poor and relatively fit and well
> *(1997:16).*

While such a political economy perspective points to the nature of production which once underpinned the social construction of age-based dependencies, within the conditions of post modernity patterns of consumption rather than production are argued to predominate as markers of social identities. For elderly people it is precisely through those goods and services that a more malleable passage through the life course is promised. Here the health club and its entailments have an iconic status, but additionally, Featherstone and Hepworth (1995) suggest, since the 1970s other goods and services associated with an active lifestyle - particularly those to do with the travel and leisure industries - have also been harnessed for the promotion of positive images of aging.

In their analysis of the changes which have taken place in the magazine for retirement planning, significantly entitled *Choice,* Featherstone and Hepworth describe how, through its articles and advertising, it has worked to reconstruct the 'image of aging as a vigorous, lively and above all enjoyable pathway to self-realization' (1995: 40). However, they also note that the imagery which such magazines promote is targeted at the 'young old' rather than those whose aging has carried the body beyond repair. The dominant image is of ' the body as a machine which can be serviced and repaired, and the array of products and techniques advertised, cultivate the hope that the period of active life can be extended and controlled' (Featherstone and Hepworth,1995:44). Finally, they note that the absence of adequate income may inhibit many elderly people from pursuing the consumer values within which such a new vision of aging is being shaped, a point echoed by Sawchuck:

> When marketeers talk about a seniors market they're talking about a small privileged sector of that age group with money to spend, a segment who have had the opportunity to build up assets and equity, savings and bonds
> *(1995:182)*

Thus the 'choice' and agency promised by postmodern accounts of aging must, we suggest, be tempered by the inequalities of income and of health which continue to produce considerable variations in the experience of aging and thus to offer rather different prospects for individuals with respect to the changing social identities which accompany the aging process

## TOWARDS THE EMBODIMENT OF AGED IDENTITIES

What then can such an acknowledgement of the variability of health status among older adults (Blaikie, 1997), contribute to our exploration of the relationship between aging and identity? The free paper *Mature Tymes* (sic) offers us a moment of reflection, a paper which as its name suggests, addresses people in the later part of the life course, those over 50. Alongside articles on finance, travel and entertainment, adverts for holidays and financial planning vie with those for body maintenance - vitamins to ' unlock the pain in your joints' and reclining chairs, the deluxe version coming complete with 'double arm storage, modem access, 10 motor adjustable massage, hands-free phone, privacy handset, heat system in seat' (November 2000). One advert stands out, however. A large black and white insert for a company calling itself 'Independence Ltd' offers a range of products aimed at enabling the individual to cope with or disguise the impact age is having on their bodies. These products include: arch supports for the feet, big toe straighteners, toe relief pads, incontinence pads, a 'helping hand' to assist those who have difficult with reaching or bending, hold up stockings for women with poor circulation and to ward off thrush or cystitis, support belts for lumbago sufferers and hernia trunks for men. In addition, the availability of single leg tights, which allow women to only replace one leg of a laddered pair at a time, ensures that the clothed body will also be properly maintained in times of economic hardship.

What view of old age does such an advert evoke for the reader? On the one hand, the reader is presented with a view of aging as a process of relentless physical decline wherein the body, willy nilly, and without let or hindrance will begin to ache, creak, leak and will eventually become immobile. On the other, that products available to cope with the body's new demands, should the individual choose to purchase them, offer older people a degree of choice. Literally they can buy their physical, and therefore also social 'independence'.

Encapsulated, then, in this single advert is the argument we are advancing here. While Jenkins (1996) suggests that individual identity can only make sense in relation to social identity, the reverse is also true. Social identities only come into being through their embodiment by individuals. Thus ' the social is the field upon which the individual and collective meet and meld' (Jenkins 1996:17). And thus we come to know that we are aging through our embodiment which, in the social, conjoins with ideological and economic structures - for example, the expectation that 'disorderly' organic processes and weakening bodily boundaries will be kept under control; and that older people will invest resources in the prolongation of their physical independence. In this way, the *Mature Tymes* advert frames aging as a threatening social and physical process to which the individual responds and in whose body these processes meet.

Such expectations are, of course, socially constructed in and through particular social contexts and practices, forming the backdrop against which everyday life unfolds. Citing the family as the location for the learning of age-specific identities, Farmer (2001) examines the changing role of grandparents. She argues, for example, that the earlier age of death among previous age cohorts means that baby-boomer grandparents often grew up in families which lacked role models for grandparenting. In addition, medical and technological change has made the parenting skills of the 1960s redundant, while the growing involvement of male parents supplants the practical and emotional support once expected of older family members. On the birth of her first grandchild Farmer therefore realised that, 'in reproductive terms, things had moved. I was now firmly in the back seat. This I had to work out, painfully, over the coming days of cooking and cleaning at my daughter's house' (Guardian, 18.1.01).

If, however, we consider the family more broadly as a key site through which aged identities are brought into being (Hockey and James 1993), what becomes apparent is the way familial identities are founded within the context of ideas of independence and dependency. Within western industrial societies in particular, and as a by-product of the growth of individualism, adulthood is held to represent the pinnacle of independence (Hockey and James 1993). Childish dependency on parental care gives way to independent adulthood but may then lead on to a form of role reversal whereby children take on the role of caring for and protecting their parents. Describing the shifting and varied patterns of embodied father-daughter relationships over the life course, Sharpe (1994) cites the words of 54-year-old Richard who describes the changing relationship he has had with his daughter over the course of their lives together. Significantly, he invokes a range of 'familial' identities and genealogical positions in order to portray the changes in their relationships, changes which centre on the practices of care and protection through which the idea of 'the family' is held to be enacted:

> you could argue that our relationship has gone through a series of changes. To begin with I was the father and she was the daughter. Then we were like brother and sister really. And I suspect now it's gone right round and she's more like a mother to me, because she tends to keep an eye on me. tried to steer me in the right direction. She is inclined, probably because in some respects I am somewhat of a child, to be a little more mature than I am. So it has gone through this metamorphosis from father and daughter to mother and son almost.
> *(1994:151)*

Whilst in this example the reframing of a 'father-daughter' relationship as one of 'son-mother' is not seen as particularly problematic, once physical dependency becomes extreme in deep old age, such shifting identities and roles may become more problematic, since they appear to project very elderly people into a child-like state. Infantilisation, which draws on the positive childhood imagery of growth and development is one way, we suggested (Hockey and James 1993), in which any decline and loss of independence towards the end of the life course is rendered conceptually less problematic and disturbing. The wrinkled and arthritic body's manifestation of dependence is reframed, and a new identity produced through treating such physical dependency as if it were akin to that exhibited by children, a process which can however be experienced as deeply humiliating by both carers and very elderly people themselves. One daughter describes her own ambivalent feelings about this role-reversal:

> I looked after him quite recently...He was like a child. he is quite happy for me to wash him, etc. He has no embarrassment. I find my feelings are very confused now. He needs me to help him. I look at his face and find it so hard to believe nothing is happening behind his expression. I keep thinking how appalled he would have been at the thought of my doing what I am now doing with him
> *(Sharpe 1994:160)*

Though such strategic re-identification of very elderly people as child-like may in some instances enable those adults who are in their middle age to offer more effective care through distancing the emotional context surrounding the loss of ability and competence, the moral and ethical consequences of such a perception are profound. And not only for very elderly people themselves. There is, for example, considerable leakage of this child metaphor from its usage for very elderly people to the wider community of older adults, embracing those who still lead active and independent lives. As noted, this leads to a subtle but wide-spread age-based discrimination within western industrial societies such that the adjective 'silly' often accompanies that of 'old' and that a person may be already considered 'too old at 58 ' (Bytheway 1995, Hockey and James 1993).

## UNDERSTANDING IDENTITIES ACROSS THE LIFE COURSE

As we have suggested, a life course perspective which dealt with aged identities solely in terms of collectives and structures does not allow us to answer our question: how is it that we know that we are aging? The social structuring of age, by whatever means, is insufficient as an account of how the individual - whether child or adult - identifies themself as aged or aging. Thus, to simply work at the level of categorical identities is to fail to get to grips with the *process* of identification itself - i.e. the way it is that social *and* individual identities are inhabited and come into being.

As noted at the outset, models which posit movement between static categories tend to privilege the power of the social structures among and between which the individual is moved, a cognitive privileging which is highly problematic. Categorical or nominal identities - such as that of child, youth, middle-aged person, elderly person - can only ever be virtual identities for the individual for they do not map easily onto the experience of the individual who, in memory or imagination, or in some bodily difference, may fail to live up the requirements of the category to which they might belong on the basis of age and generation. In this sense, they do not have 'life' outside of the person, for these identities only become meaningful in terms of the individual's response to them. Thus, though people may share the same nominal identity they may have very different experiences of it, for it is in and through social interaction with others that the individual comes to an understanding of the social identity which he or she inhabits. Indeed individuals may choose to actively resist the age-based identity which others would impose upon them, for example, by maintaining the style and regime of exercise associated with younger adulthood until well into later life, so re-configuring not only their social presence but also, indeed, the body itself. Thus, across the life course there is a continual process of tacking back and forth which ensures that the embodiment of social identity is at one and the same time a 'referent for individual continuity, an index of collective similarity and differentiation and a canvas upon which identification can play' (Jenkins 1996: 21). And this process is eminently social - indeed it *is* the social - for 'social identity is never unilateral' and must always be validated by others (Jenkins 1996:21).

In addition, however, we must also recognize that age-based categories themselves change in nature across time. One of anthropology's key contributions has been the ethnographic material it has provided in support of arguments that age-based categories are not simply biologically based but are instead the product of particular culturally located historical moments. This is not simply to argue for the preeminence of purely discursive models of aging or for identity as infinitely variable. The cultural diversity of the 'natural' categories of age is not an identity pick-and-mix selection standing outside the self as a source of lifestyle choice. Rather, they are in some ways the reverse: as we have suggested here, a less often remarked aspect of the dialectic of identification is that, through their embodiment of the nominal identities of 'child' or 'old person', individuals themselves help re-make and reconstitute in a recursive pattern the very nature of that nominal identity. In other words, it is through experiences of a 'critical lack of fit' that individuals come to contribute to the process of identity formation which constitutes the social world.

Therefore in sum: to fully understand the process of aging across the life course and how this process of identification takes place, requires us to adopt an approach which privileges neither the individual nor society in terms of the ways in which identity is assigned, achieved or experienced. The identity which is seen as unique to the individual, on the one hand, and the identity which is seen as shared, collective and social, on the other, have to be understood as not only both 'intrinsically social' but also as 'routinely related' to one another, such that the processes ' by which they are produced, reproduced and changed are analogous' ( Jenkins 1996:19) . And, as we have argued, intrinsic to such a view is, therefore, the embodied nature of identity. It is primarily the process of embodiment which enables and facilitates the links between social and individual identities.

## EMBODIED MEMORIES

One further consideration which arises out of the perspective that we have been developing is the role which memory and imagination might play in allowing access the experience of embodied identification across the life course. As noted, integral to the question of how we know we are aging is the issue of how we experience the passage of time. However, in coming to terms with aging, we need to consider not just time's passage in the moment, but also the mechanisms through which we survey a temporal landscape made up of both past and present, the twin realms of the memory and the imagination. Intersecting in the present, it is the conjoining of our remembered and projected selves which produces our current, age-based identity. When we consider the process of aging across the life course, however, it becomes apparent that the relationship between our past and our future *in* the present takes on different qualities at different times in our lives. Thus, at times of crisis, loss or extreme age, the self we know and remember threatens to founder, a new and *un*welcome future self taking shape in our imaginations. This may be a self abandoned by a partner in divorce or death; a self robbed of an occupational identity; or indeed a self bereft of mobility, continence and even the ability to think coherently.

That there are other ways in which we might apprehend aging becomes apparent, therefore, once we reverse our temporal orientation, away from the future and toward the past. Memories and mementos fix for us moments in time past. They reveal to us the time that has elapsed and, as we think of that time, so, through memory, we potentially apprehend the temporal flow of the life course. The seaside souvenir made of shells, gathering dust on the shelf, focuses our attention. It recalls a time *then* - that beach holiday in Brighton with the children - and reminds us of the temporal distance between then and now – a point in time when our youngest child is about to embark on a university career.

Drawing on the work of the French sociologist Violette Morin, Hoskins (1998) asks about the relationship we have to such objects and makes the distinction between biographical objects - those which are centred on the person, and public commodities - those objects which have a more generalised public significance. The difference between them, as she points out, is not however intrinsic to the object but, importantly, what we, as individuals, do with the object and how the object figures in our lives. Thus the shell souvenir of Brighton was, until bought by the child, simply a publicly available commodity. Once brought home gleefully, kept for many years on a bedroom shelf until finally forgotten and disregarded, it can however be transformed from an impersonal and tacky souvenir into an important biographical object, an object through which a life can be recalled, changing identities recorded. As Hoskins notes 'biographical objects share our lives with us and if they gradually deteriorate and fade with the years, we recognise our own aging in the mirror of these personal possessions ' (1998:8)

However, more public commodities, too, can chart the aging process for, even though we might not possess an object and make it integral to the private world of a home and family, we may nonetheless still recognise our aging selves through our memory of a long-forgotten object or a place. Thus, pictures of the Rotunda Tower and Snow Hill station in Birmingham, push-button telephone boxes in museums and 45 rpm records in second-hand shops, memories of frozen Jubbly drinks in triangular wax cartons, platform cork-soled shoes and midi-skirts, all remind the 47 year old woman of a childhood and adolescence spent in the Midlands in the 1960s . They underscore for her the aging process by reminding her of the passage of time between then and now. And as Zonabend (1984) describes, rose cuttings swapped between households, and then nurtured into matures bushes, map out in their blooms, whole sets of close-knit generational identities within a small French village.

Thus, in line with such views, Antze and Lambek (1996) argue that 'memory serves as both a phenomenological ground of identity. and the means for explicit identity construction'(1996:xvi). However, as they go on to point out, the role of memory in identity construction is always ambiguous since unconscious processes of selectivity, besides those of simple memory loss, work to shape particular "truths" about ourselves, truths which are devised to both fit, or indeed contrast, with who we now think we are:

> If I am constituted by what I remember, what about all that I do not remember but that I know, because of other sources including my common sense tell me, must have been mine? Or what about that which I remember but would prefer to forget? Was that awkward adolescent really me? Can I still be him?
> *(1996:xvi)*

Central to the argument put forward by Antze and Lambek (1996) is, then, the notion that memory is a discourse of identity, serving to construct and reconstruct identities. In this view memory , therefore, becomes more than a way of accessing the past but is also fundamental to the present, and by implication to the future, for memory has an important part to play in the subjective experience of the here and now: 'who people are is closely linked to what they think about memory, what they remember, and what they can can claim to remember'( 1996: xxi).

In relation to questions of aging and identity across the life course, this is a critical insight. It helps explain the wide variety of subjective experiences of aging that can be found in the literature, helps to demolish arguments which still claim some utility for static aging categories in gaining an understanding of the life course and its transitions and lends further support to the argument we have been advancing here: that social identities across the life course have to be understood in terms of the particular embodied experiences of individuals in particular social and cultural contexts. If our present knowledge of our 'selves' as aged beings is, in part, a function of our memory of ourselves at previous ages then, clearly, it matters a great deal both *how* and *what* we remember about those life course moments. It is *this* which is significant for our understanding of our present 20, 40 or 60 year old selves.

Steedman (1986) makes this point explicitly in her autobiographical account of a working class childhood. She explores her own and her mother's lives in parallel, to argue, against those who have generalised about working-class childhood in a way that is never done for middle class childhood, for the importance of working with the complexity of the life course, *as it is lived out by individuals*. Thus, Steedman describes her mother as someone 'born into the old working class', yet, as a woman, not fitting into this lifestyle. On the contrary, she was a working-class Conservative, a woman who took up the ideas of the Food Reform, 'wanted a New Look skirt , a timbered country cottage, to marry a prince'(1986 : 9). In recalling her own childhood, as the child of such a mother, Steedman says that,

> it seems now to have been a joyless childhood. There were neighbours who fed us meat and sweets, sorry for us, tea parties we went to that we were never allowed to return
> *(1986:44)*

However, though as an adult it appears thus, Steedman insists that she does not '*remember* the oddness' (1986:44, emphasis in original). The oddness is an adult reconstruction of the bare facts of a past; her *memories* are, instead, of 'playing Annie Oakley by myself all summer long in the recreation ground, running up and down the hill in my brown gingham dress, wearing a cowboy hat and carrying a rifle' (1986:44).

This raises questions, therefore, about the salience of memories of the life course for our experience and understanding of the aging process. Within psychotherapeutic regimes of governance and control of the 'self' (Rose 1989), the life course is understood as essentially unidirectional - 'childhood' experiences shape those of 'adulthood ' - and thus present identity as having its foundations in the past. However, what work on memory reveals, and accounts such as Steedman's (1986) make clear, is that, although by looking back to the past we do *know* that we have aged, understanding that as an experiential process involves more than simply memory. It includes making comparisons between then and now and using our present knowledge and standpoint to make sense of and interpret past events. The process and experience of aging is not *remembered*, then, as an orderly transition or rite of passage between a series of aged social identities across the life course, however much we like to think of it as such. Moreover, this knowledge is accessed by a constructed narrative of comparison which continually tacks back and forth, between memories of the past and our present lives, between who one was and who one now is. This suggests therefore that, in the last analysis, the *experience* of aging - like that of time passing - is essentially imperceptible; all that we can know about aging are its effects on the mind and body, its identity outcomes and social consequences.

## CONCLUSION: THE BODY SPEAKS

As we have suggested, the processes of change which aging brings to the physical body are, unless through accident or ill health, generally imperceptible on a day to day basis. Only once a larger span of time has passed might the body's aging be consciously registered. At 40 years old a single grey hair may stay unseen or be slyly removed but, ten years later, a greying head of hair has become resistant to such strategies and is taken as a sure and certain symbol that one has aged. However, individual bodies differ in the ways and the extent to which time and age leave their mark and make their alteration. Age-based rituals of transition - from formal rites of passage through to simple birthday celebrations - therefore mark, first and foremost, changes in social status or position, for the simple numerical accounting of time passing may tell us little about the physical state of the body. Thus it is the body itself that both offers and denies us access to knowledge of our aging.

There is however a somewhat curious relationship between the physicality of the body and the process of embodiment with regard to the aging process, particularly in contemporary industrialised societies. In contrast to previous generations, numerical age has become invested with such extensive bureaucratic and symbolic power that - at all ages - the denotation of a person's age has become seen as indicative of their personhood, permitting and denying access to different kinds of social arenas. The relentless and irreversible determination of the aging process, which inexorably moves us from birth to death, means that the calculation of time passing in terms of years lived through appears to offer a way to cognitively regulate and chart that passage, through linking physical progress and decline to the tread of advancing years. And yet, at the start of the twenty-first century, this very physicality of the body's life course is becoming a less and less firm indicator of age-based ability. With better state provision of health and welfare regimes, advances in cosmetic and orthopaedic surgery and a more concentrated concern for individual health and fitness, the aging body is being made, and literally remade, to resist and challenge the aging process. For many theorists, such developments suggest therefore that the patterning of the life course which aging brings has no longer the same inevitability as it once had, and personal choice and life strategies are flagged as offering alternative routes and regimes. But how far is it the case ? Does not the experience of embodiment tell us that we are aging ? To answer these questions we return, once more, to the questions of structure and agency addressed throughout this chapter.

Core to our argument is the triangular relationship between the body, the self and society. Fundamental to this are three propositions. First, that aging can only take place at the site of the body. Second, that embodiment necessarily brings with it the social experience of aging. Third, the biological fact of aging means that individuals move, inexorably, from birth to death across the life course. Thus, our argument does incorporate what Nicholson (1995) terms a biological foundationalist perspective in that, at some level, it acknowledges a grounding in the 'given' of the aging body. This is not, however, the same as giving biology a determining role. Rather, we have taken the aging body into account in our recognition of the three fundamental issues outlined above. Our argument has been, therefore, that embodiment across the life course has to be understood in terms of an active self inhabiting a body within particular social structures, producing and reproducing those structures as a set of particular cultural understandings of the aging process.

For older people, therefore, the body as it now is offers a contrast to the body as it was: through photographs of the body at a younger age and through embodied memories of what the body had, at some point in the past, been able to accomplish. Thus it is that, by looking back and recollecting, the present and the future become framed by a sense of loss - the loss of earlier competences, looks or accomplishments. And it is through such comparisons, between then and now, between what was and what now is, that the time that has elapsed becomes understood and explained in terms of the physical deterioration which the aging process brings.

# REFERENCES

Antze, P. and Lambek, M. 1996. *Tense Past: Cultural Essays in Trauma and Memory*. London: Routledge.

Baxter, P.T.W. and Almagor, V. editors. 1978. *Age, Generation and Time*, London: Hurst.

Blaikie, A. 1997. 'Age consciousness and modernity: the social reconstruction of retirement'. *Self, Agency and Society* 1(1): 9-26.

Bytheway, B. 1995. *Ageism*. Buckingham: Open University Press.

Craib, I. 1998. *Experiencing Identity*. London: Sage.

Featherstone, M. and Hepworth, M. 1991. 'The mask of ageing and the postmodern lifecourse'. pp. 143-157 in *Becoming and Being Old: Sociological Approaches to Later Life* edited by B. Bytheway, T. Keil, P. Allat and A. Bryman. London: Sage.

Featherstone, M. and Hepworth, M. 1995. 'Images of positive aging: a case study of *Retirement Choice* magazine', Pp 29-47 in *Images of Aging: Cultural Representations of Later Life* edited by M. Featherstone and A. Wernick. London: Routledge.

Farmer, P. 2001. 'I didn't have a clue'. *Guardian* January 18.

Giddens, A. 1991. *Modernity and Self-Identity*. Oxford: Polity.

Goffman, E. 1961. *Stigma: Notes on the Management of Spoiled Identity*. Englewood Cliffs, NJ: Prentice Hall.

Goffman, E. 1971. *The Presentation of Self in Everyday Life*. Harmondsworth: Penguin.

Hall, S. 2000. 'Who needs "identity"?' Pp 15-30 in *Identity: A Reader* edited by P. du Gay, J. Evans and P. Redman. London: Sage.

Harper, S. and Laws, G. 1995. 'Rethinking the geography of ageing'. *Progress in Human Geography* 19(2): 199-221.

Hockey, J. and James, A. 1993. *Growing Up and Growing Old: Ageing and Dependency in the Life Course*, London: Sage.

Hoskins, J. 1998. *Biographical Objects: How Things Tell the Stories of People's Lives*. London: Routledge.

Jenkins, R. 1996. *Social Identity*. London: Routledge.

Lakoff, G. and Johnson, M. 1980. *Metaphors We Live By*. Chicago: University of Chicago Press.

Lee, L. 1969. *As I Walked Out One Midsummer Morning*. Harmondsworth: Penguin.

Mead, G.H. 1934. *Mind, Self and Society: From the Standpoint of a Social Behaviourist*. Chicago: Chicago University Press.

Nicholson, L. 1995. 'Interpreting gender'. Pp 39-67 in *Social Postmodernism: Beyond Identity Politics* edited by L. Nicholson and S. Seidman. Cambridge: Cambridge University Press.

Radcliffe-Brown, A. 1929. 'Age organization terminology'. *Man* 29:21.

Roseneil, S. and Seymour, J. 1999. *Practising Identities: Power and Resistance*. London: Macmillan.

Sawchuck, K.A. 1995. 'From gloom to boom: age, identity and target marketing'. Pp 173-187 in *Images of Aging: Cultural Representations of Later Life* edited by M. Featherstone and A. Wernick. London: Routledge.

Sharpe, S. 1994. *Fathers and Daughters*. London: Routledge.

Sontag, S. 1978. 'The double standard of ageing'. Pp 72-80 in *An Ageing Population* edited by V.Carver and P. Liddiard. Milton Keynes: Open University Press.

Stamp, P. 1999. 'Power to the elders: the politics of ageing amongst the Kikuyu women of Kenya'. Pp 161-184 in *Children and Old Age: Equals or Opposites?* edited by J.Poulsen, S. Mellemgaard, N. de Coninck-Smith. Odense: Odense University Press.

Steedman, C. 1986. *Landscape for a Good Woman*. London: Virago.

Talle, A. 1993. 'Transforming women into "pure" agnates: aspects of female infibulation in Somalia'. Pp 83-106 in *Carved Flesh Cast Selves* edited by V. Broche-Due, I. Rudie and T.Bleie. Oxford: Berg.

Turner, B. 1995. 'Aging and Identity: Some reflections on the somatization of the self'. Pp 245-262 in ) *Images of Aging: Cultural Representations of Later Life* edited by M. Featherstone and A. Wernick. London: Routledge.

Turner, V. 1967. *The Forest of Symbols: Aspects of Ndembu Ritual*. Ithaca: Cornell University Press.

Van Gennep, A. [1908] 1960. *The Rites of Passage*. London: Routledge & Kegan Paul.

Zonabend, F. 1984. *The Enduring Memory: Time and History in a French Village*. Manchester: Manchester University Press.

# CONCLUSION

# Chapter 11

# RETHINKING AGENCY IN LATER LIFE

## *Emmanuelle Tulle*

## ABSTRACT

This collection is about rethinking the ways in which we make sense of social action or agency in later life. The contributions in this collection challenge traditional academic approaches to the study of later life, which, arguably, often deny older people agency. I have argued elsewhere (Tulle-Winton 1999) that social gerontology, and the wider society, should be more reflexive and rather than contribute to the continued marginalization of older people, should draw attention to the extent to which the latter's actions may be understood within the set of normalizing discourses which people have to manage and negotiate as they get old. The purpose of this collection is to continue this process, by providing philosophical, theoretical, conceptual and empirical direction for a reflexive social gerontology. This chapter will argue that the management of later life has become complex, caught as it is within a broad discourse which continues to construct old age as a time of decline and dependency but has shifted the burden of responsibility for the avoidance of decline onto individuals. Agency in later life thus seems to be restricted to techniques of self-government (Tulle and Mooney 2002), which, perversely, constitute people as old, rather than allowing them to resist the more challenging aspects of growing old. The proliferation of the discourse of activity and of anti-aging strategies further marginalizes the very old or very ill whose potential for agency is masked by eroded cognitive and physical competence. And yet, even then the obsession with activity which (Katz 2001/2) documented elsewhere is itself subjected to normative restrictions. Thus the experiences of those who choose to use their bodies in very active ways at an advanced age, such as Masters elite runners, are also invisible empirically and theoretically. I will close this collection by arguing that on the basis of evidence presented so far social gerontology needs to be more imaginative. This can be achieved on three fronts – firstly by fighting for the economic viability of later life and reducing structural inequalities, secondly by recovering agency where normative definitions of agency in later life forbids it, especially in the face of bodily and cognitive deterioration and thirdly, by suggesting ways of aging which are not premised on its denial.

## INTRODUCTION

The discursive context in which later life is experienced has been undergoing some shifts. The creation of retirement and the decommodification of old age has enabled people to envisage their later years without fear of destitution (Phillipson 1998). However these processes have also stoked ancient fears about physical and intellectual decline in the later years. These fears have colonized public policy and the individual management of everyday life. Thus much public policy is currently designed to avert the fiscal bankruptcy which apparently awaits advanced economies in response to the increase in the number of older people and increased longevity. In fact, it appears that the current discourse of old age has foregrounded anti-aging as a response to the cost and personal decrements of senescence, but also as a challenge to ageist practices, and to a large extent this has been lent intellectual credence by gerontological research and recommendations (Katz 2000).

But when we resist age, what is it exactly that we are resisting and how effective is it? Can we reduce agency to anti-aging strategies? In what follows I will explore critically how we might understand agency in later life. I will revisit theoretical ground covered elsewhere to show that gerontology contributes to the discourse of age by 'problematizing' or creating old age as the legitimate object of policy intervention and that it places particular responsibilities on individuals to self-govern, that is to act in accordance with orthodox knowledge about how one ought to be old. Thus a key outcome of discourse is the creation of normative identities, that is the transformation of people into subjects (Barry, Osborne and Rose 1996). Thinking about agency, therefore, what subjectivities are created by the dominant discourse of age, especially as they pivot around anti-aging?

## AGENCY IN LATER LIFE

Do older people have agency? How can we define and bring to the surface agency in later life? Is it simply the ability to 'act independently [...] of any overarching social structure' (Blaikie 1999: 3)? In our later years, the ability to act independently is not necessarily relevant, possible or even desirable. We cannot think about the experience of later life outside of structures, especially as these structures may themselves exert an overwhelming influence on older people's ability to 'act independently'. For instance, there is a plethora of constituencies with an interest in charting what the appropriate conduct during the later years ought to be, ostensibly to improve the lives of other people, but also as a way of regulating populations (Dean 1999). A related issue is to identify who defines agency and to examine the purpose of dominant ways of framing agency. Thus thinking about, and researching, agency in later life entails an interrogation of the wider cultural, political, economic and social structures, but also of the knowledge that has accumulated about the later years. Whilst here I may contradict myself by claiming that we cannot make sense of agency without considering structures, I am in fact arguing that we cannot simply equate agency with the ability to act independently. I would argue that doing so would cause us to collude with the government of older people (Foucault 1997b), and especially with the neo-liberal project which promotes the individualization and privatization of everyday life (Dean 1996). It is not simply the actions of people which are regulated but also their souls (Rose 1990). To enable me to develop these ideas further, I would like to return to a critique of gerontology which I developed in an article published in *Ageing and Society* (Tulle-Winton 1999) because it is relevant to an analysis of and search for agency.

Therefore I now turn to the discourse of later life.

# GERONTOLOGY AS DISCOURSE

I want to examine the direction taken by gerontology, as an academic activity designed to accumulate knowledge about later life, to respond to the difficulties associated with being old. I am particularly interested in its role in providing a critique of the wider context in which later life can be experienced. Why is it useful to conceptualise gerontology as discourse?

As I have shown elsewhere, Foucauldian tools of analysis are useful to bring out the role played by gerontology in producing 'truths' about old age and aging and how in the process it may provide the critic and social actors with ways of resisting its 'hegemonic' tendencies.

As with other social sciences, social gerontology should produce a theoretical understanding of the ways old age is experienced, shared with a desire to improve the lives of older people. I am not convinced that it has done that however.

In contrast I am arguing that gerontology has been implicated in the development of the dominant discourse of age. It has significantly contributed to the production of knowledge which mirrors understandings of aging and old age based on its pathological characteristics. Far from being value free and irrelevant to everyday life, much of the knowledge produced by gerontological endeavours has been widely disseminated and 'internalised' by a range of social actors, from policy-makers to individual agents. In particular it has contributed to the regulation of the behaviors and aspirations of people as they age.

## Foucault and Power

Foucault's analysis of power is particularly useful to show the regulatory role played by social gerontology, but also as opening a window onto ways in which a distancing from this discourse could take place.

As I have shown elsewhere Tulle-Winton 1999 and Tulle and Mooney 2002), Foucault (1994) offers a useful analysis of power. For Foucault (1997a) power is diffuse, it is dispersed in the social organization along a series of networks. Three aspects are interesting about this particular approach to power. Firstly, as society is relational, regardless of their social location, social actors are implicated in a range of networks of power. Secondly, power is not evenly distributed and social action bears the imprint of these uneven power relations. Thirdly, power relations are in constant flux. There is nothing permanent about them and the direction of power can be reversed or at any rate diverted.

Power relations are exercised and dispersed through the formation of bodies of expert knowledge which act as bearers and producers of truth about external reality and social actors. These bodies of knowledge exert power on social actors by both objectifying and subjectifying them. Thus we become the object of scrutiny by experts and by the same token we govern our own behaviours within these frameworks. We, as social actors, engage in our own 'government', that is we make decisions about the conduct of our own lives in the context of the neo-liberal project. It is from these twin processes that we derive, partly, our own sense of self and understand our place in the social sphere. In other words, discourses contribute to our own subjectification. These processes persist as we age and take on a particular complexion, especially as they are underpinned by bodily deterioration.

## Resisting Discourse

There appears little room in this framework for an understanding of what (Fox 1998) called 'human intentionality' or agency. Does gerontology not offer a way out of its own discourse? Foucault (1976) argues that his analysis of power allows for the possibility for resistance and change. Because power is not embodied in a monolithic entity but is the outcome of uneven social relations, it follows that it can be challenged, set off course or resisted. For Foucault resistance is, therefore, constitutive of power and is the seat of indeterminacy in social action. Thus perhaps the discourse itself may offer a way out after all and we may be able to recover agency in the lives of older people by taking a reflexive stance in relation to gerontology.

## The Problem with Old Age and Aging

Understanding gerontology as discourse allows us to posit a link between the accumulation of 'scientific', orthodox knowledge about old age and the lived experience of aging. So what does gerontology know about aging and old age?

We do not know when old age starts, that is when aging turns into senescence. Haber (2001/2) and Katz (1996) have traced the modern concern with old age as a discreet part of the lifecourse to its medicalisation from the end of the 18$^{th}$ Century onwards. During the development of biomedicine and clinical observations, old age became viewed as a time of disease and aging as pathological decline which affected not only the workings of the body but also cognition. Haber (2001/2) argues that the modern problematization of old age as a disease state and therefore as something to be eradicated, coincided with wider concerns in the US and some European countries with the management of increasing numbers of old people in the population. Thus the old were numerous and they were sick. We can see that the current preoccupation with resisting aging and old age, as the force driving both public policy and individual behaviour, has a long lineage.

Despite (and because of) the setting up of welfare resources and the exercise of public policy designed specifically to deal with the problems of old age, there is continuing anxiety in the rich West about the demographic trends identified more than a century ago and about the fiscal bankruptcy that they presage if nothing is done about the problem. Thus greater affluence and better health have not shielded older people from being caught up in a discourse of decline and dependency and from being constructed as a burden. The solution to the problem of old age then is two-fold: eliminating aging and giving the responsibility for this process to individuals as they age.

## Biology and Medicine

Eliminating aging is proving difficult, primarily because there continues to be uncertainty about the start of old age. This is reflected in efforts currently in progress in modern biology to search for the biomarkers of aging, that is a set of objective thresholds at which changes in functioning would be consistent with a significant increase in morbidity, deterioration of function and risk of death which could be said to constitute senescence (Butler and Sprott

2000). However, these biomarkers are not yet forthcoming. What is now gaining acceptance however is that senescence takes place at the cellular level of the organism 'in a hierarchical, dynamic and interacting network whose functional integrity progressively deteriorates with time' (Cristofalo, Gerhard and Pignolo 1994). Thus biological aging is not linear but locates itself in the organism in different areas in an increasingly synergistic fashion. The latter helps explain why, as we get older, we are at greater risk of multiple pathology and death, but it does not provide an instrument which would help punctuate the aging process on the basis of age. Nor do we know why cells become more prone to pathology as they age.

Furthermore there is a debate currently taking place in medicine about the best way to deal with aging. Some are advocating its eradication through a range of pharmacological interventions and the recourse to new biotechnologies. This approach is premised on the anti-aging medicine, construction of aging and old age as disease and intervention mirrors orthodox approaches to disease. For instance, Klatz (Klatz 2001/2): 2) claims that artificial organs 'would make replacement body parts readily available' and would lead to 'gains in human longevity'. He also argues that this would help 'avert the financially, socially, and medically burdensome task of caring for the swelling aged population' (p 1).

This has come under fire in other parts of the medical research establishment. Butler (2001/2) is very critical of anti-aging medicine and argues that it misleads people into believing that aging can be cured. Operating on the premise that aging increases the risk of illness and rather than advocating its eradication, he opts for the management of longevity, within the natural confines of the human lifespan. In other words, the target is to improve the health status of people as they age. This would involve identifying which processes lead to deterioration in the organism and how they lead to illness. The neuroendocrine immune system has been advanced as a possible site of deterioration and, thus, intervention. Butler (2001/2) claims that 'serious' medicine takes a more comprehensive view of intervention, advocating improvements in disease prevention, lifestyle habits as well as environmental changes. The aim of intervention, it is claimed, is to 'extend life within what appear to be genetically determined limits, through control of the myriad diseases that afflict humanity, and through direct intervention in the biological processes of aging' (Butler, 2001/2: 2).

Despite the disagreements (and I will leave it to the reader to reflect on the actual difference between the two positions), it is clear from the current state of research in medicine and biology that aging is attracting an increasing amount of interest amongst the funders of research (although Hayflick (2001/2) thinks the funding is mis-directed) and private medical practitioners and that there is a belief that it is desirable to arrest or even overturn biological aging. But these interventions raise a number of ethical issues which are not always addressed in the biomedical literature. A very basic question would be: if we do not know when senescence starts, when do we intervene? Furthermore most of the therapies advocated by these protagonists are not yet available, yet alone known, to the majority of older people whose encounters with medical professionals tend to be more perfunctory.

## Welfare

The economic and social management of old age has until the late 70s been the remit of welfare institutions. Blaikie (1999) has argued that welfare has been the key framework (beside biomedicine) within which the social problems of old age have been identified and appropriate responses devised. Powell and Biggs (2000) add that it is also the prime site in which old age is 'performed'. This has been an ambiguous project however: on the one hand the problems of old age, through welfare, were a collective responsibility, but on the other hand, they have contributed to the economic, social and cultural marginalization of old people: retirement and exclusion from the labour market has led to the mass decommodification of older people and their consequent dependency on public funding (Estes, Swan and Gerard 1984); (Phillipson 1998 and Walker 1980). This, in turn, has fuelled the discourse linking old people with poverty, illness, disability and social disengagement (Powell and Longino Forthcoming), (Tulle-Winton 1999).

However the idea that supporting older people should be a collective responsibility has been under threat with the rise of neoliberal policies. Katz (2000) and Tulle and Mooney (2002) have shown that, in response to population aging and the fiscal crisis of the late 70s and early 80s, old age has been reconstructed as a private problem. No longer can people rely on the State for economic support or to address their health problems. They must plan ahead and prevent dependency on the State. This can be done in several ways: by buying private pension schemes, by moving to age-appropriate housing where the physical decrements of old age will be more manageable, by taking private medical insurance and by adopting healthy lifestyles.

## RESISTING OLD AGE?

We have already seen that discourses can be resisted, or that through discourse, existing power relations can be challenged and modified. Does gerontology itself contain the key to a challenge to the dominant discourse of old age? In order to uphold any strategy of resistance as valuable and truly liberating, one that has the potential to change for the better the conditions in which people become older, we must identify the target. Gullette (1997) has argued that old age is trapped in a discourse of decline which alienates older people from the mainstream of society and from themselves. What is to be resisted? There are several candidates: physical and intellectual decrements, poverty and inequality, negative attitudes towards older people, the lack of social and cultural resources, the individualization and privatization of later life.

Strategies for dealing with the management of the later years have become commonplace. Some theoretical developments, such as Disengagement Theory (Cumming and Henry 1961), Activity Theory (Havighurst and Albrecht 1958), Continuity Theory (Atchley 1989) or Successful Aging (Baltes and Baltes 1993), have focused on ways of adapting to later life. The latter seem to be located on a continuum, ranging from total disengagement to busyness. Disengagement Theory recommends complete acceptance of social and cultural marginalisation. Activity Theory, Continuity Theory and Productive Aging reject cultural marginalisation by advocating a life of continued *activity*, albeit unremunerated activity.

Successful aging refers to the ability to adapt to the decrements of old age and loss, not by following externally set normative criteria but by an individual process of coming to terms with the decline of opportunities and achievable life goals. This can be achieved through 'sensible' and efficacious lifestyle choices aimed at fulfilling one's health and welfare needs.

## Resisting What?

These understandings of later life have come under a lot of renewed scrutiny recently (see Biggs and Katz in this collection) and their propensity to produce normative statements about what later life ought to consist of has been highlighted. The physical, psychological, social and aesthetic decrements which accompany aging appear to be the prime targets of these theoretical accounts. They offer ways of making the best of a bad deal, without examining the structural and discursive context in which people disengage from social life or remain active, why some people may experience aging as biographical disruption (Bury 1982) or what might facilitate the continuation of longstanding interests and practices. They do not explore the socially constructed barriers which may speed up attrition in functioning. Nor do they explore the level of 'compulsion' involved in opting for active, productive aging, rather than disengagement.

Katz (2000) has shown that older people are no longer shielded from the obligation to remain active. Welfare systems measure activity in the lives of older people and people themselves are encouraged to engage in a range of activities, especially in retirement communities or day centers. What however is no longer encouraged is the pursuit of what he terms 'anti-activity activities' (p. 143), such as napping or introspection, as these are seen as inimical to an ethics of activity and independence.

Thus activity can be understood as a technique of the self, because it is related to the wider aim of eliminating dependency and postponing disability. Through the regulation of their everyday lives, active older people are fulfilling the goals of neoliberal ideology and becoming good citizens: The promise of liberation from the personal decrements of later life is part of a broader project of ensuring that as few people as possible rely on public resources for the continuation of their lives and the personal fear of physical deterioration. They are therefore engaged in what Foucault (1997b) called 'government'. Government refers to the concurrent control of populations and of interiority. The outcome of government is the individual as subject of government, whose self is shaped by specific projects of government. Government takes place when experts make recommendations about what we ought to do, but also when we, as social actors, reflect on what we ought to do (Tulle and Mooney 2002) and act accordingly. This task is facilitated by the cultural primacy given to youthful and aesthetically pleasing bodies.

Arguably, most of the strategies of resistance to decline appear to amount to techniques leading to normative constructions of the self. These strategies are consonant with a definition of agency as the ability to act independently, by postponing senescence or, when that can no longer be done, by remaining financially independent of collective forms of support. Thus they do not pose a fundamental challenge to the discourse of decline, the regulation of older people and the production of subjects. Nor do any of these strategies address social inequality in later life, inequality among older people on the basis of age, class, gender and ethnicity or inequality between decommodified people and those still active in the labour market. In the final analysis, these strategies do not help resolve the tension which exists between the declining body (its sensed reality and the available cultural meanings attributed to it) and the self. I will now turn to an examination of agency amongst two contrasting groups of older people.

## AGENCY IN ACTION

My research has focused on exploring the link between agency and resistance. Two projects with an ostensibly divergent substantive focus can nevertheless be brought together, in order to examine the impact of the discourse of aging and old age on the management of everyday life. The research summarized below was conducted in central Scotland in 1997 (age-appropriate housing) and Autumn 2000 (Masters athletes) and in both cases the data were obtained in life history interviews.

*Age-appropriate Housing* - This project examined the pathways to retirement and beyond of people who had retired less than 10 years before the research, and especially the move to specialist accommodation upon retirement (Tulle-Winton and Mooney 1997). A very small sample of nine informants aged between 60 and 73 provided material rich enough to explore theoretically the ways in which they engaged with the dominant discourse of age which gave primacy to successful aging, old age as obsolescence and the privatization and individualization of the management of risk entailed in potential bodily deterioration. The informants had all recently moved to smaller, 'age-appropriate' accommodation, usually an apartment of recent construction, from a large house. Three informants had chosen to live in specialist accommodation, that is accommodation with warden support. The rest lived in 'mainstream' housing.

Apart from one married couple, the informants were from professional backgrounds or in business and still affluent. Seven informants had lived in owner occupied properties since marrying. One woman, who had never married and whose early professional training required a lot of travelling, had lived in privately rented apartments until advised by a friend to buy property only a few years before moving to a sheltered apartment. She had MS and used a walking frame and electronic buggy to move around. Another woman had lived in privately rented tenement apartments in the late 40s and early 50s and then public housing until her second marriage in the early 70s. At that point her material circumstances improved considerably (her new husband was a wealthy businessman) and they lived in owner occupied houses or expensively rented apartments. Finally one couple lived in privately rented and then public housing until 1981. That year they bought their large semi-detached house from the local council under the Right-to-Buy scheme. Selling this house in 1996 allowed them to release enough equity to buy their pensioners' apartment outright. Unlike the other informants they spent their working lives in manual occupations. They used his small occupational pension to pay for the monthly maintenance charge which covered a part-time warden, an alarm, buildings maintenance and repairs.

A range of issues arose in the interviews - all had moved, of their own volition, either forced by illness and disability or in anticipation of restricted mobility. Therefore they appeared to engage in age-appropriate behavior (Tulle and Mooney 2002). They had used equity released from the sale of a large house to buy – outright – a property with features normally associated with the management of later life. The new property was smaller than the house previously sold, within walking distance of shops and public transport networks, and it was protected by security devices or a warden. The informants themselves appeared to conform to the discourse of age – they kept active, helped in this way by their affluence, and where physically able they continued to drive a car. Lastly they were satisfied with their decision to move house, in that they appeared to justify it on grounds of their age.

However, in other ways, they resisted the discourse of age. One couple specified that the security device was not for personal protection (consonant with the construction of older people as victims), but to protect their property from the risk of burglary during their numerous absences. Those not already in sheltered housing, on the whole refused to contemplate one such move. Sheltered housing was too closely associated with impending physical frailty, primarily because the accommodation itself was too small, but also because it reinforced spatial and cultural marginalization. In addition it was perceived as a poor investment: expensive to buy, especially in relation to the quality of the accommodation, but also expensive to run, as it attracted monthly charges which could be increased without any account taken of the fixity of income in later life. Nevertheless, the need to plan for greater physical restrictions was ever present in the informants' minds but had not been acted on. One couple had taken the precaution of putting their names on the waiting list for a publicly funded sheltered apartment, because they refused to use their savings to fund their later years. Another couple had taken steps to sell some of their assets to their daughter for the same reason. And, despite their affluence, they all expressed loyalty to public pensions as a safety net.

*Masters Elite Runners* - The issue of control is also highly pertinent, but in a different direction, in the lives of a contrasting group of people: Masters elite runners, that is athletes who compete in the Masters age categories, which start at 35 for women and 40 for men (there is no upper limit but those set by the athletes themselves).

I carried out life history interviews with 21 male and female athletes aged 48 to 86. The majority (14) were long distance runners and the others track and field athletes, specializing in sprinting and jumps. Only five of the informants had retired from their sport, because of illness, but these informants, who were all male, maintained some involvement with athletics, in coaching or administration, and they all continued to engage in physical activity, albeit at considerably reduced levels. Nevertheless they were more athletically active than contemporaries without any history of athletics. Long distance runners ran between 35 and 80 miles a week – in fact the greatest weekly mileage was covered by a 70-year-old male runner. Track and field athletes and long distance runners trained at least four times a week, and competed several times a year, in some cases, at the height of the season, every second weekend. They had all reported achieving personal bests in their 40s and 50s, even among those with a lifelong history of athletics. The majority of long distance runners had run marathons at some point in their career, a discipline which most took up as Masters athletes, rather than as senior runners.

Involvement in athletics at elite level inevitably increases the risk of injuries and, as survivors, they had been relatively free of serious, career threatening problems. Nevertheless, accidents, overuse or wear and tear injuries had brought them in contact with medical professionals, amongst whom, on the whole they had found mostly hostility. The exception was a 67-year-old female sprinter who continued training despite arthritis in her hip, with the support of her family physician and physiotherapist.

Another interesting feature of these people was the willingness with which they were prepared to dedicate a large proportion of their daily lives to the pursuit of their sporting career (Nash 1979). A training session could take in excess of two hours, repeated six or seven times a week. Travelling to international competitions would occupy a whole weekend, and longer if competing outside Europe or in a championship spread out over several days. Runners took their running shoes even on holiday and ran every day. If the opportunity arose, athletes would reduce their work schedules to dedicate more time to their sport. Thus, one male informant, who was in his mid-50s, had been made redundant from a well-paid job and was only looking for part-time employment. Another male runner refused the offer of working a longer shift, which would have meant waiting till the evening to go out training.

Unlike the other informants in the retirement research, these people resisted what was expected of them by lay people and professionals alike. One 65 year-old male informant had been advised by his physician to give up running and take up a more sedate pursuit, such as bowling, in effect asking him to engage in age-appropriate behavior. One female ultra distance runner was expected by her friends to give up running when she turned 50. Although this was presented (and interpreted by the informant) as a joke, the making of the joke itself nevertheless resonates with wider expectations of age-appropriate behaviour, a point which was not lost on her.

But it was more than disengagement which was at stake: they were also challenging beliefs widely held among lay people and medical professionals that aging bodies should not be subjected to physical exertion and that injuries in later life cannot be remedied. The informants showed that with careful management of their bodily capital (Tulle 2003), by resting, pacing their participation in competitions and managing injuries, they could continue training intensively and break age-adjusted records. The 86 year-old male still held the world 70-75 age group 10km record which he broke at the age of 70. However this record was under threat from another informant who was training to break it, despite having experienced a heart attack several years previously.

So, on the surface, these athletes appeared to engage in self-government – they kept active and busy after retirement, and they were physically fit. They were conscious that they 'looked' healthier than their physically inactive contemporaries and therefore fulfilled their obligations to prevent illness and disability and in the process reduced dependency on health resources. On the other hand, by disciplining their lives and their bodies in this way they challenged assumptions of appropriate behavior in later life. Their busy-ness was a-typical, simply because it was focused on the body. They also found themselves denied health resources. Consequently, like most senior athletes, they had to resort to private treatment, mixing orthodox and alternative forms of healing.

From these experiences, we could conclude that agency is resistance to bodily aging itself. Thus being independent and self-reliant, and engaging in anti-aging practices, such as remaining active and managing the outward signs of aging, would offer an effective challenge to the dominant discourse of age which associates aging with inevitable decline, dependency and obsolescence. The responsibility to 'address' the problems of old age is placed on individuals, but the problematization of old age is carried out mainly in structures, like medicine and welfare and wider political goals.

However there is something unsatisfactory about this. The empirical evidence shows that anti-aging practices do not include challenging the spatial marginalization of older people into the home or in retirement communities. Furthermore, the encouragement to be active is circumscribed within very strict boundaries of appropriate bodily experience – thus, rather than stating 'I'm not old' (Thompson, Itzin and Abendstern 1990), some people would rather use the expression 'I'm not too old' to stake a claim to a different use of their bodies, one which, as embodied by long distance runners or track and field athletes, challenges traditional views about what can be accomplished by older bodies. Conversely, other people may want to claim that they are 'old enough', that is old enough to disengage from the pursuit of active aging and from the pursuit of individual responsibility, and staking a claim to collective forms of support.

Lastly the possibility for agency is premised on cognitive competence. Thus people who are in the advanced stages of brain pathologies are denied volition in their actions and their self is assumed to have disappeared (see Kontos in this collection).

I would argue that gerontologists need to work towards a new understanding of agency. This is premised on a different research agenda and a different way of theorizing, one which, Bourdieu (2000(1972)) argues, questions the foundations of the objective knowledge constituted in discourse, in this case gerontology. Science, whether of the natural world or of the social, should engage in an examination of 'its conditions of possibility' by redirecting its focus towards structures on the one hand but, just as importantly, towards the 'dispositions' that they foster. In other words, structures are involved in the constitution of orthodox knowledge about the social world and they map out what it is possible to accomplish. Orthodox forms of resistance to aging, encapsulated in anti-aging or active aging strategies, do not challenge the dominant discourse of age. On the contrary they lead to orthodox forms of subjectification, through the government of dispositions relevant to the achievement of the successful or good ager and through continued participation in consumption, of goods and services. In other words, they constitute social actors as old.

## Resisting the Individualization of Later Life

Thus a new research agenda – and a reconstruction of agency - would focus on both collective and individual challenges to cultural marginalization and self-government. As we have already seen, conceiving of strategies of resistance within collective structures may be fruitful, for instance through new social movements. The U3A or the Elderhostel movements (see Katz and Laliberte-Rudman and Moody in this collection) appear to fulfill current political rhetoric about the desirability of lifelong education, but instead challenge educational orthodoxy by refusing to model third age education on mainstream 'adult' education, which would be oriented towards a traditional curriculum, and would be supplemented by a well organized research programme. By rejecting assessment and the awarding of diplomas and degrees, they also challenge the instrumentalist relationship between education and the production of marketable skills, but also the concept of education as progression towards higher levels of enlightenment and specialisation. Furthermore these new institutions tend to be organized and managed by older people themselves and they foreground solidarity and public visibility.

A similar interpretation of Masters athletics is possible. Continuing to run into old age is not an anti-aging practice and there are at least four factors which may favour such an interpretation. Firstly, although the organization of the Masters scene appears to mimic that of senior athletics, in fact it does not, nor can it possibly aspire to it. It is entirely based on an awareness and acceptance of attrition in bio-mechanical functioning. In races, Masters runners may aim to run faster than the rest of the field. However they are also separated into specific age-groups and therefore have to contend with expectations of achievements based on decreases in performance. Thus runners might not win a race overall but they might win the race in their age-group. On both a personal and a cultural level it makes the encounter with bodily aging inescapable. Far from inducing negative feelings in the runners however, the separation into age-groups provides the spur for continued competitiveness, gives meaning to training and encourages athletes to 'look forward' to aging, that is, to move to a new age category, in the hope that they may dominate this new age-group for a period of time. Secondly, by providing a framework in which older athletes can continue to perform at high levels of achievement and competitiveness, Masters athletics challenge the restricted and restrictive boundaries placed around older bodies in encounters with lay and professional actors. Thirdly, older athletes re-colonize the streets when they go training outside, in this way resisting the marginalization of older people operated in their exclusion from the streets and other public spaces. Some prefer to run independently, usually out of a rejection of what they perceive to be the overconstraining of age-adjusted times. Nevertheless the rejection of the formal athletic structure provided by the Masters movement does not constitute resistance to the aging body. It is simply another modality of responding to biological change.

In both examples and the examples highlighted by fellow contributors, agency is defined by agents themselves and its modalities are informed by a critique of what one might call their 'enfeeblement' by hostile structures.

## CONCLUSION

What this collection has sought to do is map out the discursive context in which later life is experienced and to explore the possibilities for agency. But what has emerged is not simply a retelling of stories of everyday living or a description of the structures within which these lives are conducted. There is a consensus developing here and elsewhere in the literature that discussing agency cannot be conducted without a critique of these structures. These structures, which I have argued, contribute to and constitute the discourse of old age, provide us with ways in which we devise strategies for the everyday management of our lives and they are informed, produced and reinforced by the pronouncements of experts on the problems of age but also in our own appropriation of these pronouncements through techniques of self-government. Thus the discourse of old age maps out a space, or conditions of possibility, for imagining what later life might consist of. What we have found here is that this space has hitherto been too narrow, confined largely to ways of imagining old age premised on its denial. Thus a premium has been placed on the extension of midlife, the erosion of the visible signs of age and the rejection of dependency. This fulfills the neoliberal project of shifting the responsibility for the management of the decrements of old age onto private individual themselves, at the expense of collective forms of support or the nurturing of interdependency. And it is fuelled by the old desire to eliminate old age altogether through biotechnological interventions. The danger however is the social, cultural and increasingly economic marginalization of very old people – and this is a worrying trend, given that more of us will live for a very long time.

Nevertheless, much as we may dislike these trends, they provide the context in which lives are led and, as social gerontologists, our job is to explore in detail how social actors operate within it. Thus our focus here was not on making normative pronouncements about the 'best' ways to manage old age and the self – this would yield a restricted and restrictive account of agency, one which would focus on the lack of agency or the encouragement to stay active and independent for as long as possible. Also such a stance would lead us to take issue with many of the people whose stories have been gathered here.

Instead, this collection aimed to unlock, bring to the surface, social action in all its diversity, and especially to find it where we would least expect to find it – because we too are subjected to the discourse of old age, or simply because some social actors are literally out of sight, such as Wahidin's elder female prisoners or Conway's older woman isolated in a deprived housing estate. We are not denying that as we age, the risks of bodily and cognitive malfunction will increase. Nor are we ignoring the hostility of the world in which people become older. In fact, it appears that agency is located less in the pursuit of an ageless body (people find ways of aging well in spite of their physical decrements) and more in the battle against the discourse of age itself and the structures in which the discourse is played out and disseminated.

Thus what we are trying to do is to find chinks in the discourse through which resistance can be undertaken and agency reclaimed. Our theoretical engagements seem to draw us inexorably towards a critique of political projects which, whilst they may offer opportunities for self-fulfillment, are only available to those who can afford it or for those who never grow old. Aging into very old age appears to remind those who contemplate entry into it first hand of the need for others, that dependence or perhaps interdependence is a socially valuable asset and that poverty is an ever-present risk which perhaps should be borne collectively. There are other issues which none of the contributions has addressed, like those arising from becoming older as a member of a minority ethnic group or in countries with crumbling or non-existent industrial and welfare structures.

Nevertheless, despite this lacunae I would argue that throughout this collection we have fulfilled Mills' (1967) vision of sociology as the examination of the interplay between personal troubles and problems of milieu, in the pursuit of improvements in the lives of individuals and the experience of aging into old and very old age.

# REFERENCES

Archley, R. 1989. "A Continuity Theory of Normal Aging." *The Gerontologist* 29: 183-190.

Baltes, P. B., and Baltes, M. M. (Eds.). 1993. *Successful Aging: Perspectives from the Behavioral Sciences*. Cambridge: Cambridge University Press.

Barry, A., Osborne, T., and Rose, N. (Eds.). 1996. *Foucault and Political Reason: Liberalism, Neo-Liberalism and Rationalities of Government*. London: UCL Press.

Blaikie, A. 1999. *Ageing and Popular Culture*. Cambridge: Cambridge University Press.

Bourdieu, P. 2000(1972). *Esquisse D'une Théorie De La Pratique, Précédé De Trois Études D'ethnologie Kabyle*. Paris: Seuil.

Bury, M. 1982. "Chronic Illness as Biographical Description." *Sociology of Health and Illness*. 4:167-182.

Butler, R. 2001/2. "Is There an Anti-Aging Medicine." *Generations* 25:63-65.

Butler, R. N., and Sprott, R. L. 2000. "Biomarkers of Aging: From Primitive Organisms to Man." Tucson, Arizona: International Longevity Center-USA.

Cristofalo, V. J., Gerhard, G. S., and Pignolo, R. J. 1994. "Molecular Biology of Aging (Ui: 94151716)." *Surgical Clinics of North America* 74:1-21.

Dean, M. 1996. "Foucault, Government and the Enfolding of Authority." in *Foucault and Political Reason: Liberalism, Neo-Liberalism and Rationalities of Government*, edited by N. Rose. London: UCL Press.

Dean, M. 1999. *Governmentality: Power and Rule in Modern Society*. London: Sage.

Estes, C. L., Swan, J. H., and Gerard, L. E. 1984. "Dominant and Competing Paradigms in Gerontology: Towards a Political Economy of Aging." pp. 25-36 in *Readings in the Political Economy of Aging*, edited by C. L. Estes. Farmingdale, N.Y.: Baywood.

Foucault, M. 1976. *Histoire De La Sexualite: La Volonte De Savoir*. Paris: Gallimard.

Foucault, M. 1994. "Sur L'archeologie Des Sciences: Reponse Au Cercle D'epistemologie." pp. 696-731 in *Dits Et Ecrits*. Paris: Gallimard.

Foucault, M. 1997a. "The Ethics of the Concern for Self as a Practice of Truth." in *Ethics: Subjectivity and Truth, the Essential Works*, edited by P. Rabinow. London: Allen Lane.

Foucault, M. 1997b. "On the Government of the Living." in *Ethics: Subjectivity and Truth. London*, edited by P. Rabinow. London: Allen Lane.

Fox, N. J. 1998. "Foucault, Foucauldians and Sociology." *British Journal of Sociology* 49:415-433.

Gullette, M. M. 1997. *Declining to Decline: Cultural Combat and the Politics of the Midlife*. Charlottesville, Va: University of Virginia Press.

Haber, C. 2001/2. "Anti-Aging: Why Now? A Historical Framework for Understanding the Contemporary Enthusiasm." *Generations* 25:9-14.

Havighurst , R., and Albrecht, R. 1958. *Older People*. New York: Longmans.

Hayflick, L. 2001/2. "Anti-Aging Medicine: Hype, Hope, and Reality." *Generations* 25:20-26.

Katz, S. 1996. *Disciplining Old Age*. Charlottesville, Va.: Virginia University Press.

Katz, S. 2000. "Busy Bodies: Activity, Aging and the Management of Everyday Life." *Journal of Aging Studies* 14:135-152.

Katz, S. 2001/2. "Growing Older without Aging? Positive Aging, Anti-Ageism and Anti-Aging." *Generations* 25:27-32.

Klatz, R. 2001/2. "Anti-Aging Medicine: Resounding, Independent Support for Expansion of an Innovative Medical Specialty." *Generations* 25:59-62.

Mills, C. W. 1967. *The Sociological Imagination*. London: Oxford University Press.

Nash, J. F. 1979. "Weekend Racing as an Eventful Experience: Understanding the Accomplishment of Well-Being." *Urban life* 8:199-217.

Phillipson, C. 1998. *Reconstructing Old Age: New Agendas in Social Theory and Practice*. London: Sage.

Powell, J. L., and Longino, C. L. J. Forthcoming. "Embodiment and the Study of Aging." in *The Body in Human Inquiry: Interdisciplinary Perspectives to Embodiment*, edited by V. Berdayes. New York: Routledge.

Rose, N. 1990. *Governing the Soul*. London: Routledge.

Thompson, P., Itzin, C., and Abendstern, M. 1990. *I Don't Feel Old: Understanding the Experience of Later Life*. Oxford: Oxford University Press.

Tulle, E. 2003. "Sense and Structure: Towards a Sociology of Old Bodies." pp. 91-104 in *The Need for Theory: Critical Gerontology for the 21$^{st}$ Century*, edited by S. Briggs, A. Lowenstein and J. Hendricks. Amityville, N.Y.: Baywood.

Tulle, E., and Mooney, E. 2002. "Moving to 'Age-Appropriate' Housing: Government and Self in Later Life." *Sociology* 36:683-701.

Tulle-Winton, E. 1999. "Growing Old and Resistance: Towards a New Cultural Economy of Old Age?" *Ageing and Society* 19:281-299.

Tulle-Winton, E., and Mooney, E. 1997. "Talking About Yourself: Becoming Old in Urban Scotland." Paper presented at the Reclaiming Voices Conference: Ethnographic Inquiry and Qualitative Research in a Postmodern Age. University of Southern California, Los Angeles, Ca.

Walker, A. 1980. "The Social Creation of Poverty and Dependency in Old Age." *Ageing and Society* 1:73-94.

# CONTRIBUTORS

Simon Biggs PhD is Director of the Age Concern Institute of Gerontology, King's College, London, UK. He is an executive member of the European Masters Programme in Gerontology. He has previously worked as a policy adviser and as a community psychologist and has written widely in the areas of social policy, social theory, aging studies and professional identity.

Steve Conway PhD is a researcher in the School of Social Sciences and Law, University of Teesside, UK. His academic research has been mostly concerned with social attitudes to ageing, illness and death. He is currently engaged in evaluative work and the management of researchers related to the evaluation of several Sure Start programmes in Middlesbrough and in the Redcar and Cleveland areas.

Mike Hepworth is Emeritus Reader in Sociology at the University of Aberdeen and Visiting Professor of Sociology at the University of Abertay Dundee. He is a By Fellow of Churchill College, Cambridge, and a member of the Academy for The Social Sciences. He is a member of Age Concern Scotland, The British Society for Social Gerontology and the British Sociological Association. His main research interests are the sociology of the body and the sociology of aging and he has published widely in these areas. His latest book is *Stories of Ageing,* a study of images of aging in popular fiction.

Jenny Hockey PhD is Professor of Sociology at the University of Sheffield. Trained as an anthropologist, she has published widely on ageing, gender, health, death and dying, death ritual and memorialisation, and bereavement. Her most recent books include: *Death, Memory and Material Culture,* Berg 2002 (with Elizabeth Hallam) and *Social Identities across the Life Course,* Palgrave 2003 (with Allison James). Her current research includes 2 ESRC funded projects: on heterosexuality, and on the destinations of ashes removed from crematoria.

Allison James PhD is Professor of Sociology at the University of Sheffield. She has worked in the sociology/ anthropology of childhood since the late 1970s and has helped pioneer the theoretical and methodological approaches to research with children which are central to the new childhood studies. Her current work explores aspects of law and social policy as it relates to ageing and the social and cultural construction of models of 'the child' and of 'childhood' within the life course. Her most recent books include *Theorising Childhood* (1998) with C. Jenks and A. Prout, (Polity Press) and *Research with Children* (2000) with P. Christensen (Falmer Press).

Stephen Katz PhD is Professor of Sociology at Trent University, Peterborough, Canada. He is the author *of Disciplining Old Age: The Formation of Gerontological Knowledge* (1996). He has contributed chapters to critical gerontology texts such as *Figuring Age: Women, Bodies, Generations* (1999) and *Handbook of the Humanities and Aging* (2000), and journal articles to *Generations, Journal of Aging Studies, Journal of Women & Ageing* and *Journal of Aging & Identity.* He is currently completing a book on cultural ageing and lifestyle.

Pia Kontos PhD is a Postdoctoral Fellow at the Toronto Rehabilitation Institute, Canada. Her research was supported by the Alzheimer Society of Canada and the Institute of Aging (Canadian Institutes of Health Research). Her interests are in social theory of the body, critical gerontology, and ethnographic methods. She has published articles in the Journal of Aging Studies, Ageing and Society, and Philosophy in the Contemporary World.

Deborah Laliberte-Rudman PhD is Assistant Professor at the School of Occupational Therapy at the University of Western Ontario, Canada. Her interest in examining discursive constructions of later life initially stemmed from her work as a clinical occupational therapist in a geriatric rehabilitation unit, and was further heightened through her Masters work which involved a phenomenological study of the meaning of activity for community-dwelling seniors. Her doctoral dissertation focused on examining the contemporary 'government' of aging within the Canadian context, with a particular focus on the interconnections between neoliberal political rationality and discursive constructions of subjectivities for retirees.

Charles F. Longino, Jr. PhD is Director of the Reynolda Gerontology Program at Wake Forest University. He received his PhD from the University of North Carolina at Chapel Hill, and has also taught at the University of Virginia, Kansas and the University of Miami before coming to Wake Forest. He is the current editor of the *Journal of Gerontology: Social Sciences,* and is president of the Association for Gerontology in Higher Education in the United States. In the early 1990s, he served as North American Chair of the International Association of Gerontology, through the 1993 world congress in Budapest. He is interested in modern theory, and in the consequences of population change.

Harry R. Moody PhD is currently Director of the Institute for Human Values in Aging and Senior Associate at the International Longevity Center in New York City. He is known for his work in older adult education and is currently Chairman of the Board of ELDERHOSTEL, the world's largest education-travel organization. Moody is the author of many articles and books in gerontology including *Ethics in an Aging Society* (Johns Hopkins University Press, 1992) and *Aging: Concepts and Controversies* (Sage, 2002). A graduate of Yale with a PhD in philosophy from Columbia University, has Dr. Moody taught at Columbia, Hunter College, New York University, and the University of California at Santa Cruz. He currently edits an international newsletter, "Human Values in Aging" (*valuesinaging@yahoo.com*)

Chris Phillipson PhD is Professor of Applied Social Studies and Social Gerontology at the University of Keele where he directs the Institute of Ageing. He has published numerous books and articles on a variety of aspects of ageing. Recent work includes *Reconstructing Old Age* (Sage, 1998), *The Family and Community Life of Older People* (co-authored, Routledge, 2001), and *Transitions from Work to Retirement* (Policy Press, 2002). He is currently involved in an ESRC-financed project investigating problems associated with social exclusion in old age.

Larry Polivka PhD has served as Director of the Florida Policy Exchange Center on Aging at the University of South Florida since September of 1992. Prior to directing the Center on Aging, Dr. Polivka worked at the State of Florida's Health and Rehabilitative Services as Assistant Secretary for Aging and Adult Services from August 1989 through September 1992 and as Policy Coordinator for Health and Human Services, Office of Planning and Budgeting, Executive Office of the Governor from August 1988 through August 1989. Dr. Polivka received his Ph.D. in Sociology from Florida State University specializing in urban and political sociology, social theory, and applied social science.

Jason L. Powell PhD is Senior Lecturer in Social Policy in the Department of Sociology, Social Policy and Social Work Studies at the University of Liverpool, UK. His research interests extend to wider social theory, power, helping professions, and old age. He has authored and co-authored almost 50 publications world-wide. He is a regular invited speaker at US and UK universities on his research. He currently serves on several international editorial boards, *namely Language, Society and Culture* (Australia), *Sincronia: Journal of Social Sciences and Humanities* (North America), *Journal of Aging & Identity* (USA) and *Social Science Paper Publisher* (Canada). He is currently writing a book on Foucault and aging, and conducting work on technological innovation, old age and higher education in the UK.

Emmanuelle Tulle is a Lecturer in Sociology in the School of Law and Social Sciences at Glasgow Caledonian University, Scotland. She has a long standing interest in later life, both empirically and theoretically and publishes regularly in academic journals and edited collections. Her empirical work has spanned a broad spectrum, covering various aspects of social work, retirement housing and now sport. She is currently engaged in a piece of research examining changing bodily capital among veteran elite runners. She has contributed to new theoretical developments which combine perspectives drawn from critical gerontology, social and sociological theory, the sociology of the body and, more recently, the biomedical sciences.

Azrini Wahidin PhD is a lecturer in the School of Social Policy, Sociology and Social Research at the University of Kent, UK. Her teaching and research interests are; elders in prison, the female prison estate, the body, identity, the performativity of sexuality and foucaudian theory. Her thesis on female elders in prison is the first of kind to look at this growing population. She is currently working on a project entitled 'Against the Law -Growing up Gay Pre 1967 Sexual Offences Act. She has published in various journals including *Sociology, Time and Society* and the *Journal of Aging & Identity*.

# INDEX